Praise for *In*

This is a breath-taking treasure trov_____ ,voan share their lives'
work in developing, practising and teaching the art of supervision. They describe
in detail not only the models they have developed and the principles behind them
but how they teach them – right down to the detailed design of their programmes,
the exercises and experiments they use – and even the recipes for the cakes Joan
bakes for the participants.

But not only that. The book is a delightful read – it zings engagingly along,
full of stories and vignettes, quotations and anecdotes. One feels privileged to meet
the authors in all their humanity – their mistakes as well as their brilliance, their
feelings and their experience. I feel deeply appreciative.

Professor Charlotte Sills, Ashridge Business School and Metanoia Institute, London

I am struck by the authors' generosity in providing a detailed 'warts and all' account
of each course, together with their own experiences, reflections and learning. This
is a golden treasury of ideas, examples and food, both for thought and in the form
of recipes for the cakes offered at the courses.

I shall return to the book regularly in order to savour each reflection and
continue learning from the wisdom and humanity contained within it.

**Els van Ooijen, psychotherapist, counsellor and supervisor in private practice
in Bristol, a former visiting lecturer to the counselling and supervision courses
at the University of South Wales, and author of (among other books)** *Clinical
Supervision Made Easy*

A wise, loving, and penetrating book about supervision by the acknowledged masters
in the field. Unmissable.

Dina Glouberman, psychotherapist, author of *The Joy of Burnout* **and Co-
Founder/Director of Skyros Holidays**

Here supervision is not a job to be done, or a set of techniques to be played with, or
an expert guiding the faltering footsteps of a trainee. Nor is it a management tool for
ensuring practice is done properly. It's a meeting place of equals where practitioners
'sit at the feet of their own experience' and, in relationship with one another, delve
deeply and reflectively into their work.

**Michael Carroll PhD is former Visiting Industrial Professor at the Graduate
School of Education, University of Bristol, and author of** *Effective Supervision for
the Helping Professions* **(among many other publications on the topic)**

Dedication

To Ben, Joe, Sam and Zac

IN LOVE WITH SUPERVISION

CREATING TRANSFORMATIVE CONVERSATIONS

ROBIN SHOHET AND JOAN SHOHET

First published 2020

PCCS Books Ltd
Wyastone Business Park
Wyastone Leys
Monmouth
NP25 3SR
contact@pccs-books.co.uk
www.pccs-books.co.uk

In Love with Supervision:
creating transformative conversations

British Library Cataloguing in Publication data: a catalogue record for this book is available from the British Library.

ISBN 978 1 910919 51 4

Front cover illustration by Steve Mepsted
Cover design Jason Anscomb
Typeset in-house by PCCS Books using Minion Pro and Myriad Pro
Printed in the UK by TJ International, Padstow

Contents

Acknowledgements

Where to begin? Parents, friends, colleagues, family? We would like to start with the Richmond Fellowship therapeutic community, where we first received and gave supervision, and gratitude to the late founder, Elly Jansen, who had the wisdom to realise how important staff training and supervision are. And then to Peter Hawkins, who was part of introducing a supervision policy to the organisation and has taught us a huge amount in this field. Several of our exercises came from him and we particularly appreciate his contribution to our combined book *Supervision in the Helping Professions*.

Over the years we have been in several peer supervision groups, but the most recent one feels like it could be lifelong. Thanks to David, Charlotte, Jochen and Ben for your support around this project. A special thank you to Ben, who has written our foreword.

In terms of colleagues, we would like to thank all those who have contributed to the edited books *Passionate Supervision* and *Supervision as Transformation* – namely, Jochen Encke, Julie Hewson, David Owen, Sheila Ryan, Joe Wilmot, Anna Chesner, Jane Read, Michael Carroll, Ann Rowe, Richard Olivier, Fiona Adamson, Alan Rodgers, Judy Ryde, Mary Creaner, Christina Breene and Nicole Coombe, all of whose ideas have influenced our thinking around supervision.

Several people have looked over early drafts: Christina Breene, Dina Glouberman, Rachel Lovie, Peter Reason, Charlotte Sills, Ben Fuchs, David Owen, Jochen Encke, Jenny Mitchell and, finally, Bronwen Williams, who came just at the right time and was an excellent midwife.

Our training groups have been largely run through the Centre for Supervision and Team Development (CSTD), and thanks to our associates in CSTD London – namely, Ben Fuchs, Joseph Wilmot and Steve Page. Also, thanks to Alison Stephenson, our administrator, who has been core to our centre thriving in the way it has.

The Work of Byron Katie, and her ways of working with core beliefs, has had a big influence on both of us, both personally and professionally.

Several people have provided writing venues over the years: Robin Coates, Steve Guest, Andrea Borwell-Fox in Malvern and especially Angus Marland and Elizabeth Tonsberg – their B&B, Scourie Lodge, in the far north of Scotland, was the birthplace for this book.

Chapter 9 has been almost exclusively written by participants on a bespoke course. Thank you Liz, Kirsti, Gary, Karin, Cassie and Mike. Also thanks to Sue Haycroft for writing your experience of the residential course.

Catherine Jackson at PCCS Books commissioned this book and thanks to her for her patience and shrewd editorial eye – with that, we knew the book was in safe hands.

We would like to thank Nigel Hamilton, who founded the Centre for Counselling and Psychotherapy Education (CCPE) and whose venue in Paddington has provided such a good place to hold our training, and to Christine Keeves, who has liaised with our adminstrator.

We would like to appreciate our families. In family constellation terms, we honour our ancestors, and our parents in particular. We would like to thank our four children for sharing some of their lives with us – particularly Joe Wilmot, who has taken up the mantle of supervisor and trainer with CSTD London.

And finally, thank you to the residents at the Richmond Fellowship from whom we learnt so much, and to our clients, supervisees and those who have come on our courses. You have enabled us to keep learning.

Preface
Michael Carroll

Robin and Joan have a creative way of turning supervision on its head, as this new book testifies. They are creative in finding alternative ways into what supervision means and how it can be used in everyday life, as well as in professional practice. They are artful in 'manufacturing uncertainty' as a way of learning, in embracing the opposite as a method of connection and in holding contradictions together as a journey or pilgrimage towards what is real. They are like good hunters who honour the kill and use every part of it. For them, nothing goes to waste, nothing is ignored, nothing is unimportant. 'Stay with it, notice it and allow it to become your teacher' is their motto; 'Whatever is happening between us *is* supervision.'

In this book they wander into places other writers on supervision fear to tread. Here supervision is not a job to be done, nor a set of techniques to be played with, nor an expert guiding the faltering footsteps of a trainee. Nor is it a management tool for ensuring practice is done properly. It's a meeting place of equals where practitioners 'sit at the feet of their own experience' and, in relationship with one another, delve deeply and reflectively into their work. Robin and Joan's first aim is to banish fear – fear of being vulnerable, of being known, of being found out, of not knowing, of getting it wrong, of being shamed – and this gives the supervisor and supervisee the relational flashlamps to shine into the corners of their work with compassion, understanding and, indeed, love. 'Supervision as meeting otherness with compassion' is how it is explained here.

Joan and Robin mine out and present 23 principles or foundation stones that guide supervision. They then offer us their training programmes as ways of seeing how these principles work in practice. These chapters on their trainings are veritable treasure troves of ideas, exercises, reflections and readings on various aspects of supervision. If one of our aims as teachers and trainers is to give away knowledge and skills, then Joan and Robin have been selfless in doing this. So much of what is here you could take to create your own learning space. As long as you don't forget that it is all 'relational'. Just as life happens in relationships, so does supervision. This book is the Martin Buber book on supervisory relationships where the 'I/Thou' relationship is core. It's a testament to their generosity that they even share some of the recipes for the cakes they bake for participants on their courses.

Joan and Robin have gathered their learning from more than 40 years (each) of supervising, being supervised, training in supervision and writing on supervision, and present that wisdom to us here. *In Love with Supervision* is an unusual title, you might think. But it captures the content well. If transformative conversations are the stuff of supervision, then, for them, the supervisory relationship is the superglue that holds it all together. In their words: 'In the giving, receiving, training and reflecting on supervision, we have come to see it as a form of spiritual practice, with awareness, inquiry and relationship at the core. And community.'

Michael Carroll PhD
Michael is former Visiting Industrial Professor at the Graduate School of Education, University of Bristol, and author of *Effective Supervision for the Helping Professions* (among many other publications on the topic).

Foreword
Ben Fuchs

This book is, first and foremost, a story of relationships. Joan and Robin's work grew out of their relationship as a couple, their relationships with colleagues with whom they have pioneered this work over the past 40-plus years, and their relationships with their supervisees and students, all of which provide the rich and varied context that brings their work to life.

I have known Joan and Robin since 1992. One thing that has stood out for me in that time is their fearless commitment to surfacing and shedding light on the deeper truths of the human condition and on the complexity of human relationships. This may appear at times like compassionate support, and at other times like uncompromising challenge, but it is always intended to shed light on those parts of ourselves that we may avoid. It is how they express love.

One of my earliest memories of receiving supervision from Joan is when I told her about something I wanted to change in myself. She said: 'I'll take that as a 50% true statement.' In a flash, I realised that, if the statement were 100% true, we would not be having this conversation, as I would have already made the change. By gently pointing to my unconscious ambivalence, rather than taking sides in my internal conflict, she invited me into a deeper relationship with myself.

Over the years we have become close colleagues and share a longstanding, regular peer supervision group. Their approach to supervision and to life is relational. With this book, they provide an intimate account of *how* they approach training others to have transformative conversations and become relational supervisors.

The term supervision is traditionally associated with oversight that in some way provides safety, assurance, regulation or control. It implies a power relationship in which the supervisor has formal or informal authority over those being supervised. This definition is most often used wherever there is an element of governance or management oversight of a person or activity. It is still the most common association.

More recently, another definition has grown out of clinical practices such as counselling, psychotherapy, social work and nursing. In this context, supervision is more of a reflective practice for continuing professional development – a way to support those doing emotionally laborious work. It is often associated with a teaching or mentoring relationship, with less experienced clinicians working under the supervision of someone more experienced. Robin and Joan were some of the early pioneers in developing this type of supervision and embedding this approach into a range of professional practices.

Their work now extends well beyond its origins in the clinical setting. Like many valuable bodies of knowledge, insights that emerge from one field often find fertile ground in other fields. The essential lessons of clinical supervision can be applied to any activity or occupation. It is the practice and discipline of self-reflection and facilitated inquiry into the dilemmas that can arise wherever human psychology plays a part. In this regard, supervision can be seen as a lens, a way of looking at any situation and oneself; a way of being in the world; a way of seeing with new eyes.

The move from regarding supervision as a concept of oversight and control to the ways in which it is practised by the authors is a fundamental shift in thinking. The idea of a reflective practice where we inquire into our own internal motives, feelings, attitudes and assumptions *in the presence of another*, in order to increase self-awareness, may seem fairly common practice today. However, this was not the case until relatively recently. Outside of a small subculture, self-examination was seen as suspect, or even threatening. Today, self-awareness is expected both in our personal relationships and for most professional roles. People who lack this capability are seen as missing an essential skill for adult life in the modern world. Like most cultural change, this shift to a more psychological language and a growth mindset has happened gradually. Yet, the way people today think and speak about themselves, other people and their relationships has changed over the past 40 years.

To understand the authors' thinking, it's helpful to consider their formative context. Born in the post-war years, they participated in many of the social changes of the 1960s and 1970s. Their generation experienced freedoms, opportunities and social mobility unknown to previous generations. Supported by a new post-war contract between state and citizen that created access to free health care (including birth control), higher education and affordable housing, their generation critiqued and challenged the traditional power structures and social norms of the day. In the process, they brought new thinking into the arts, education, health and social care.

In 1970s London, psychiatry and psychotherapy were going through a period of innovation and experimentation. Psychology broke out of the clinical mental health context. The pursuit of personal growth and expanding one's potential gained in popularity. Therapy and training centres sprang up, offering an eclectic choice of teachers, modalities and theories to choose from. This spirit of freedom and experimentation created something of a 'Wild West' personal growth movement.

The anti-psychiatry movement offered an alternative narrative about mental health, redefining 'normal' and thinking systemically about the environmental determinants of psychological health in the wider society. These ideas were instrumental in turning public policy away from large residential asylums and provided the academic ballast that gave rise to therapeutic residential communities. It was in one of these communities that the ideas underpinning this book were first developed.

It is easy to forget, from today's perspective, just how different and disruptive to the status quo many of these ideas were at the time. They challenged the conventional thinking of the day, particularly in the fields of education, social work and mental health. What may seem fairly conventional today in the fields of coaching, counselling and psychotherapy has been distilled from these radical roots.

Concepts such as self-awareness and feedback are so ingrained today that it's hard to imagine that, until recently, these were terms greeted with incomprehension and suspicion outside of some small professional circles. Work-based learning and development, now a massive industry, was viewed as remediation for those who lacked the competency to do their jobs. Development was seen as something that applied to children until late in their teens. As fields of study, adult developmental psychology and adult learning are relative latecomers.

Psychology, once the preserve of psychiatrists and small pockets of intelligentsia, is now mainstream. The language of personal development is everywhere. People talk about their feelings and inquire into others' feelings. In fact, keeping things bottled up, once considered a virtue, is now often seen as a problem. Psychological concepts and language are part of our everyday vernacular.

When viewed retrospectively, the emergence of professions such as psychotherapy, coaching and supervision can seem like a natural flow of events. But until recently these were not considered legitimate 'professions' in the sense of having professional bodies or any official status. Over time, they have become more self-regulating, with their own professional membership bodies, as well as more recognised by mainstream society. Yet, in becoming more mainstream, there is also the possibility that some of the ideas that form the roots of these professions can become diluted, as the price of mainstream acceptance.

As senior practitioners, Joan and Robin have been important contributors to this cultural change and the mainstream adoption of psychological concepts. They have continued to be seminal voices in the development and articulation of supervision for more than 40 years. During this time, they have remained true to the origins of their work and to the values with which they have contributed to shaping the field of supervision as it is practised today. They are uncompromising in their commitment to their values.

Their approach to writing this book reflects their style of working. Rather than follow the usual formula, laying out theories and models and adding stories of how well these concepts have worked in practice, they have chosen to describe the training they do, step by step, warts and all. They reflect on what they do and the thinking behind it as the reader is taken through the theories that underpin their work. They offer detailed descriptions that demystify supervision training and make it very accessible, including detailed examples of what happens in real life, where the best laid plans are thwarted and where people are caught in the grip of their misperceptions and judgements. The authors offer examples that are the essence of supervision, where unconscious processes surface unexpectedly and so-called mistakes become opportunities for genuine transformative learning.

With so many books on supervision now available, this one stands out both for its original voice and for its practicality. It takes the reader on a journey to help them understand the developmental process of *how* people learn to see through the new eyes of supervision and gain insights into becoming both a supervisor and a supervisee.

Ben Fuchs
Ben is a leadership and organisational development practitioner, coach and supervisor, senior consultant for the King's Fund and Associate Faculty with Ashridge Business School and the NHS Leadership Academy.

Part 1
Sources

1

Supervision: a way of life

Once upon a time, a very strong woodcutter asked for a job with a timber merchant. The pay was really good and so were the working conditions. For those reasons, the woodcutter was determined to do his best.

His boss gave him an axe and showed him where he would work.

The first day, the woodcutter felled 18 trees.

'Congratulations,' the boss said. 'Go on that way!'

Motivated by the boss's words, the woodcutter tried harder the next day, but he could only bring down 15 trees. The third day he tried even harder, but he could only manage 10 trees. Day after day, he finished with fewer trees.

'I must be losing my strength,' the woodcutter thought. He went to the boss and apologised, saying that he could not understand what was going on.

'When was the last time you sharpened your axe?' the boss asked.

'Sharpen?' said the woodcutter. 'I've had no time to sharpen my axe. I've been so busy trying to cut trees.' (Anderson, 2017)

We see supervision as a way of life. As we stand back and find a different perspective on the work we do, we learn skills that can apply to all aspects of our lives. What we have seen in ourselves and others is that, when we are most stuck, we can most grow if we have a space to reflect with another who will both support and challenge us. We would love everyone to have this opportunity, regardless of the work they do. As the story above implies, taking time out can enable us to renew our energy and bring a greater clarity to our work.

In this book we are describing our work as supervisors, supervisees and trainers of supervisors. We share techniques and exercises and also some of the philosophy behind our work. By doing so, we hope to inspire you to say, in the immortal words from the film *When Harry Met Sally*: 'I'll have some of what she's having.'

The idea of taking space to reflect is, for many, still quite radical, although less so now than in the mid-1970s, when we first started this work. Now mindfulness, reflective practice, coaching, counselling, therapy and supervision – all of which to different degrees encourage reflection – have become more established. However, we wonder if that acceptance has come at a price. In any movement, after a period of initiation, charisma and pioneering, there comes an impulse to put the original ideas into some formula. And in doing so, some of the freshness is lost. It also means that a certain orthodoxy can creep in and structures develop to ensure that guidelines and rules are being kept. This is neither bad nor good; it is just how things develop. We want here to share some of the original inspiration that drove our work.

This reflection takes place through a conversation with another or others. Supervision is a very particular kind of conversation but, as in any conversation or relationship, there are factors that can help to make it more easeful and useful, and some that might contribute to one or both parties holding back. We teach different techniques for facilitating the supervisory relationship, but ultimately good relationship goes beyond technique and what emerges is fresh from being in the moment together. As psychologist Sarah Rozenthuler writes in her book *Life-Changing Conversations*: 'True dialogue is, in its best moments, techniqueless' (2012: 6). Our wish is for both supervisor and supervisee to feel free to express themselves and, from the quality of their presence together, make the space for something new and perhaps life-changing to emerge.

We see the book as relevant to all supervisors and supervisees, no matter what their experience. Viktor Frankl (1946/2004) described freedom as the capacity to pause between stimulus and response. We see supervision as a way of familiarising ourselves with that pause, so we can listen at a deep level – listen, in fact, to the spaces between the notes as well as to the notes. In the same way that we practise this in supervision, we can apply this too to other aspects of our lives.

A graduate from our courses told us that the most important thing she had learned was to trust herself. It is what we would want for anyone and goes beyond supervision, into our lives. In describing our courses, which are very largely experiential, our wish is to show how to create some of the conditions for that trusting of self to happen. Since the 1970s, when we started, research, books, courses, models and theories on supervision have mushroomed, and there is a potential pressure for a novice – or even experienced – supervisor to feel they have to know the field; a pressure to try 'to cover the world with leather' rather than 'wear your own sandals'. This does not preclude knowing more about the field, but it reminds us that we take ourselves wherever we go and that this is a process that never ends, however experienced we are. In the following section, we will say a little about the selves we are taking with us.

Therapeutic community background

We met in 1976, at a half-way house for people coming mainly out of psychiatric hospital. It was run as a therapeutic community and was part of an organisation called the Richmond Fellowship, which at the time had 21 such houses all over England and Scotland, mostly for people leaving hospital, but also for recovering drug addicts and alcoholics. The founder, Elly Jansen, was a pioneer. She took the Mental Health Act of 1959, which advocated treating mental illness in the community, and acted on it by setting up these therapeutic communities. The particular house we were helping to run was the senior staff training house, where staff from other houses were sent for training. This included how to introduce a supervision policy in their own houses. So, as well as doing supervision ourselves, we had to have a clear idea of how to teach it to others.

There were four of us, all in our 20s, in the senior staff team. We were responsible for 24 residents and a staff team of 12, if we included trainees from other houses and students on placement. We were able to create processes for running community meetings for up to 40 people, as well as theme groups, therapy groups and work groups (where the residents were taught practical skills in preparation for their re-entry into so-called normal life), learning groups for staff and case-study meetings, and for providing counselling and, of course, supervision. We instinctively knew that we needed to model taking care of ourselves and one of the ways we did this was through individual and group supervision. This taking care of *ourselves* resourced us for the job of providing a safe container in which the residents could heal and learn to take care of *themselves*. In taking responsibility for our own self-care, we modeled the residents taking responsibility for themselves and each other. What we learnt there has stood us in good stead throughout our working lives, and we are immensely grateful to all those who participated in our time there. I (Robin) think that I would probably have burnt out were it not for my regular supervision, and my subsequent work is partly motivated by my wish to give back what I received.

The 1970s was a time of great excitement, therapeutically. We would liaise with other therapeutic movements and bring back the learning to our team. It was a time of anti-psychiatry, the Cassell Hospital, the Henderson Hospital, the Arbours Association, and the Philadelphia Association founded by RD Laing, all run as therapeutic communities. Laing wrote extensively on schizophrenia and suggested that so-called mad people were more sane than supposedly sane people, as they saw through the madness of society. The ideas that floated around were very optimistic – that therapy could be done outside the mental hospitals, in communities, and with specialist crisis intervention teams. Family therapy was taking off, to replace what was seen as outdated one-to-one analysis, and all sorts of new therapies were crossing the Atlantic from the US. It was the beginning of the growth movement and our residents benefitted (or not, as the case may be) from being rebirthed, psychodramatised and Gestalted.

And yet there were gaping holes in what we did. Sexual abuse had not emerged as a likely causative factor in psychiatric problems, and there was one resident who, in retrospect, we think was either consciously or unconsciously trying to tell us about her abuse as we look back and try to decode what at the time we thought of as 'psychotic imagery'. How many others did we miss because of our ignorance? We will never know.

We, with Peter Hawkins, left the Richmond Fellowship in 1979 and went on to form the Centre for Supervision and Team Development, where we were later joined by Peter's wife, Judy Ryde. In about 2008, after 30 years, we two couples went our separate ways, but much of the content of our courses was formed together.

Robin's story

Aged 14, I picked up one of my father's books on psychology and knew immediately I wanted to work in that field. A futile attempt to go into the family business of law was quickly aborted and, at university, I changed courses to read psychology. However, before I joined the Richmond Fellowship in my late 20s, I had two experiences that have shaped all my work.

The first was eating cannabis – eaten because I did not smoke – in Israel, at the age of 21. I went psychotic for a couple of hours and was worried that the police would come and cart me off to hospital or, worse, prison for having this illegal substance. Then I suddenly heard myself say, 'There is no fear. The fear is inside me.' What ensued was complete peace, which lasted for weeks. I saw that, regardless of what was happening externally, fear was much more of an 'inside job' than I had realised. I was at the time in my final year at university and I refused to do a project on psychological measurement, and instead wrote 50 quotes on love, saying that love was the only intervention that made sense to me and it could not be measured. I look back and ask myself how I had the nerve and got away with it. The psychotic experience was, however, very useful in my work with the residents in the therapeutic community as I was able to describe psychosis from my own experience. Later, I overheard two residents in the therapeutic community talking to each other about me, saying, 'He's one of us.' I took this as a huge compliment.

The other experience was of going to India in the search of Truth (a very 1970s thing to do) and finding it (or something, anyway) in a way I did not expect – namely, through an attack of hepatitis. As I lay in hospital in Sri Lanka, my money stolen, no means to contact anyone, with a temperature of 104°, I thought I might die there, alone. I noticed that I had no fear. I woke up again in complete peace and left hospital against the advice of the doctors but feeling an inner strength that I knew would see me through.

I crashed soon after, and realised I was going through what is called a 'spiritual bypass' – that is, avoiding my psychological problems by trying to transcend them with spirituality. So, I went into therapy. From there I found the Richmond Fellowship, luckily (and only just) as a staff member, not a resident.

Since then, numerous experiences have contributed to the courses we run. In the 1980s, I discovered a book called *A Course in Miracles* (Foundation for Inner Peace, 1996), of which a central tenet is that everything comes from love or fear. This echoes the biblical statement in 1 John 4:18: 'Perfect Love casteth out fear.' The lessons in this book have been one of the inspirations for the courses I run on 'Love and Fear in Supervision'.

The other huge influence has been *The Work* of Byron Katie,[1] who suffered extreme problems with depression and paranoia (are psychiatric problems an entry requirement into this work, I wonder?) until one day she awoke and realised that all her thinking had been not true. She developed a line of inquiry, which she teaches all over the world, that asks us to investigate our thinking. You will see her form of Socratic questioning appear particularly in the 'Love and Fear in Supervision' workshop description. Her ideas are quite radical in that they ask us to question absolutely everything. I am Robin, a supervisor, a son, a man, a father – is that true? Don't take anything for granted. In the stripping away of concepts, beliefs and identities, something new and fresh can emerge.

These experiences, and many others, have reinforced my wish to sit outside mainstream thinking. It took me a while to realise that much of mainstream thinking scared me. I saw it as leading to a conformity that could result in mass psychosis, as in Nazi Germany or Rwanda, and I had plenty of my own to cope with, thank you very much. Belonging implied conformity and, for better or worse, I could not take that route, although again I have been humbled to discover that I am far more conforming than I wanted to believe. Nevertheless, some of our work does sit outside the mainstream, and we invite you to be open to it, even when you do not always agree with us, and see if there is anything that could be of use to you.

Finally, a friend once (quite scathingly) remarked. 'If it moves, Robin will supervise it.' I believe that being a supervisor fits my temperament. I have a need to understand situations from different perspectives. For me, supervision creates a space in which we can inquire into human behaviour on many levels: intrapersonal, interpersonal, group, intergroup, organisational and societal. All of these are, I believe, encompassed by a spiritual approach in which we have the opportunity to go past a sense of separateness, past the problems by which we and others are defined, and reach a deeper truth where we recognise our interconnectedness.

Joan's story

I have worked as supervisor for more than 45 years and will probably continue doing it for the rest of my life, in some way or another, as it is where I feel most myself. The Seven-Eyed framework (see Chapter 4), which we developed in the 1980s, reflects in many ways how I perceive life. The place you are looking from

---

1. www.thework.com (accessed 13 September 2019).

influences what you see, and there are many angles from which to look at any person, situation, theory or opinion. The model invites a looking at the whole system within which any relationship or interaction is happening.

I have seen the world systemically as long as I can recall. I remember, at primary school, one boy, Colin, was put in the corner most days for being naughty. I somehow knew that he was getting into trouble for our naughtiness, as well as his own, although I couldn't have put it into words.

To paraphrase the poet David Whyte (2001), we are always standing on the shoulders of our ancestors: He writes: 'Our work is a measure not only of our own lives but of all those who came before us and created the world we inherit' (p92).

And as I write this, and consider my early life and family, I think I am beginning to catch sight of why I am a supervisor.

I was born by Caesarean section and spent my first three weeks of life in hospital, in the nursery, being brought to my mother only for feeding. That was the thinking in those days. I was my mother's first live birth. Previously she had had two miscarriages and her first child, a boy, died an hour after his birth because she had been refused an elective Caesarean (prescribed by her GP) by the hospital, on religious grounds. I was told that, after the death of his son, my father went into the hospital, lifted up the doctor who had refused the Caesarean by his lapels and said, 'Don't you ever treat a woman like that again.' My father died at the age of 32, when I was nearly two and my sister was seven weeks old. I think this precipitated in me a sense of loss, combined with a wish to inquire into meaning. Another important event was my half-brother taking his own life when he was 32. I could not help him to detach from his beliefs.

So, as I look back now, I am sensing a pattern emerging of unexamined core beliefs – religious, medical, patriarchal, familial and societal (I was born 22 days after the end of the Second World War) – coupled with fear, denial and faulty thinking, running our family. Supervision and the role of supervisor have given me permission to examine these core beliefs and go anywhere in the service of my own work and of helping to develop other people's. In my family, work was our survival and also an expression of our creativity, identity and joy. I was born at a time when, because of the war, women could no longer be kept down as second-class citizens; we could no longer be put back in the box, and work was how we were going to stay out of that box, however long it might take.

I see how the time, class and culture I was born into has shaped me and pointed me in certain directions. My siblings and I were the first generation to go to grammar school, and from grammar school the way out into the world was university. I became a social worker. It was the longing for freedom, unavailable to my ancestors, that moved me. I entered social work in the second half of the 1960s, when the humanistic movement was bursting into our world. It was in my first field social work job, in a large mental hospital, that I first experienced reflective, time-to-think supervision on a weekly basis, and found it so essential in terms of what are still its three main foci: management, education and support. I must have breathed it in and seen it as a cornerstone of work-life.

From there, I followed my first husband into residential social work – or, more specifically, a therapeutic community, the Richmond Fellowship. This was a time where there was freedom to rethink ideas, beliefs and perceptions about mental health and mental illness. I stayed there for seven years and the learning was immense. As Robin has described, besides being a therapeutic community, we were the training house for the other residential staff, so we were required to design and deliver programmes for both residents and staff.

At this point I will refer to just one of those learnings. We discovered that, if there was a disturbance around a resident that was causing a problem in the community as a whole, we should not focus on the resident first as the problem. We needed to stop what we were doing, have a staff meeting and look at what we had become unconscious of. When we found that, the resident would usually settle. If this did not happen and we couldn't hold them, we would recognise that it was we who had not grown enough in that area, and we recognised our failure. We hold the same view in relation to the students on our courses. We look to ourselves first, to identify what we might be doing to co-create the block or failure. We will describe our approaches to assessment later in the book. In the therapeutic community, we had to maintain the house physically as well as emotionally, so there were very real boundaries to hold us to account, such as finances, meals, accommodation, the health of our residents and our own, and the consequences if we lost touch with reality.

Writing my story here led me to wonder why I have a job with such an obscure name that is so difficult to describe. About 10 years ago, I was in South Africa with a South African friend, who raised money to support a school for disabled children there. Twice I was asked what I did for a living. The first time I floundered for the words to describe it, saw the blank expression on the face of the person who had asked me, and rapidly changed the subject. The second time I was talking to a man who had been a politician during Apartheid. When he heard what I did, he said, 'I wish I had had some of that when I was a politician.' It seems that part of writing this book is to convey what this man had intuitively grasped – namely, supervision's potential relevance to all walks of life.

Here is my longhand attempt to convey the essence of supervision, taken from *Passionate Supervision* (Wilmot, 2007: 88):

> I am trying to explain the inexplicable. I see supervision as a hologram
> in which each moment contains everything that needs to be embodied,
> felt and known. The different worlds of the client, supervisee, supervisor
> and the outside world are simultaneously mirroring and co-creating
> each other. Supervision offers us the opportunity to become present to
> that moment of awareness, to slow down so that the wound, disturbance
> or disconnection that seems to be breaking everything and us apart is,
> instead, the road back home.

I have tried to trace some of the influences on my choice to make supervision part of my life's work. Of necessity, the description is incomplete. Over the years, my thinking has expanded, but I believe that presence, a wish to enquire, seeing a situation from many perspectives, helping people connect with their passion for work and being able to have good conversations are the essence of supervision, and this is why my enthusiasm is as strong now as it was 45 years ago.

Outline of the book

In the next chapter we outline 23 principles that form the basis of our work. In writing this book, we realised how much the courses have been informed by our life experiences and belief systems. Our wish is to make these explicit and, in doing so, help you, the reader, understand something of the foundations of our courses.

In Part 2 we describe five of the courses that we have been running, mostly through the Centre for Supervision and Team Development (CSTD) since 1979. Over the years, we have added to and changed them to fit our current thinking, and no doubt will continue to do so. They are, for the most part, described as if we were talking to the group, and you might like to do some of the exercises with a partner or partners. As well as describing the exercises, we have included some theory, philosophy and experience, to share some of the thinking behind them. Some of this can also be found in other books Robin has co-written and edited.[2] However, how it is presented here, through the medium of participation in a supervision course, is, as far as we know, new.

We start with a description of our first course, which we call our Core Course. It is built round the acronym CLEAR, which stands for Contracting, Listening, Exploring, Action and Review. In many ways, the course is about undoing, realising how much baggage we carry into supervision and helping us to let go of what might no longer serve, so that we can approach the work freshly, with what in Zen is called a 'beginner's mind'.

The next course we describe is based on the Seven-Eyed Model, which grew out of our work at the Richmond Fellowship. This is a map of the supervision process, looking at client, supervisee and supervisor and the system in which all are involved. We think this model has stood the test of time because it is, in fact, more of a map than a model, and as such it can be used by supervisors of any theoretical orientation. Over the years, we have added exercises, just as we might add details to a map, but the territory has remained the same. A particular delight for us was when a colleague, Joseph Wilmot, found himself teaching a group of IT workers who had been sent on a one-day supervision course. They thought of supervision as irrelevant to their work. However, he managed to get them very excited about it by framing the organisation's IT system as their 'client'

---

2. See *Supervision in the Helping Professions* (Hawkins & Shohet, 2012), *Passionate Supervision* (Shohet, 2007), *Supervision as Transformation* (Shohet, 2011) and *Clinical Supervision in the Medical Profession* (Owen & Shohet, 2012).

and helping them to see how this 'client' was seen by others and how they could help integrate the 'client' more into their organisation (see Resources, p209).

The Group Supervision Course developed in part out of a supervision group for trainees that Robin ran back in 1978. He just assumed that the way to work was with the group's here-and-now responses to the material that was being presented by the supervisee. Over the years, we have expanded the range of skills and interventions, but the here-and-now responses of the group remain the foundation on which the other techniques are built. We include material on group dynamics, highlighted by exploring difficult situations in supervision groups. We emphasise the importance of safety in group supervision – we have found that, when there is a clear contract and structure, the wisdom inherent in the group is free to emerge. In the final day of the group course, we expand the focus to look at supervision in organisations.

The Advanced Course is the final three days of the 12-day training and is run as a learning community where some of the sessions are run by the students. Much of the content of the first two days of this course involves the use of video and a technique called Interpersonal Process Recall (IPR), and in delivering it we continually learn new ways of deepening the experience for us and our students. We describe the source of this work and why we make it such a central feature of the course.

After students have completed the four courses, delivered 50 hours of supervision and received 10 hours of supervision on their supervision, they arrange with us the first of two individual tutorials to embark on their certificate process. In the first tutorial, they review the training and their supervision practice, and we go through together the inquiry form described in Chapter 7. They will complete this with a supervisor, two supervisees and a peer. In the second tutorial, they share the results of these conversations. We have found that the conversations they have had almost invariably deepen their relationships with all four people.

The last workshop described, 'Love and Fear in Supervision' (Chapter 8), is usually a one-day course and contains many of the exercises we have developed over the years. It implicitly outlines a philosophy of relationships that go well beyond supervision. Robin has described above a little of how he came to his ideas about love and fear, and on this course we look at how fear can creep into the supervisory relationship, overtly or quite subtly. By shining the light of awareness on some of the fears, course participants – supervisors and supervisees – find themselves more willing to take risks with each other, thereby strengthening their relationship, which, as we have said, we believe forms the core of our work.

Next, Chapter 9, 'The Beast from the East', describes a bespoke course where the same students did all four modules together. There were times when we thought the course would implode. This chapter mostly comprises accounts written by the students on the course, and is included here as an example of how failure, which we would consciously seek to avoid at all costs, can lead to transformation.

We have labeled the final, concluding chapter in this section (and the book) 'Beyond otherness', to suggest that, if we go beyond individuality and recognise our interconnectedness, this will lead us naturally into relationship and community. As such, the idea of going beyond separation can act as a powerful resource in a fragmented world. We have put this idea into practice by setting up the Interdependent Supervisors Network, as a community of supervisors. We end with a quote from one of the founders of humanistic psychology in Britain, John Rowan, which reminds us of the spiritual potential in supervision.

Finally, this brings us to why we have decided to write this book. To put it bluntly, we would like everyone, no matter what their work, to have a space to reflect. As Carroll (2011: 19) writes:

> Reflection is the ability to examine, to observe, to look at, to review, to evaluate, to interrogate, to assess, to question and to own our own thinking.

As the story about the woodcutter shows, on efficiency grounds alone, it works. But we believe a space to reflect can also reduce burnout and restore joy and creativity to our work, which occupies so much of all our time. So, we would like to be part of spreading the idea as widely as possible.

If we see part of the work of supervision as a way of helping the supervisee be present with their client, and in their work generally, then we give ourselves permission to go wherever we and the supervisee might think is relevant to achieve this aim. We particularly focus on how our core beliefs can stop us being present, and as such interfere with our work. Our focus is to examine the thinking and emotional ground behind behaviour and choices.

So, besides offering some practical exercises, we wish to see people giving themselves freedom in their work. This may mean uncovering some of the ways that we restrict ourselves, whatever the outside circumstances. Many of the beliefs that we hold have been swallowed unconsciously and limit us more than perhaps we realise. By bringing them into consciousness, we can free ourselves and, therefore, potentially, our supervisees and clients. For this reason, we say that supervision is more than just supervision; it is a way of enquiry that has relevance to all aspects of our lives. Bill Shankley, the late manager of Liverpool Football Club, was asked if he thought football was a matter of life and death. He replied: 'It's more important than that.' We feel the same about supervision.

In these descriptions of our work from the last 40 years and more, we hope some of our sheer delight in supervising and training supervisors comes through. We have been fortunate in that, by and large, we were free to forge our own path around supervision, when it was still in its infancy. Now that the field has 'grown up', we want to transmit some of that original sense of discovery and excitement, and share why, even after all these years, we still want to go on supervising and teaching. We say that we would like to live more often as we find ourselves being in supervision: non-judgemental, curious and playful. We teach what we need to learn.

References

Anderson B (2017). *Sharpening your axe: a leadership lesson.* [Online.] NetGain Technologies; 28 August. www.netgainit.com/sharpen-your-axe (accessed 22 November 2019).

Carroll M (2011). Supervision: a journey of lifelong learning. In: Shohet R (ed) (2011). *Supervision as Transformation: a passion for learning.* London: Jessica Kingsley (pp14–28).

Foundation for Inner Peace (1996). *A Course in Miracles.* New York, NY: Viking Penguin.

Frankl V (1946/2004). *Man's Search for Meaning.* London: Rider.

Hawkins P, Shohet R (2012). *Supervision in the Helping Professions* (4th ed). Maidenhead: Open University Press.

Owen D, Shohet R (eds) (2012). *Clinical Supervision in the Medical Profession.* Maidenhead: Open University Press.

Rozenthuler S (2012). *Life-Changing Conversations.* London: Watkins.

Whyte D (2001). *Crossing the Unknown Sea: work as a pilgrimage of identity.* New York, NY: Riverhead.

Wilmot J (2007). *The Supervisory Relationship: a life-long calling.* In: Shohet R (ed). *Passionate Supervision.* London: Jessica Kingsley (pp88–110).

Core propositions and principles

In Chapter 1, we described how we came to supervision and our belief that supervision is relevant to anyone, whatever their work, and also that many of the lessons we can learn from supervision are relevant to life. In this chapter, we describe some of the principles that have informed our work. Often these are implicit in our teaching; here, we are aiming to be more explicit. While many of the principles are self-evident, some are jumping-off points for a deeper dialogue. There may be others that are important to you that we have not included. This will always be work in progress for all of us.

1. Know yourself

Our starting point for this chapter is that we bring our life experiences and belief systems into everything we do. Obviously, this includes our work as supervisors. Our belief is that the more we are aware of our life experiences and how they have shaped us, the less likely we are to act them out unconsciously, and the more we are able to use them creatively. Both of us have described in the introduction some of our formative influences. However, we know that, however much we try to look at our early influences, we will still have blind spots. Part of the role of supervision is to uncover these blind spots. They are personal and also cultural. As a rule of thumb, if something is causing us difficulty, it may be due to a blind spot or a core belief of which we might have been unaware.

An example of this comes from our work in the Richmond Fellowship therapeutic community. We were discussing a resident whose behaviour we all found difficult. We slowed ourselves down and, to our surprise, realised we each found him difficult in a different way. This alerted us to how much we were projecting on to him. We learnt to question each other about anyone with whom we were having problems, such as, 'Does this resident remind you of anyone?' or, 'Can you think of a time when you have felt similar feelings?' or, 'How are you like them?'

Here is an example from private practice.

> Mary was a very caring therapist who held her boundaries. Yet, when she
> worked with Jack, she seemed to lose herself, even to the point of allowing
> him to telephone between sessions, which she had never done with any
> other client. She was uneasy about this but felt she could not help herself.
> The simple question, 'Does he remind you of anyone?' was enough to take
> her out of her trance and see how much the client reminded her of her
> father. She was the only person in her family who could manage him; that
> was her role. She could not believe she had not seen the connection for
> herself, but it is hard, if not impossible, by definition, to see our own blind
> spots. It is like expecting to see the back of our heads. This brings us to core
> beliefs, which can also be very hidden, posing as self-evident truths.

In their book *How Can I Help?*, Ram Dass and Paul Gorman write (1985: 191):

> Without minimizing the external demands of helping others, it seems fair
> to say that some of the factors that wear us down, we have brought with us
> at the outset.

2. Examine your core beliefs

Part of the function of supervision is to unearth some of the beliefs that might be
affecting us in ways that do not serve us. Many of our core beliefs were probably
made as a survival mechanism when we were young, and are taken as truths. A
core belief might be, 'I have to manage everything myself' or, 'I am on my own
in life' or, 'People will let you down in the end.' These beliefs may be operating
below the level of consciousness or seen as self-evident truths, and obviously
they will affect all relationships, not just supervisory ones. We see supervision as
an opportunity to investigate some of them, both for the supervisees and their
clients, and to see how much they might be influencing us in unhelpful ways.

> Courtney came to supervision exasperated with his client. What was
> bothering him most was that the client was lying about his drinking.
> Without condoning the client, the supervisor spotted that the degree of
> feeling could point to a core belief. In this instance, the core belief was that
> people should not lie. The supervisor asked if Courtney had a belief that
> people should not lie. Courtney said that was obvious, and the supervisor
> asked him if he had ever lied, adding that he knew he (the supervisor) had
> lied and doubted if there was anyone on the planet who had not. Courtney
> smiled and saw that he was asking something of his client that he could
> not do himself. The supervisor said that it might still be appropriate to
> challenge the client, but it would be done from a place of empathy rather
> than judgement.

As we have mentioned above, any difficulty with anyone or anything can point to a core belief. We all have them, but bringing them to consciousness can help to free us.

3. Use inquiry to spot and challenge biases

Inquiry can support us to peel back the defences we all maintain, often with the 'help' of our core beliefs. To challenge these beliefs, we ask such questions as, 'Is it true?' and 'Can you really know that?' We are not asking people to change their beliefs; we are asking them to inquire into the assumptions that can separate us from others who have different assumptions. We have found that core beliefs have often been formed as a survival technique at a time when we felt helpless. Formed initially to protect us, they become part of our identity and can alienate us from people who have transgressed one of our 'rules' – as we saw in the case of Courtney above. As supervisors, we listen carefully to the presentation of a case. We listen to generalisations, diagnoses and judgements and see if we can help the supervisee go behind them.

> On a supervision training, a member of the group presented a boundary break by her supervisor. The group were visibly shocked and supported the presenter in condemning her now ex-supervisor. The trainer sat back and waited, and then offered a possible explanation of what might have been happening. 'It seems that the group is very much on your side. I wonder if there are other ways of looking at this?' The mood in the group changed as they realised that they had taken the so-called facts of the case at face value. The trainer challenged the presenter with, 'It seems you want support in looking at this from your point of view. The need to be right seems part of the human condition, but my experience is that things are not that simple. I think it might be more useful to you and to all of us if, in any difficult situation, we concentrated on our own contribution.' The presenter was able to own that she had never felt comfortable with this supervisor and that she had used the supervisor's behaviour to get out of the relationship. She had felt dishonest, so was seeking support from the group by placing the supervisor in the wrong, rather than admit she didn't have the courage to challenge her.

What we have noticed in supervision and in many aspects of our work – and, indeed, our lives – is how much the other person is inviting us to take sides, and how important it is not to collude with that. (Gossip often provides that function of making the other look wrong.) In our descriptions of the courses in the chapters that follow, we show in more detail how we use inquiry. We have mentioned the need to be right and there is a quote from the Sufi poet Rumi (2004) that supports us in the pursuit of inquiry:

> Out beyond our ideas of rightdoing and wrongdoing, there is a field. I will
> meet you there.

4. 'Enter a relationship without memory, desire or understanding'

This is a quote from Wilfred Bion (1967). What we take this to mean is that, without memory, we see the person as they are now, not blinded by our history of similar relationships or the history we have shared, as they are bound to be different in some way, however subtle. Heraclitus, a Greek philosopher born in 544 BCE, said, 'No man ever steps in the same river twice for it's not the same river and he's not the same man.' An exercise for the supervisee is to share previous experiences of supervision. If these experiences were not good, this could affect their approach to the current relationship, perhaps making them too guarded. If good, they might compare their present supervisor unfavourably with previous ones. Of course, it is very difficult to enter a relationship without memory, but asking this of ourselves encourages us to be more present to what is. A teacher colleague was talking about this to us and described the surprise of one of her pupils, who had behaved in a disruptive way the day before, when she was pleased to see him the next day. His comment to her was, 'You come in fresh each day, Miss.' In other words, she was not holding on to what had happened between them the previous day.

Entering a relationship without desire describes how we often bring to a relationship our expectations that the other person will change. We think this is true of many relationships, not just supervisory ones. One of the questions we ask a supervisee when they are stuck is to name three ways in which they would like their client to be different.

> A trainee supervisor complained that his client wasn't changing. The supervisor realised that the supervisee was not actually interested in the client, but in their changing, because it would show what a good therapist he was. She asked him to just observe his client and then, in the next supervision session, asked what he had observed. All he could report was that he observed that the client was not changing. She repeated the instruction and, in the next supervision, again asked what he had observed. He said simply, 'Her hands.' And this was the beginning of a shift from a desire or investment for the client to change to simple observation. (Shainberg, 1983)

Entering a relationship without understanding relates to recognising how little we in fact do know. It seems most of us feel a need to know. Enabling the supervisee (and us) to stay in a place of not knowing is uncomfortable, as the world seems to demand answers – but, if we don't, it can lead to a situation where, as Peter Senge (2006) wrote, 'Today's problems are a result of yesterday's solutions.' When we don't fall for the illusion of knowing, we are less ready to leap to a quick fix or jump in with a strong opinion.

> There is a very ancient Chinese Taoist story about a farmer in a poor country village, where he was considered very well to do, because he owned a horse that he used for ploughing and for transportation. One day his horse ran away. All his neighbours exclaimed how terrible this was, but the farmer simply said, 'Maybe.'
>
> A few days later, the horse returned and brought two wild horses with it. The neighbours all rejoiced at his good fortune, but the farmer just said, 'Maybe.'
>
> The next day, when the farmer's son tried to ride one of the wild horses, the horse threw him and he broke his leg. The neighbours all offered their sympathy for his misfortune, but the farmer again said, 'Maybe.'
>
> The next week, conscription officers came to the village to take the young men for the army. They rejected the farmer's son because of his broken leg. When the neighbours told him how lucky he was, the farmer replied, 'Maybe.' And so on.

There is also a temptation to fall back on rules that seem to offer a certain sense of safety. We like this quote from Anthony de Mello (1985: 74): 'Obedience keeps the rules. Love knows when to break them.'

Barry Mason (2015) has written a paper called 'Towards Positions of Safe Uncertainty'. Unsafe uncertainty throws us into panic and survival mode. With certainty, we are closed to new ideas and sure we are right. This can very easily lead to feeling threatened when our beliefs are questioned. Safe uncertainty provides the space for questioning to happen. Supervisor and supervisee enter a world where new possibilities can emerge. Zen Buddhists talk about being willing to have a beginner's mind – to see with fresh eyes. There are times when what we think we know can get in the way. It seems as if the human mind demands explanations and is constantly searching for them, and when we believe we have found them, we can cling to the feeling of security, overlooking or blocking out anything that will unsettle us.

> Explanation sets the need for further inquiry aside… It does not invite us to rethink what we thought we knew. (Carse, 1986: 125)

5. Use the here and now

As trainers we find ourselves in a paradoxical situation (see principle 7 below). We offer techniques, theories, maps and models but, we remind people of the importance of entering the here and now, which is beyond technique. A technique to enter the here and now would be an oxymoron because we would not be in the here and now if we were to deliberately call upon it. However, we can encourage people to lose their fear of not knowing, of being stuck; we can emphasise the value of waiting, of trusting the moment and the relationship. We see this in drama or jazz improvisation, where the need to control is surrendered. In improvisation, one of the necessary elements is sensitivity to the moment and to the other person. Pre-planning will tend to ruin the scene. You can find a more detailed discussion about how improvisation can be used in supervision in the Resources section at the end of the book (see p226). We will give plenty of examples of using the here and now in supervision in the Courses section that follows, but here are three examples – one from therapy, one from training and one from supervision .

A client came from 200 miles away to see a therapist who had been highly recommended. The therapist listened and said nothing. After a few minutes, the client asked for a response. It did not seem to be what was being asked for, but the therapist trusted himself enough to respond simply with, 'I have nothing to say.' Whereupon the client exploded, saying that he had made huge sacrifices to come. The therapist said, 'Now you are angry, I feel engaged. I wonder what that means to you.' The client then said he had been very angry because he did not feel he needed therapy and had been pushed by friends to come. The therapist used his here-and-now experience, even though it did not initially make much sense.

Joan was asked part-way through a training, 'How do you create safety in supervision?' Initially, she was going to offer some theory, but instead she asked, 'How are we doing it now?' The members of the group began to be conscious of how they were managing safety now, particularly focusing on cues in their body that they had not consciously noticed, and began to articulate them. The attention to the here and now demonstrated that safety is a process rather than a state of being.

Joan was working with a client, with whom she had a good working relationship, who was complaining about unfair practices in her workplace that affected her ability to contribute as much as she could and wanted to. She then listed some of them. They all seemed very valid and Joan was about to explore with her how she could address them, but instead asked, 'Is there anything unfair happening here?' The client sat up in her chair and said vigorously, 'Oh yes! You know all about me and I know nothing about you.' This led to a lively exploration of what was in the room in the here-and-now relationship, which also resourced the client, in a more immediate and embodied way, to address the issue in her workplace. It was only something that Joan had learnt from psychoanalysis – that whatever the client is talking about outside the room is most likely to be in the room – that led her to make the intervention. There was nothing apparent to Joan that would have suggested the issue was also in the room.

6. Everything can be reframed

Reframing helps us to move to new possibilities. It stops us getting into over-simple cause-and-effect ways of looking at a situation and increases our repertoire of interventions as we look from different perspectives and encourage the supervisee to do likewise. So, the classic dictum of mistakes being opportunities would be an example of reframing. Once the reframe has happened, the supervisee is able to give themselves new options.

> A very effective reframe occurred when Robin was seeing a client who professed herself to be in love with him. She would bring presents and confessed to driving past the house from time to time. Robin asked Joan for some supervision as he felt quite invaded. When he told her the details, Joan said, 'What a generous woman. She declares herself and makes herself vulnerable.' Robin was very touched by Joan's genuine appreciation and her reframe of the client's behaviour. That simple reframe completely changed his approach to the client as he saw that Joan's version was so much kinder than his version and just as true, if not truer.

> Joan was running a one-off group supervision in a school. She started the group by inviting each person to share their name and what they hoped to get from the group. Half-way round, a teaching assistant said she didn't want to be there; it was a waste of time. Joan's response was to say, 'It sounds like it is really important to you not to waste time.' The woman's response was a heartfelt, 'Oh yes,' and she then proceeded to talk about the seven-year-old boy she felt she should have been with, in the classroom, instead of the group supervision she had been required to attend.

7. Encourage paradoxical thinking

The idea that something can be true and not true at the same time allows for ambiguity, or not-knowing. In the words of Lao Tzu, the ancient Chinese philosopher: 'Those who speak do not know. Those who know do not speak.'

Paradox helps us to move beyond either/or to a place of both/and. When we are stressed, we want solutions to move us beyond our anxiety – we want the fix. Paradox enables us to see things from many perspectives. Robin's client (above) is both invasive *and* generous. Paradoxical thinking also invites humour as we simultaneously take ourselves seriously and laugh at ourselves. It can help us move beyond the mind that is attached to duality – black or white, right or wrong. In paradox, we try to move beyond the simplistic and, in the famous Zen saying, contemplate the sound of one hand clapping.

A technique I (Robin) often use in training is to challenge a group by saying, 'You are all frauds. And I obviously include myself.' Because I can say this without judgement, recognising my own talent for self-deception, there is usually relief and people share the different ways in which they have been pretending. Here we have the paradox that owning the fraud can make us genuine. I love paradox because with it we can trick the mind and open up to new ways of looking. It offers a reframe to a mind that thinks in terms of either/or.

8. Everything is data

A friend said, 'Don't use the word data. For some of us, particularly in the NHS, it has bad connotations – collecting data at the expense of relating.' However, we are using it differently and in some ways this expression sums up in three words much of what we have been saying so far. What we mean by this phrase is that, once we enter the supervision space, everything that happens is there to be understood and appreciated. Everything is material for us to question and work on. If, for example, a mobile phone goes off, we notice the impact it has on us and the other, rather than see it as just an interruption. If a supervisee makes a supposedly bad intervention, we look at what was going on at the time rather than judging. We are curious about everything that happens and encourage the supervisee also to be curious. As you can imagine, this affects our approach to supposed mistakes. It gives us an opportunity to reframe what is happening, and this ability to reframe, as we have suggested above, is a core skill. The idea that everything is data also encourages witness consciousness – it encourages us to stand back and look rather than simply react.

> A supervisee brought to supervision a client who persistently arrived late. She was very angry with her client and felt she was being tested. She reported that this phrase, 'Everything is data,' came into her head, much to her annoyance as she thought that the expression was a bit trite. However, she noticed a softening in herself, and she began to observe the client and her own reactions more carefully. Finally, she was able to say to her client, 'I notice when you are late, I have a mixture of reactions. I have felt annoyed, messed around. I have felt as if I am being invited into the role of Critical Parent (Berne, 1986/61). But actually, if I observe my reactions more carefully, I notice I feel sad.' Whereupon the client burst into tears and said that was how she felt at the school gates, when her mother was always the last to collect her. A new depth came into their relationship.

> A supervisee insisted on having her mobile phone switched on during supervision. Holding the idea of 'everything as data', rather than asking her to turn it off, the supervisor wondered if she would be willing to explore what that might mean. When she agreed, he wondered if she needed to be needed. She realised this was true, and spontaneously switched her phone off.

9. Our feelings can be a very important resource

Building on the example above, where the supervisee felt messed around but took the time to go deeper to notice her sadness, we can use our feelings to understand more of our clients' and supervisees' experiences. We might initially not understand what is happening. We just feel the impact.

During our training, we suggest to trainee supervisors that it is essential that they be willing to feel useless at times. Their supervisees will feel like that, and unless the supervisors are willing to feel those feelings, they are too removed from the clients' and supervisees' experiences. Of course, if they feel like that a lot of the time, then there is a real possibility of burn-out. But feeling useless, for example, is a very important piece of data. Robin will go further into this in Chapter 9, 'The Beast from the East'.

A psychoanalytic concept called projective identification (it is quite simple, despite its name) can help with understanding feelings that seem confusing. It posits that what we cannot integrate in ourselves, we attempt to make others feel. It is a very early form of preverbal communication. A baby will communicate its distress so that the mother will pay attention and will feel compelled to act on her feelings. The baby somehow transmits the feeling of distress into the parental figure. (Obviously this is not done consciously – it is an evolutionary survival behaviour.) So, if we take fear as an example, the theory of projective identification will suggest that those who cannot/will not feel fear seek to make others feel it. We instinctively know bullies are cowards, making others feel their fear. Understanding the dynamics of projective identification can help us understand others better, as we register their impact on us (see Shohet, 2018). Relating this to supervision, what the client cannot feel, he or she puts into the supervisee, and what the supervisee cannot process or integrate, they put into the supervisor. The supervisor's job is to notice this as data and find a way of using it for the benefit of the supervisee and client. And the more self-knowledge the supervisor has, the more capacity they have to use themselves as a resource. Feelings also bring us into the here and now.

10. Intent and impact are easily confused

Building on the discussion about the impact someone might have on us, a very useful distinction that can help to clear up misunderstandings in all areas of life is to differentiate between intent and impact. If I ask how you are, my conscious intention is to make contact. The impact on you might be to feel invaded, so you reply, 'Mind your own business,' and I feel hurt and misunderstood. If both parties are willing to explore, they might discover their unconscious intents and core beliefs. Breakdown of relationships of any kind can sometimes be understood by looking at the intention of communications and its impact and seeing if they are out of sync.

> A new supervisee came to a fairly recently qualified supervisor whose own supervisor had let him find his own answers. The supervisor really liked this approach and assumed his new supervisee would too. However, things were not going well; the supervisee was obviously not feeling he was getting what he wanted. It took a bit of unpacking, but it turned out that the supervisor thought he was giving space for the supervisee to find his own way, and the supervisee felt that the supervisor was withholding and was not really interested in him or his work.

11. Distinguish between content and process

Very often a supervisee will want to give us a lot of detail about the case, the supposed facts. There are several reasons why we should interrupt this way of presenting. The facts may be selective, often just focusing on pathology and not including strengths. They may have unconscious and cultural bias. The supervisee is in control and reporting the known, whereas in supervision the aim is to help them see the client with fresh eyes. By moving the focus from content to process, the supervisor will notice the impact that the supervisee is having on them in the here and now. They might notice, for example, that they feel distanced by the over-reporting and wonder what this could mean. They are moving from content – the story – to process the impact in the here and now.

In group supervision especially, we suggest that the group regularly feeds back the impact of the case that the supervisee is bringing. When supervising, we state very clearly that we will interrupt the content and look at the impact on the group, and we invite our trainees to do the same.

> A supervisee in group supervision we ran together wanted to tell us the whole story – to give us the facts so we got a fuller picture. It was quite difficult to interrupt him, but even when we did, and we fed back the impact he was having on us, he ignored our feedback and continued his narration. Finally, the group leader wondered aloud about the process – it seems, she said, as if the supervisee is insisting on being in control and is not open to feedback, and she wondered if this was how the client was. The supervisee paused and said that was exactly right; with this client, he could not get a word in edgeways. We thus moved from content to process. The supervisee became more open to the feedback and we tentatively suggested that the client was frightened of being misunderstood so felt they had to give the whole picture. This resonated with the supervisee, who agreed that he had this fear too.

12. Be willing to look at the shadow side of everything (including yourself)

The 'shadow' is a concept introduced by Carl Jung, founder of analytic psychology. We all have blind spots and parts of ourselves that we want to disown. Usually these are more unpleasant traits, like envy, greed or hatred. This leads us to develop a mask in order to present ourselves in the best possible light and keep some of our more undesirable qualities hidden beneath its surface. This in turn leads us to project the disowned parts of ourselves onto others. An interesting exercise is to think of someone you do not like, for whatever reason, and put down three of the qualities that you least like, and then own them as your own.

Above, we looked at intent and impact and how that can lead us to shadow, to the parts of ourselves that we prefer to keep hidden from others (and ourselves). The impact I have on others (especially those I don't like or don't like me) may tell me more about myself than it says about my friends. I might think, for example, that I am helpful, but when my offers of help are refused or resented, that might tell me that I have different motives (intentions) than I realised. By definition, we cannot see the back of our head, which others can see. The so-called helping professions have their shadows, and an excellent book on this topic is *Power in the Helping Professions* (Guggenbuhl-Graig, 1971). Here is a quote from it:

> No one can act out of exclusively pure motives. The greater the contamination by dark motives, the more the case worker clings to his alleged objectivity. (pp9–10)

The book is a challenging read, as the author looks at the shadow side of the teaching, social work, medical and psychotherapy professions. In *Supervision in the Helping Professions* (Hawkins & Shohet, 2012), we included a chapter on 'Why am I a Helper?' to describe some of these common shadow motivations, like patterns of rescuing learnt from childhood, a need to feel useful, an urge to help people who are disadvantaged because it makes us feel OK about ourselves, and having a mission to save the world.

> A placement supervisor, Jane, was furious with her supervisee. 'I have gone out of my way to make her placement easy for her, been available for her whenever I could, and her feedback to her college is that I was not at all helpful,' she told her supervision supervisor. The supervisor said she could understand Jane's feelings, but perhaps Jane was not really giving her time and energy but simply making a psychological contract in which she offered help in order to get the reward of appreciation. (A psychological contract is a set of promises or expectations that, unlike formal contracts, are usually tacit and implicit.) This came as a shock to Jane, who was initially indignant but then saw how much she wanted to be liked and appreciated – that her 'help' had a shadow side.

13. Nothing is just personal

This is basically a systemic worldview. It recognises that we are all connected and affect each other and, therefore, through projective identification, we may carry feelings for others. In a family, for example, the supposed difficult child might be reflecting a problem in the marriage or the family generally. In her introduction, Joan mentions Colin, the boy in her nursery school who was taking the punishment for the so-called naughtiness of the whole class. For many of us, because of the current zeitgeist, it is quite a stretch to move from an individualistic worldview to a systemic one. Taken at a societal level, psychiatric patients might be thought of as taking on all our madness that we do not want to look at (see Szasz, 1961, 1970; Laing & Esterson, 1964). This viewpoint takes into account context and relationship and gives them more importance than they are accorded in a simple, individual perspective. It reduces the likelihood of blame because it asks us to search for a deeper understanding of all the contributing factors in the field. And it moves us towards the idea of community, which recognises that we all affect each other and in some way are responsive to each other and responsible for each other. We cannot *not* be in relationship with each other.

> A supervisor had been asked to work with a team that was full of conflict. The presenting issue was the conflict between two members of staff, which had left the rest of the staff feeling helpless and resentful. The supervisor listened and then turned to these two individuals and told them how generous they were. 'There is obviously a lot of anger in the team that can be hidden because you are willing to carry it for the rest of the team,' she said. Whereupon the two members said to their colleagues: 'That makes sense. It is almost as if we are being set up to carry your issues. You are pretending we are the problem and we have bought into it.' Wider, organisational issues that had been masked by the focus on the conflict between the two members within the team now surfaced. Here, the supervisor used a combination of reframing and moving from what looked like an inter-personal issue to looking at the wider system, which was initially the team, and subsequently the whole organisation.

> In another piece of work with a different organisation, the supervisor was shocked by how vicious colleagues were to each other, especially to the team leader. He went to his supervisor and said: 'I can't work with these people. I feel physically sick to watch them attack each other like that.' His supervisor listened and said, 'People don't want to be like that. I think they might be carrying something for the organisation.' This rang true. They were the student counsellor team and were being unconsciously used by the organisation as its emotional dustbin while it went through a very difficult time. This insight seemed to have the effect of helping them reflect and not identify with and absorb the rage and helplessness that was in the wider system. They no longer needed to act out the feelings on each other and became a valued resource for the organisation.

14. Slower can be faster and more effective

If we rush to a solution because of a need for a quick fix, then we will not have taken the time to look at the whole system. Parts of the system that have been neglected have the potential to sabotage. Action at all costs is replacing thoughtful assessment of the whole picture. The job of the supervisor might be, among other things, not to collude with that picture, but to slow things down.

> A social worker was threatened with violence by an angry father because the social worker, as the father saw it, was threatening to take his son into care. The supervisor did not jump straight into action but took time to look at the case from many different perspectives and encouraged the supervisee to do the same. This led to the social worker seeing the place of the father in the family system. Their seeing the situation from the father's perspective enabled the situation to be diffused. The father was included in the decision-making, instead of being avoided and his wishes overruled.

15. If anything appears to go wrong, there may be some unacknowledged fear in the system

The issue of fear – acknowledged and unacknowledged – will be explored more in Chapter 8, 'Love and Fear in Supervision'. Briefly here, we have found that anger, blame, criticism and judgement can be traced back to fear, and uncovering this can help to move the situation and relationship on. I (Robin) was once asked by a lawyer to describe supervision, and I said: 'It's about helping to uncover the fear in a system.' This helped him reframe the difficulties he was having in his organisation. Part of our work is helping people recognise how similar our fears are, despite appearances. We believe it is not the fear itself that creates the problem but the failure to recognise it and inability to share it, which is also culturally reinforced.

> I (Robin) was once asked to do a supervision training day for psychologists in the NHS. I thought the day had gone well until one of the group commented, 'You know, we won't be able to use any of this in our work. It's far too risky.' I saw that I had fallen into a common trap in training, of giving a good experience on the day but not paying enough attention to how participants will carry the learning over into their day-to-day practice. It turned out that many participants felt that their jobs could be at risk because of cuts and were intent on keeping their heads down. I apologised to the group and said I had not paid enough attention to the cultural forces in the system.
>
> Sometime later I was asked to work with a team that was going to have to lose two staff members because of cuts. I started the day with: 'I take it as a given that you are all scared. You don't know whose job will go so you are very available to being split, not trusting each other and being competitive

and secretive. I could look at you as a team that is not working well, or a team that is dominated by survival issues. I prefer the latter and so I want to hear from each person what strategies you use when you are severely stressed. For example, do you switch off, gossip, drink, overwork, blame?' Gradually, each person shared their survival strategies, and this enabled them all to see how the others behaved – hitherto seen as dysfunctional – in a new light. Another outcome was that they all agreed to take a pay cut if it meant that no posts would be lost. They had moved from an isolated fear position to thinking collectively.

Making it safe to share fear is, we believe, an important part of any training or groupwork. It is also probably the main reason for unresolved conflict of all kinds. Our experience is that, once fear is named and normalised (ie. we all feel it), then relationships – whether they be one-to-one, group or organisational – can move onto a deeper, more intimate footing.

16. We can all feel exposed in supervision – both supervisor and supervisee

What we bring to supervision are situations where we are stuck or uncertain. It is easy for the supervisor to forget how exposed the supervisee might feel. The supervisor may focus on their wish to be helpful and forget that the very act of supervision can raise authority issues from childhood. They might see the supervisee as resistant – and we think it is important to be able to reframe resistance (see principle 17 below). In Chapter 3, 'The Core Course', Joan writes about vulnerability in any learning situation. Many of us have to some extent been traumatised by our education system, and perhaps shamed or made to feel inadequate, and can regress into our child behaviour when learning as adults.

It is also easy to forget that the supervisor can feel vulnerable too. In a managerial situation, they could be squeezed between the demands of the organisation and the needs of the supervisee and are having to implement policies they might not fully agree with. On our training courses, we have seen how gossip can lead trainees to choose particular supervisors and not others. Supervisors can also be held accountable for their supervisee's work. All these factors make it very important that supervisors themselves are in supervision.

17. Honour resistance

A useful starting point here might be to say there are no resistant supervisees. Of course, there are supervisees who appear to behave in a resistant manner. However, resistance can be reframed in many ways, starting with looking at ourselves as supervisors/trainers, rather than focusing on the other person, whether they are supervisee or client. Here are some questions that can be used as a form of self-supervision (for more on this, see Breene (2011) and Shohet (2012):

- What have I not understood about this person and their situation?
- Have I underestimated the power differential between us?
- What parts of the system have we not taken into account that either of us might be carrying?
- Is the supervisee mirroring or acting out resistance in their client or in the system?
- Has the supervisor a dual role – like managerial or assessor – and how might that be affecting them?
- Is it safe to talk about difference, whether it be race, gender, class or any other?
- Am I judging them and what does that say about me?
- Am I similar to them? How?
- Might they be frightened, and if so, can I come alongside that?
- Might I be frightened?
- How can I reframe their behaviour?
- Is their apparent resistance honouring their strongly held beliefs (like the example Joan gave about it being important to make good use of time)?
- What haven't I appreciated about them?
- How is their resistance a form of supervision to me?
- What can't we/I talk about in the session?
- What rules of mine are they breaking?

Here is an example:

> In their first session together, the supervisor got a picture of the supervisee's work and explained how he worked, and they contracted times, costs and his cancellation policy. In the second session, the supervisee was late. When asked about this, the supervisee became very defensive and said that the supervisor did not appreciate how far she had to travel and that, in fact, she was not sure that they were a good match. The supervisor was shocked and felt impelled to become defensive himself, but stopped and said: 'I think it might not be just the travel I haven't appreciated. Would you be willing to say if there is something else I haven't understood?' The supervisee said that the supervisor had not seemed interested in her and she felt he was going through the motions. He said that yes, he had not felt very engaged in the first session but had thought it too early to feed it back, and he really appreciated her honesty and her ability to pick up his feelings. She then shared that she had been on antidepressants and was thinking of quitting her job. Perhaps the supervisor had picked that up and that was why he had not been engaged? He replied that yes, that did make sense, but he still

wanted to apologise for not trusting himself or her to feed back what he had picked up. This conversation marked the beginning of a transformation in the supervisee, who came off the antidepressants, stayed in her job and became team leader. (Shohet & Wilmot, 1991: 95)

A second example:

A client talked about tracing his family in his therapy session. The therapist had done this himself and tried to be helpful by making some suggestions about how to go about it. The following week the client had indeed found out some interesting material, but seemed rather flat about it; he wasn't as pleased and excited as the therapist expected. This alerted the therapist to ask if there was something in the previous session that he (the therapist) had missed or not understood. The client said that, at the time he had been pleased with the therapist's suggestions, but then felt that the joy of discovery was not all his. The therapist agreed and apologised.

18. See all students as 'A' students

We recognise how vulnerable we can be in supervision and in any learning situation, and that assessment can multiply our anxieties. Our wish is to minimise these anxieties as much as possible for our trainees (and ourselves). To do this, we have borrowed from the work of Ben Zander (Stone Zander & Zander, 2000) the idea of seeing our course participants as 'A' students before we even start on the training. As with all the other principles, this can be applied to all walks of life. Zander proposes that we give an 'A' to the waitress who serves us, or to other drivers on the road. It is an attitude of mind that, he argues (and we have found), brings out the best in others.

The practice of giving an A transports your relationships from the world of measurement to the world of possibility... When you give an A, you find yourself speaking to people not from a place of measuring how they stack up against your standards, but from a place that gives them room to realize themselves. The A is not an expectation to live up to but a possibility to live into. (Stone Zander & Zander, 2000: 26)

It is potentially our most controversial tenet and will challenge many people's core beliefs around measurement, success, merit, comparison, competition and so on. In Chapter 6 (pages 161–162), we give an example of how this worked for us on a postgraduate diploma supervision course. To briefly summarise it here, we announced to the students that they had passed their live supervision sessions before they had actually completed them. The students were initially very relieved, but almost immediately suspicion and core beliefs emerged – 'This a hoax', 'What does this say about the course?', 'I need to work for my grade, not have it given to me.' However, once these were surfaced, the students relaxed and were free to give each other useful and robust feedback about their work, knowing that it would not lead to another student failing the course.

Seeing all students as 'A' students can become a self-fulfilling prophecy, just as the opposite can be true: when we look for faults, we find them, and even make them more prominent. If we believe that all students are 'A' students and that it is our job, as trainers, to find a way to bring out their potential, then, paradoxically, because there is no question of any student failing the course, and as the above example illustrates, we feel freed to be more challenging and we find students feel freed to challenge us.

19. Appreciation is the glue that connects us

This is obviously an extension of the preceding principle of giving an 'A' to everyone we meet. We often start our courses with an exercise from Appreciative Inquiry (Cooperrider & Whitney, 2005). Appreciative Inquiry means that, when we look at any system – couple, family, team or organisation – we look first for what is working well and build on it, rather than look for a problem and try to fix it. An appreciative approach enables people to think creatively about a particular issue and approach the situation with fresh eyes. Genuine appreciation encourages people to open up. It is one of the best ways of connecting because, just as we see the best in another, we see it in ourselves.

> The head teacher of an East London comprehensive school, in an area known for violence and street crime, decided to commit himself to an appreciative approach. After two years of introducing this approach through regular meetings with staff and students, he decided to take the senior staff and students away for a residential overnight stay, along with a parent governor. This was a first, but from the previous work they had done, he knew that trust breeds trust. Halfway through the event, the trainers asked the staff and students to appreciate each other. A girl who had previously been seen as difficult at school, including by herself, turned to the assistant head teacher and said, 'You brought the light back into my life.'

> In another example, Joan was running the core supervision training where the exercise was to discover more about the supervisor's style and the impact of a particular intervention on the supervision. Joan chose only to use support/ appreciation and was paired with a member of the group who was a family therapist. Joan appreciated everything that the family therapist had done in their work with a family. At first the therapist was irritated by Joan's appreciation of everything she had said or done, as the work had not, in her mind, been going well and she felt blocked in her ability to help the family. Then she had an insight about the husband, who was resistant to coming and angry in the sessions. Through Joan's appreciation of what she had done, the therapist

looked with new eyes at the husband's position and understood how he felt a failure because he was having to come to family therapy and have experts do for his family what he felt he should have been able to do himself. She saw she hadn't appreciated what it was costing him to come and his courage in coming and how she could appreciate him for doing that.

20. See the possibility of failure from many different perspectives

Even though we consider all our students to be 'A' students and we use an appreciative approach, the students on our courses may still hold a fear of failure – they may be assessing others or are being assessed in another capacity. We could say that failure is an important part of learning, but the survival mechanism in most of us will not hear that. However, we can use many of the above principles to help us look at failure from other perspectives. We could see failure as belonging to the system, which includes us, the trainers. The person who might be thought to be failing could be carrying something for the all the course participants. We could think of failure simply as data. We could try to work through it in relationship with the other party or parties, paying close attention to any fear we might have missed. We could examine our core beliefs about success and failure. We could explore how each of us feels about failure – is there anything we have not felt able to own that we are getting the other to feel and act out? We could think about how the failing person could, paradoxically, be the one with most to teach us. We could think about how important it is that we approach the whole idea of failure without memory, desire or understanding. We could ask ourselves what we might have missed in the contract (the next principle below). We could look at how unacknowledged fear and vulnerability in the system might be contributing to the apparent failure.

> In the final module of one of our courses, we were seriously wondering about whether we could award our certificate to a student. She was very insightful and perceptive, and we had not predicted the possibility of failure. However, watching a video of her work on the final course, we experienced her as very critical and wondered how safe her supervisees would feel to bring their shortcomings to her. We took this as our failure to have spotted this before; this was our cue to work on ourselves. Were we like this trainee? In how many ways? How safe did we make supervision for our own supervisees? Did our critical parts leak out in supervision? Was this student a mirror to this aspect of ourselves? Had she carried something for the whole group? The next day we watched the video with the student and, as she saw herself on the video, without much prompting, she told us a story about her family history that helped both her and us make sense of her overwhelming critical part. There was a softness about her after that, which we and others noticed and appreciated.

21. Pay careful attention to the contract

We have often found, when there is a breakdown in the supervisory relationship, it is useful to go back to the contract and ask what both participants might have missed. For example, we have noticed supervisor and supervisee often collude at the start of supervision to avoid difficult topics like cancellation fees. The supervisee might have idealised the supervisor, which was bound to lead to disappointment (as in all relationships). Or perhaps some part of the system was not brought into the room and is now acting as a ghost? What about confidentiality? Is the supervisor's contract with the supervisee or with their employing organisation who is paying their fee? Is any assessment involved? How do you review your work together?

Here is an example of using contracting as a container for team dynamics:

> A consultant was brought in to work with a team in conflict. They had barely started when one of the team criticised a colleague who had arrived late. The consultant stopped them and said that, although he recognised there was conflict within the team, the only person they were allowed to challenge at this stage was him. Otherwise, it would be just more of the same of what was already going on. He said he would find ways of reframing the conflicts as this was part of his job. He added that he wanted an agreement that no one would walk out, as doing so would just recycle the conflicts, as people would have feelings about the person who had left. He explained that it is when things become really difficult that the potential for change can occur, as they would know from their client work.

We have also found it useful to distinguish between the overt contract and the psychological contract. We often see the psychological contract at work in couples therapy, where unconscious 'deals' between the partners have not been kept – for example, 'You were supposed to make me happy.' In supervision, the psychological contract between supervisee and supervisor could be, 'You are here to solve my problems,' and the supervisor might buy into that and try to be too helpful. At work an employee might do a lot of uncontracted overtime and feel furious that they have then been refused time off to go to their children's Christmas show. An unnegotiated psychological contract has been broken. A feeling of being let down can be traced back to a psychological contract. Whether we recognise it or not, we are making these contracts in supervision and elsewhere. In Chapter 3, we describe an exercise designed to make some of this psychological contracting more explicit.

22. Being able to comment on the relationship is key

Apart from self-supervision, supervision takes place in relationship, so all of the previous 21 propositions take place within that context. Our belief is that humans want to join with each other. Issues of power, difference and fear can get in the way if we let them. The skill of the supervisor is to make the relationship safe enough for both parties to share their vulnerabilities together. Without a trusting relationship, supervision can be a power struggle, a form of 'snoopervision', or a collusion. So, it is important to look at the factors that contribute to a good relationship and what might get in the way. These include the wider system in which the supervision takes place, the supervisee's previous histories of giving and receiving supervision and their history with authority figures; how fear can enter the relationship without either participant fully realising, and how that fear can be brought into consciousness and transcended (see also proposition 15). This too is potentially useful for all relationships.

We have included in Chapter 7 an inquiry form that we ask students to complete with two supervisees, their supervisor and a colleague or peer when they have finished the final course. This form can be adapted for any relationship. The power of using it is illustrated in the following example:

> The supervisee had asked her supervisor if they could do the form together as part of the course. The first question asks the supervisee to give an image of their relationship with their supervisor, and she said, 'Cat and mouse.' The supervisor said that the image had resonance but he did not like it as it placed him in the role of the mouse, and he asked the supervisee to expand. She put it back to the supervisor and they realised the cat and mouse relationship was happening now. The supervisor had sometimes felt uncomfortable without being able to put his finger on why, so he was glad that the power battle could be named explicitly. A more trusting relationship developed.

23. Supervision as spiritual practice

> Is it possible that adopting a supervisory attitude, viewing supervision as a reflective process that allows participants to think deeply and vulnerably about life and values, work and career, relationships and connections, might make an immense difference in how participants live? (Carroll, 2001: 77)

Carroll writes about the distinction between 'functional supervision' – that is, supervision as technology – and a 'philosophy of supervision' – that is, supervision as a way of being. He writes about the 'outside-in supervisor' – the technician who is doing something to someone else – and the inside-out supervisor, who knows that the beginning is always with the self.

We have come full circle with our propositions and are here going back to the first one, which is 'Know yourself'. We thought that the final proposition would be on the supervisory relationship, but we noticed how often we say that what we have written applies also to life outside supervision. So, we are also looking at what might stop us being present in our lives, as well as in supervision. And it then becomes apparent that supervision can be seen as a form of spiritual practice – a place of inquiry beyond technique, beyond training. We offer it as one of the reasons we are still passionate about our work and can maintain the freshness with which we started.

We are inevitably a product of our time. We have already alluded to this in the introduction in describing our therapeutic community work in the 1970s. We come from a time when there were experiments in education – the work of Paulo Freire (Darder, 2000), and of AS Neill at Summerhill (1960); the *Plowden Report* (Central Advisory Council for Education, 1967), which foregrounded the needs of the primary school child (and which most teachers today have not heard of), and John Holt's ideas in his book *How Children Learn* (1967) and *How Children Fail* (1964). In adult education, Carl Rogers (1969) was pioneering bringing therapeutic principles of self-direction into education at all levels. While recognising that the teacher/educator has to hold the space, all of these put the student more in charge of their own learning than does conventional pedagogy. These writers were often criticised, but their ideas are dear to our hearts. The courses we teach are designed specifically for the students to learn supervision, and this is what the overt contract says. But the process, or implicit contract, is for them to feel safe to question us, and for us not to overwhelm them with content; for us to support them to feel in charge of their learning as much as possible; to encourage peer learning, build a sense of community from the outset and, as we mentioned in the introduction, to model trusting the students so they can trust themselves and, by extension, their supervisees. That is the destination. In the following pages we will describe the journey.

References

Berne E (1986/61). *Transactional Analysis in Psychotherapy.* London: Souvenir Press.

Bion W (1967). Notes on memory and desire. *Psychoanalytic Forum* 2(3): 272–273, 279–280.

Breene C (2011). Resistance is a natural path: an alternative perspective on transformation. In: Shohet R (ed). *Supervision as Transformation.* London: Jessica Kingsley (pp162–180).

Carroll M (2001). The spirituality of supervision. In: Carroll M, Tholstrup M (eds). *Integrative Approaches to Supervision.* London: Jessica Kingsley (pp76–90).

Carse J (1986). *Finite and Infinite Games.* New York, NY: Free Press.

Central Advisory Council for Education (1967). *Children and their Primary Schools (The Plowden Report). A Report of the Central Advisory Council for Education (England).* London: HMSO.

Cooperrider DL, Whitney D (2005). *Appreciative Inquiry: a positive revolution in change.* San Francisco, CA: Berrett Koehler Publishers Inc.

Darder A (2002). *Reinventing Paulo Freire*. Boulder, CO: Westview Press.

Dass R, Gorman P (1985). *How Can I Help?* London: Rider.

de Mello A (1985). *One-Minute Wisdom*. Anand: Guiariat Sahitya Prakash.

Guggenbuhl-Graig A (1971). *Power in the Helping Professions*. Dallas, TX: Spring Publications.

Hawkins P, Shohet R (2012). *Supervision in the Helping Professions* (4th ed). Maidenhead: Open University Press.

Holt J (1967). *How Children Learn*. New York, NY: Pitman Publishing.

Holt J (1964). *How Children Fail*. New York, NY: Pitman Publishing.

Laing RD, Esterson A (1964). *Sanity, Madness and the Family*. London: Penguin Books.

Mason B (2015). Towards positions of safe uncertainty. *InterAction: the Journal of Solution Focus in Organisations* 7(1): 28–43.

Neill AS (1960). *Summerhill: a radical approach to child rearing*. London: Penguin Books.

Rogers C (1969). *Freedom to Learn: a view of what education might become*. New York, NY: CE Merrill Publishing Co.

Rumi (2004). *Selected Poems*. London: Penguin Classics.

Senge P (2006). *The Fifth Discipline: the art and prctice of the learning organisation*. London: Random House.

Shainberg D (1983). Teaching therapists to be with their clients. In: Westwood J (ed). *Awakening the Heart*. Boulder, CO: Shambhala.

Shohet R (2018). Whose feelings am I feeling? using the concept of projective identification. In: Hardwick A, Woodhead J (eds). *Loving, Hating and Survival. Routledge Revivals*. Abingdon: Routledge (pp41–53).

Shohet R (2012). Listening to resistance. In: Owen D, Shohet R (eds). *Clinical Supervision in the Medical Profession*. Maidenhead: McGraw Hill (pp143–156).

Shohet R, Wilmot J (1991). The key issue in the supervision of counsellors: the supervisory relationship. In: Dryden W, Thorne B (eds). *Training and Supervision for Counselling in Action*. London: Sage (pp87–98).

Stone Zander R, Zander B (2000). *The Art of Possibility: transforming professional and personal life*. Boston, MA: Harvard Business School Press.

Szasz T (1970). *The Manufacture of Madness*. Syracuse, NY: Syracuse University Press.

Szasz T (1961). *The Myth of Mental Illness*. New York, NY: Harper.

Part 2
Courses

3

The core course

Pulling the Chair
Beneath your mind
And watching you fall upon God
What else is there
For Hafiz to do
That is any fun in this world! (Hafiz, 2006)

Supervision interrupts practice. It wakes us up to what we are doing.
When we are alive to what we are doing, we wake up to what is, instead
of falling asleep in the comfort stories of our clinical routines and daily
practice. We have profound learning difficulties when it comes to being
present to our own moment-to-moment experiences. (Ryan, 2004: 44)

In the Core Course we enter into the what, how, why and who of supervision and
the supervisory relationship.: it is a space for you to attend to yourself and your
work. The course is experiential; it is the essentials and the essence of supervision
and, as I (Joan) believe everything is about relationship, it will mirror, illuminate,
irritate and reflect all our other relationships. It will be held by the container that
I/we create, and by the contract I and the students make together – a place where
we can reflect on our life and our work. Most importantly, we will slow down.
The intention on the Core Course is to take apart everything we know, to have
the chair pulled from under our minds and to enter into the field of not knowing.
We will look for what is called *Shoshin* in Zen Buddhism, or beginner's mind.
This is an attitude of openness, eagerness and absence of preconceptions when
studying a subject.

The Core Course is where the students and I meet face to face for the first
time, although in one sense we have been meeting for some time before. I believe
that once the booking has been made, we are connected. The course is for anyone
who is in work. Bearing in mind the story of the woodcutter that introduced this

book, it is for anyone who wants to learn how to sharpen their metaphorical axe in order to be more effective at work. It is for those who want to develop their own internal supervisor and also become a supervisor to other people and their work. As a consequence, we have students from many walks of life and with a range of experience. This makes for a rich learning community.

Each time we run the Core Course, the order in which we deliver the content is slightly different, but every course will essentially contain the exercises and structure described below. There are usually 18 participants. When we meet, our administrator has already emailed out the manual to the students – a collections of quotes, articles and exercises we have built up over 40 years. The room has been booked at CCPE, a training centre in Paddington, London, where we have run our trainings ever since we took the supervision we had developed in the Richmond Fellowship senior staff training house out into the public arena.

As I sit here and write, I reflect on different aspects of supervision. I have put these reflections in italics as they do not only refer to this course.

So what has this practice or process that we call supervision grown out of? In the last 100 years or so, it has been a key element of such professions as psychoanalysis, psychotherapy, counselling, social work, occupational therapy, speech therapy and probation. As David Whyte (2002: 93) says in his book, Crossing the Unknown Sea: work as a pilgrimage of identity, *we stand on the shoulders of our ancestors – the analysts, the therapists, the philosophers, the teachers, practitioners and supervisors that have gone before us. We honour them. I see it as a place to reflect on our work and ourselves in our work, whatever the work might be. In my career as a supervisor, I have supervised people from my first profession, social work, and since then artists, musicians, hairdressers, teachers, doctors, administrators, self-employed workers and people running small businesses; I have supervised and am supervising supervisees who are working with people in professions as diverse as the oil industry, the prison service, religious orders and a funeral parlour.*

Supervision is a space; a time to think, to bring in the witness, to honour the judge and also move beyond it. As Rumi, the 13th century poet (2004), said: 'Out beyond our ideas of wrongdoing and rightdoing there is a field. I'll meet you there.' A recent supervisee put it in terms of his right and left brain; that, when the discernment of the left brain joins the awe of his right brain, everything is presence, energising and uplifting, and when they don't it is black-and-white, right-and-wrong thinking on the one hand and exhaustion and confusion on the other. Declan Donnellan, in his book The Actor and the Target *(2002: 107–108), puts it even more strongly: 'To hold that a human being can be good or evil as part of their intrinsic nature is the very depth of sentimentality.'*

His definition of sentimentality is 'the refusal to accept ambivalence'. He goes on to say: 'We can never know, control or contain the essence of anyone, including us. We can always observe, however.' And that, I believe, is core to supervision – to see, to observe.

What is supervision and who or what is a supervisor? My experience, over the 40 years I have been receiving and offering supervision, is that, like love, it is a verb, not a noun. It is a process, a service and a relationship in which love, trust, self-belief, self-knowledge, creativity, grieving, suffering, bearing witness and attending to the context are all core ingredients.

In conversation, Judy Ryde, a fellow supervision trainer, once compared supervision to Dr Who's Tardis – it looks very ordinary and functional on the outside but when you go inside, it is vast, infinite and extraordinary. Diana Athill, literary editor, novelist and centenarian, was asked in an interview how authors could bear to have their precious books scrutinised by her. She paused and then said they seemed to value having someone being as interested in their work as they were. I see supervision like that. Peter Caddy, co-founder in 1964 of the Findhorn Foundation, a spiritual community in the North of Scotland, in his lectures, used to describe work as 'love in action', and I see supervision as bearing witness and deepening this.

Gaie Houston (1995) describes three aspects to supervision: policing, plumbing and poetry: 'Policing is the term coined to describe the aspect of supervision concerned with boundary-monitoring and the maintenance of a framework in which counselling and supervision can take place… Plumbing refers to the educative aspect of supervision in teaching supervisees how to be more effective and competent in their therapeutic work. Poetry in supervision is the creation of a space where supervisees have the freedom to explore their experience with the client. It involves the imaginative collaboration of supervisor and supervisee in gaining insight and empathy for the client. Where there have been difficulties in communication, it allows for the supervisee to regain compassion and thereby work more effectively with the client.'

I am struck that 'supervision' can still be seen as having somewhat of a policing function; the frequently quoted phrase 'a man in a white coat with a clip board' is offered up. This also reflects, I believe, an aspect of our society that favours judgement as a way of managing others and ourselves. An intimation that it might not be so, and the cost of it, comes from Malidome Some, a Western-educated author and workshop leader from the Dagara tribe of West Africa. When he attempted to explain to his village elders the Western concept of suing others for compensation, they could not grasp it. After some considerable time, one of them asked, 'How then, do these people ever learn?' In other words, we go out of relationship, the other person becomes 'other', someone to be defended against or defeated, and the cost is alienation, even if you win. More complaints procedures have been introduced into many professions, which has led to more complaints being made, but this has not, on the whole, led to resolution.

So, back to the course and some of the ways I build the container and help other people build theirs. The day before the course, I buy the biscuits and bake the cakes. The next day I arrive as soon as the building opens so I can prepare the space. The room at CCPE is beautiful – it is about 150 years old and was once the ballroom, when the premises was a private house. I arrange the chairs so that the group is facing me and, beyond me, there is the view of Regent's Canal and Little Venice. It draws my attention to how the supervisory relationship is impacted on by the context and the environment, as well as the personalities of the people involved.

I put out the hard copies of our training manual, along with copies of *Supervision in the Helping Professions* (Hawkins & Shohet, 2012). I write up the timetable on a flip chart and then overlay it with a welcome message. I am ready to host and greet the participants as they arrive.

The arrival time on the first day is between 9.30 and 10am, so that people have a bit more time to locate the training room, find their seat, drop off their bags, meet me and whoever else is on the course. I tell them a little about the layout of the building and where the kitchen, dining room and toilets are. We begin to settle to each other.

I always start and finish on time. That holds the container for the group and for me. Within those parameters, the sessions can vary in length. At 10am, I ask whoever is nearest the door to close it and I welcome the group.

First session

Paired exercise

I begin with a paired exercise. I invite the participants to turn to their neighbour and introduce themselves, decide who goes first and each spend three minutes talking about their journey and what they have left behind to get here. I say I will call the time. This gives any latecomers time to arrive – although this rarely happens, and if it does, they have usually called in to let me know. If there is an odd number and we are all there, I will pair up with the singleton; if there is someone yet to arrive, I will invite three people to join up so I am free to meet the latecomer. We need time to transition before we can fully arrive at a new place. In *The Continuum Concept*, Liedloff (1975/2004) recounts how an African tribe she visited would invite visitors to rest and eat before they did business together, which could take up to three hours. The paired exercise and the next two exercises are my shorter version.

> *When I first started as a trainer, I had some tension around anyone coming late. I used to take it personally or make it a problem. Now I find myself more in a place of 'loving what is' – the title of a book by Byron Katie (2002). This is a good place to be in any experience, I would say, and in particular in relation to being a supervisor or supervisee. Byron Katie says that all stress comes from arguing with reality. And what is this reality? Someone is late*

*when they arrive; so, let's meet each other there. However, if someone misses
more than an hour at any stage, we will together look at how this time can
be made up, as we ask for full attendance.*

I call time and ask if anyone would like to share from their exchanges. This gives
members of the group a chance to share with everyone what it has taken to carve
these three days out of their life or to discharge any stress from the journey to the
venue, or anything that is still worrying them from what they have left behind, or
to celebrate a recent event in their lives.

Postcard exercise

While they have been speaking in pairs, I have spread some picture postcards
on the floor at the far end of the room. Robin and I have been collecting these
over the years. I invite them each to choose two – one to represent their current
relationship with supervision and one to represent a snapshot of how they
are right now. I myself choose two postcards and then invite someone to start
with their name, show the group their postcards and share their associations.
So, for example, on one course, someone chose a picture of a red squirrel for
supervision, saying they came to supervision to learn about the nuts (and bolts).
To illustrate how they were at that time, they chose a picture of two children
embracing, with the caption: 'To have joy one must share it'. We then continue
round the group. Each person puts their postcards up on the wall and we leave
them there throughout the three days of the course, until the end, when they
will collect them up as part of their reviewing process. This exercise, along with
the next, 'Sparkling Moment', both originate from a course I did on Appreciative
Inquiry (Cooperrider & Whitney, 2005), which (as explained in Chapter 2) is
one of the cornerstones of our supervision practice.

> *One of the premises of Appreciative Inquiry is to wonder how we see the
> world: whether as a mystery to be embraced or as a problem to be solved.
> In offering this exercise, I want to invite the participants into the mystery
> of seeing themselves and supervision. When we enter into a learning
> environment, we can be somewhat overcome by fear of failure, past shame
> or distress from learning experiences in school, and self-criticisms from the
> voice in our head, rather than accessing our original innocence. Appreciative
> Inquiry is based on a social constructionist approach, which is that anything,
> be it a person, a group or an organisation, will develop in the direction we
> are looking. This is quite profound and simple. If we expect problems, we will
> find problems; if we look at what is working, we will build on that.*
>
> In Love's Hidden Symmetry, *Bert Hellinger (1998: 220) has an
> interesting take on problems. 'From a systemic point of view,' he says,
> 'problems are unsuccessful attempts to love and the love that maintains the
> problem can be redirected to resolve it. The therapeutic task is, first of all,
> to find the point at which the client loves'. 'When I have found that point,'*

he writes, 'then I have therapeutic leverage. By helping the client find an appropriate and mature way to love, the problem dissolves, and the same love that maintained the problem solves it.'

Sparkling Moment and Appreciative Inquiry

I suggest we look at what is working well in our work lives, using the Sparkling Moment exercise, which I learnt on an Appreciative Inquiry conference. I ask participants to form pairs and decide who is A and who B and to have a pen and paper to hand, which they can set to one side for the moment but will need a little later. I ask them to think of a 'sparkling moment' that has happened to them at work in the last week – it can be very small or monumental, whatever comes to mind. I then ask A to share that moment in detail with B for two minutes, while B listens. The listener can say 'What else?' in an inquiring tone if they want to encourage the other, but nothing else. After two minutes, I call time and ask them to reverse roles. After another two minutes I again call time and invite everyone to pick up their pens and paper, take a minute to reflect on the story they have just heard, and from that pick out two strengths or qualities that their partner has. I then invite them to share these strengths/qualities with their partner. I tell them their only verbal response to what is shared is 'Thank you' and to notice how much they take in or refuse the offering. We can often feel more comfortable with giving than receiving, especially when it is appreciative. I also invite them then to have a short conversation together about their experience of the exercise. I finish by inviting the whole group to share their qualities and their experience. What comes across in the sharing is how much people learnt and connected with each other in such a short time.

> *At this point, or maybe later in the course, I will share a little more about Appreciative Inquiry, including the following story about David Cooperrider, its co-founder (Cooperrider & Srivastva, 1987). A major Fortune-500 company (one of the top 500 wealthiest corporations in the world) decided to address sexual harassment in their workplace. They hired a very effective consulting firm to work on this issue. One day the president of the consulting firm telephoned David Coooperrider and said, 'Every single thing we've done is making things worse.' Litigation had increased, the cost to the company had increased, the numbers of people having counselling had increased, and the reported incidents of sexual harassment had increased. At the suggestion of Cooperrider, the consultants put out an invitation in the company newsletter for pairs of men and women to come to a workshop if they felt they had something to teach the world about the high quality of their co-leadership. They were hoping for maybe a dozen volunteers to share their stories, but more than 100 pairs volunteered. These pairs held a series of workshops on what made their co-working successful and, two years later, the company won the Catalyst Award for Best Organization in the Country for Women at Work.*

*This story also takes us into the world of paradox, where focusing on
what you don't want can create more of it. When he was seven, my oldest
son received a note from school that he was not to bring sweets on his first
school trip. He said he had never thought of bringing sweets and now that
was all he could think of!*

Having begun the contracting together into a learning group with the preceding
three exercises, I check in to see how everyone is doing and if they are ready
for the final exercise before we take our first break. I also ask at this stage who
already knows each other, as sometimes people have come together, or have
met on other trainings, know each other through their work or have social
connections. This helps the group to begin to talk to each other and encourages
them to trust what is.

Learning log

I invite them to open their training manuals, turn to the page with the learning
log and take between five and 10 minutes to fill it in.

The learning log is something we have devised as a warm-up and a focus for
the learning. It has the following headings, with blank spaces for the participants
to fill in:

1. Experiences of giving and receiving supervision.

*This is to put people in touch with their previous experiences of supervision
as they inevitably affect their current supervisory relationships. Good ones
have formed the basis for strong working relationships and not so good ones
may have resulted in a pullback that can be useful to share in order to move
beyond.*

2. Learning needs of the course and training
a) Personal
b) Professional
c) Clients/supervisees
d) Team/organisation
e) Family/friends

*For the last three, I am asking them to see what their clients, supervisees, team,
organisation, family and friends might want them to learn. It is useful to see if
we can see ourselves as others see us, and what others may be wanting from us.*

3. What do you have to offer?

*I want people to be in touch with their resources. When we are in a learning
environment, we can forget the richness of our life experience.*

4. What are your support systems, both formal and informal?

These can include books, nature and music, as well as people. People in the helping professions can sometimes find it easier to give than receive, which can lead to burnout, so I want to raise awareness of the importance of support.

5. How might you sabotage your learning?

Most, if not all of us, have internal saboteurs and I want these to be named and shared. They might include anxiety to 'get it right'; feeling not good enough; clinging to the known, or (one of my own) needing to cover all the bases.

Home groups

Next, I number people off into groups of three or four. This will be their home group for the three days, and they will meet at least once a day to check in with each other. I do this in preference to self-selection, because choosing and being chosen can be quite re-stimulating. This is not necessarily a bad thing but would come a little too early in the course, I think. I invite them to take five minutes each to share their needs and sabotages in their small group and then it is time for a break, to chat over tea, coffee and cake.

Sharing needs and sabotages

After about 20 minutes, we gather again to share the needs and sabotages we have discussed in the home groups and continue the work of contracting together. I write these out on the flip chart and put up the sheet alongside the postcards. These will stay up for the duration of the course. There is value in sharing our sabotages with other people and meeting and inquiring into them with humour, consciousness and compassion. We all have them and accepting them helps. Indeed, another core tenet of being a supervisor is to honour resistance; it has a purpose and we should value it, rather than try to dismiss it or bludgeon it away. The needs focus on our natural desire to learn, to stretch ourselves, to aspire. However, they can often become tyrannies. The sabotages are the strategies we have developed to defend and protect ourselves against the pain, the fear of failure and the losses we have experienced in the past.

Below are some of the needs and sabotages we've collected over the years:

- **Needs** – gain confidence; slow down; manage tiredness; to be in a supportive environment; to be challenged and know how to challenge; managing difficult supervisees; taking authority.

- **Sabotages** – not engaging; comparing; switching off; judging; inner critic; worrying; clowning; imposter syndrome; not being good enough.

In her book Education – an 'impossible profession'?*, Tamara Bibby (2010) talks about our ambivalent relationship to learning, which coming on a training course can activate – hence the invitation to share our sabotages, such as comparing ourselves or withdrawing. Sharing them softens their power; we find we are not alone, and we find we are human. We also often find these sabotages are out of date, an old habit, and we can perhaps help each other give up our beloved but redundant security blankets. Learning requires letting go of what feels like some hard-won lessons, without any certainty of where we will arrive or if we will arrive. It also involves loss. As Bibby says, 'There is the joy and sense of achievement of learning to button up your own coat but also there is the concomitant loss of having someone button it up for you' (p149). Declan Donnellan (2005: 107) puts it this way: 'The human condition is living with permanent loss and permanent rebirth', moment by moment.*

Maybe this is the moment to confess to myself and to you as reader – or (as 'confess' can have a pejorative sense) state the obvious: this training is all about our favourite topic, ourselves. If that isn't your favourite topic, it will be, because you are your responsibility. I believe you can't love another if you can't love yourself; you can't have empathy if you haven't got empathy for yourself, and, to some extent, lack of self-care is at the root of burn-out. At the end of the course, when we are looking at how people take the learning back home, we invite people to look at their support systems. My core belief is that loving yourself is essential, including loving and accepting the bits of ourselves we might find less acceptable that are often in shadow – the non-caring, non-loving bits. Paradox is in there and so we enter into the finite and infinite game of supervision.

At this point, as we are talking about such topics as failure, judgement and not being good enough, I recommend Ben Zander's YouTube clip, *Work (how to give an 'A')* (2012). I invite people to watch it that evening at home or during the course next day in one of the breaks. Zander gives all his students an 'A' at the beginning of his nine-month music training, and simply asks that they write him a letter in their first two weeks of the course to tell him how they got their 'A' and then fall deeply in love with that person who got the 'A'. *(We have referred to this in point 18 in Chapter 2.)*

The CLEAR model

Following on from the collection of needs and sabotages, I introduce the CLEAR model. This is one of the frames Robin and I use to focus on what supervision is and how we do it. It is an attempt to look at the elements involved in supervision as a way of deepening our understanding and engagement with it. Peter Hawkins developed this model in the early 1980s. It is an acronym for:

- Contracting
- Listening
- Exploring
- Action
- Review.

The acronym provides a framework for looking at the journey of the session and its elements. It is both circular and linear in that contracting, listening, exploring and action are happening simultaneously and there may be several rounds in just one session. It is also part of everyday conversation, although we don't usually analyse conversations that way. If a conversation happens between two or more people who, say, bump into each other in the street, they will have implicitly agreed to stand still for a short time and have a backwards and forwards conversation. They will be listening to each other and exploring, and they will at some time decide on an action, which could be to move off to do something together. Then there is often the briefest of reviews, which goes something like this: 'Nice to see you. We must do this more often.'

I will point out to the group at this point that *contracting* is happening now: we have implicitly agreed that I will do most of the talking and they will listen and that the topic is supervision, although we undoubtedly are carrying different and often unrecognised assumptions about the content and process of supervision.

Supervision is essentially a good conversation between two or more people. One of the cornerstones of supervision is to slow the conversation down, become curious about the relationship and enquire into what it is, when it started, who or what is in charge and what assumptions are being made within it.

Hopes and fears exercise for contracting

Next, I ask the participants to look at the hopes and fears that they are carrying as a supervisor or supervisee when they approach their first supervision session. This is an exercise to focus on the contracting part of supervision and have the students look at their assumptions and projections. I invite them to choose the perspective from which they want to explore the contracting for this exercise – that of supervisor or supervisee – and then to divide into two equal-sized groups to brainstorm:

1. What I want to happen.

2. What I fear will happen.

3. What I want to happen but will not contract for explicitly (for example, 'I want you to like me or think I am brilliant or I am your favourite.')

The two groups, supervisors and supervisees, go to either end of the room with a sheet of A1 paper to brainstorm and write up their thinking. After the allotted time, usually 10–15 minutes, I invite the two groups to face each other. I then ask each group to present what they have written for the different headings. The other group listens, staying in role, and shares the impact on them of hearing the other group's hopes and fears. Then the two groups reverse positions. We complete by de-roling and sharing some of the experience of what might be happening before supervisor and supervisee meet for their first supervision session. Participants often remark on how similar the fears of the supervisors and supervisees are and wonder how to create an environment where they might be shared.

Games, transactions and roles

This exercise naturally leads on to the last session of the morning, which looks at the 'games' we co-create to manage and control the balance of intimacy and connection and the separateness that we need, or believe we need, in our interactions with other human beings. Our meeting with another person is usually coloured by our past experiences, and in particular the past experiences that resonate with our perception of the current relationship. So, in the case of supervision, where we experience ourselves as seeking help or offering help, we may draw, unconsciously or semi-consciously, on help-seeking and help-giving relationships from the past.

Below is a brainstorm exercise we do as a whole group, which we have found illuminates how roles and transactions from the past come into play in the supervisory relationship. It also throws into relief our tendency to be drawn into certain roles or put other people into certain roles.

I put the three headings on the flip chart and ask the group first to call out the role, then what they take to that role and then what they expect to receive. These are some of the words students offer:

Helping role	What you take	What you expect to receive
Teacher	Questions, ignorance	Answers, knowledge
Mother	Hurts, wounds	Love, being on your side
Provocateur	Sameness	Rattle and shake
Friend	Concerns	Acceptance, warts and all
Big sister	Problems	Guidance, reassurance
Storyteller	Problems	Metaphor
Judge	Crimes	Retribution, justice
Priest	Sins	Absolution

It is worth noticing at this point how much we, as supervisors or supervisees, see the exchanges as one way or as mutual. So, do we see the supervisor as 'the helper' and the supervisee as the recipient of that help? A story comes to mind about this question. My two children were attending the local Steiner school and were performing in a play, which was both part of their education and a fundraiser for the school. I had contributed by helping with their costumes, making cakes to sell in the interval and giving up my evening to serve the refreshments. As I handed a cup of tea to a person on the other side of the counter, I moved out of the role of giver, tinged, I confess, with more than a modicum of martyrdom and superiority, to realising we were interdependent, equal and mutual: without her receiving the cup of tea, my offering could not happen. It is the same in the supervisory relationship: we are both helping and being helped, helping ourselves and helping the other, in the moment, in the service of simply what is.

In the course of this exploration, we can also look at whether these are confluent or collusive transactions, crossed transactions or mutual transactions and what we might discover that is new about our clients, our work and ourselves. So, for example, taking the Transactional Analysis model of Parent, Adult, Child (Berne, 1964), a supervisee might see themselves as the Child and the supervisor as a Parent who tells them what to do, and they may enter a collusive relationship in which the supervisor gives them lots of advice. A crossed transaction might be when a supervisor waits for the answer to come from the supervisee, thinking that this is an adult transaction, but is then seen as withholding by the supervisee, who thinks supervision is about being told what to do. The aim is to be in adult/adult relationship but, as we can see from the above, there is plenty of scope for transference and countertransference. So this setting up of the contract, the working alliance, takes us inevitably right into the heart of matter, the nuts and bolts and the process of supervision. The beauty of the contract is that it is both a container and a mirror; it is both holding the relationship and the work and holding up a mirror to what has been missed or marginalised or can only be accessed via the non-verbal.

I believe our greatest desire is to have clear, honest, transparent and intimate relationships. However, we often fail, interrupt or feel interrupted in this desire, and this is no less so in the supervisory relationship than it is in all other relationships. It seems that the pain, shock, trauma and unfinished emotional baggage that we humans have gathered over our lifetime conspire into a fearful, defensive, self-protective state that is expressed in reactivity and game-playing, as opposed to intimacy. Our experience is perhaps not so much either game-playing or not game-playing as that each of us is simultaneously both trying to hide and trying to make contact in our interactions with each other.

We also believe that games are co-created, so, from that standpoint, supervisor and supervisee can share ownership and grapple together with their resolution and transformation. If we see games as co-created, then we become interested in the space between supervisor and supervisee rather than locating responsibility for the games in one of the parties. We can also see the supervisory relationship as being a mirror to all the other relationships we have been and will be involved in during our work and life.

We touch on the games people play in supervision – as supervisees (Kadushin, 1976; Hawthorne, 1975), and in group supervision (Houston, 1985). There is a lot to pack into this first morning, and I find I need to remind myself, and the participants, that this is the first morning of what will be a 12-day training, and that the most important skill of supervision is the ability to *slow down*. I end the morning by drawing attention to one of the best-known games, Karpman's drama triangle (1968), with its three roles of Persecutor, Victim and Rescuer, and its companion, the beneficial triangle, to which we will return on the third day (see further below). It is now lunchtime and the afternoon is set aside for practice and experimenting, with a focus on contracting.

Afternoon

Contracting role-play

When the participants return from lunch, I have set up the room with two chairs facing each other in the middle of the circle. One is the supervisor chair and the other the supervisee chair. I have drawn a line lengthwise down the middle of the flip chart, to create two columns. One column is headed 'Explicit contracting' and the other 'Implicit contracting'. Pinned on the wall is our feedback structure (which I will explain below).

I set the scene and invite two participants into the chairs. This will be the first seven minutes of a first meeting to contract a supervisory relationship. It will be role play in the sense that the supervisor and supervisee are not going to forge an actual ongoing supervisory relationship, but it will be real play in that they will be themselves and will negotiate a contract.

I invite two participants to record what happens on the flip chart. One participant records the explicit contracting, the content, that they observe – for example, decisions about the length and frequency of sessions, the focus of the work, what the cancellation policy is and so on. In the adjacent column, the other participant will record the implicit contracting that is happening – the process, for instance, and who is taking the lead, what hopes and fears may be emerging, and what can and can't be talked about. A comparison comes to mind of piano playing: the right hand plays the tune and the left hand the accompaniment, giving colour and tone to the relationship. The other participants are invited to be observers. I give a minute's warning at six minutes and then the supervisor brings it to a close.

Feedback structure

At this point I introduce the feedback structure, and stress that it is feedback for the supervisor. Indeed, I point out that, as this course is about learning to supervise, all the practice sessions are for the benefit of the supervisor. Good supervision will happen, but the exercises and feedback are intended to offer learning to the supervisor. The feedback structure is as follows:

- One thing I appreciated.
- One thing I found difficult.
- One thing I would like to encourage.

1. The supervisor is invited to give feedback on him or herself, starting with what they appreciated about how they were as a supervisor during the session.

> The reason we ask for the supervisor to start is all of us are always giving ourselves feedback; we have a running commentary in our heads – 'the voice in our head' that rarely ceases to make judgements about our performance and, if that is not enough, anyone or anything else it can lay its hands on! We want to invite in the witness to interrupt it and we do that by bringing in appreciation. We believe that appreciation of what is working is the only way to change anything. This was illustrated for me by a support tutor in a workshop I was running who talked about a four-year-old girl she had been asked to see because of her bad behaviour. She described how no one could stand the little girl; the teacher of her next class dreaded her moving up; the parents talked about her in the playground; the other children avoided her. As the support tutor sat with her, the girl suddenly burst into tears and sobbed, 'I don't know how to be good.' All she had ever received was feedback on how bad she was; no one had ever given her any clue as to how she was good or what good looked like – what people wanted of her.

2. The supervisee next gives feedback to the supervisor, and then, finally, the observer feeds back, both using the feedback structure. We always start with the appreciation: one sentence, no clauses, explanations, justifications or going back into the content of the session. Then they add one encouragement or difficulty. One minute is enough for all three to give their feedback in the practice triads. If it starts taking longer, it usually means the triad has gone back into supervising or theorising. When we are doing it as a group, as we are here, in a demonstration, I invite feedback to the supervisor from some of the rest of the group. I finish by thanking the supervisor and supervisee for being the first to move into practice and performance and invite them to de-role and rejoin the group. I then ask the two people at the flipchart to share their observations but to direct their comments to the group or to me, not the supervisor or supervisee, to distinguish between the actual session and learning about the process of supervision and contracting.

I see feedback as relational, co-created and subjective. In my many years of giving and receiving feedback, the most useful feedback I have received is in the present and in relationship. Here, in the training, is the place to practise and develop that muscle. It is important to be clear about your intention. If your desire is to establish contact with that person and you are willing to take responsibility for your part in that, then you usually have a formula for success. You might consider using the feedback as a doorway into yourself – a mirror, in effect. Another way to put it is that any feedback we give is also about us; it takes one to know one. This is true of appreciations as well as difficulties. If you notice that your desire is to a) make the other person wrong, b) have them change, c) punish them in some way, d) vent your anger, e) manipulate or f) guilt trip, then this is a 'dump' and is usually not constructive to either party.

Practice sessions

Following this exercise, the participants will be doing their first practice sessions, so we discuss the structure of the sessions.

> **First step:** form triads. Decide who will be supervisor, supervisee and observer. All will have a chance to be in each role.
>
> **Task:** either contract with the supervisee along the lines of what happened in the demonstration, or bring a new contracting issue to the session, such as how the contract is going with a current client. The session will last seven minutes. The exercise is for the benefit of the supervisor's learning. The supervisee brings something that is live and is responsible for taking care of him or herself. The observer has chance to learn by watching and has no other task except to give a one-minute warning at six minutes and say 'Time' when the seven minutes are up.

After the seven minutes are up, each group follows the feedback structure, focusing on the supervisor. I suggest participants make a note of both the feedback they receive and that they give. As I said earlier, the feedback is always about us too.

I write the steps on the flip chart to mitigate the performance anxiety that kicks in for most people. Then, having clarified as much as possible, slowed us down so we are more present, and underlined that the exercise is for the supervisor to try things out and play/learn, not to give good supervision or solve any problems presented, I send them off to do their first session. A group of 18 will form six triads, which all fit very comfortably into the ballroom space and create a focused working atmosphere. After the first session we take a 20-minute drinks break and then resume for the other two sessions.

The commitment, good work and concentration is always high. I think by this time in the first day we have created a sense of safety and they are trusting their ability to supervise and be supervised.

After the three practices, I ask the participants to come back to the large group to share their experiences and learning and clarify the structure and the steps, as there is much to take in the first time. After that, I suggest they return to their home groups for 20 minutes of integration time and to reflect on their learning for the day. We finish back together again in the large group, when I invite everyone to share a self-appreciation. We close at 5pm precisely, and I remind them that we start half an hour earlier on the next two days.

> *A final thought on contracting. Robin and I used to establish a confidentiality contract with the groups we taught but some years ago we changed it to a good will contract. By 'good will' we mean that, if anyone refers to anything from a session, they talk about it from a place of good will. Also, as we are process supervisors and trainers, the content or the story is not usually relevant, only the process, so any comments at the level of 'He said/She said' aren't pertinent.*
>
> *I have sometimes had an in-depth conversation with a group about what we mean by confidentiality and good will. They are concepts, with all the projections and assumptions that go with that; they are also hugely contextual in that every situation is unique and needs to be attended to at that level. Sometimes in a group no one will even mention a confidentiality or good will contract. It is so implicit in the way we are together that the thought of acting any other way does not enter the field. I believe it is in our true nature and not there just because we have made a contract to make it happen. If we are contracting for confidentiality (or good will, for that matter), it is interesting to consider whether we are doing it to defend against its opposite – ie. the fear that we may gossip and our fear of being gossiped about. Are we therefore unconsciously creating separation when we thought we were creating connection? It is an intriguing thought.*

❧   ❧   ❧

Day 2

Sharing about names

I have two exercises with which I usually start days 2 and 3. Apart from the practical purpose of helping participants learn each other's names, my aim is to continue to build a learning community. In the first exercise, I ask participants to share all their names; how they came by them, if they know, and how they feel about them. Each time I start this way, I am struck by how much information and connection happens in this simple, short way of beginning. I believe there is an energy being transmitted, as well as the sharing of facts about the name. In supervision, some counsellors and therapists are required or choose not to use the client's actual name but instead choose a pseudonym, which potentially cuts us off from that form of transmission. However, I have found it still works if I ask the supervisee to share why they chose that particular pseudonym.

Open and closed questions

The second exercise is about open and closed questions. Part of working as a supervisor is to enquire and have a range of questions – or you could call them a variety of tools in your toolkit; they are a pathway to inviting the supervisee to enquire into their work and their relationship with it. Closed questions are those requiring a 'yes' or 'no' answer; open questions invite the person into a reflective, exploratory place. There is no hierarchy of which kind of question is better; what is important is the intention behind the questions, the tone of voice of the questioner and the context.

I invite one person to start by turning to their neighbour and saying good morning to them, using their name (or asking them their name if they don't remember it), and then asking whatever question comes to mind. The person replies, or not, and then turns to their neighbour and does the same thing. We proceed around the group, and I include myself in the exercise.

I complete the exercise by asking the participants their experience either as the questioner or the questioned. I ask what they discovered about themselves, particularly in terms of the intention behind their question and the impact on the receiver, and this leads on to the focus of the next practice supervision session: 'Intent and Impact'. It is also fascinating to see the attunement that happens in such a brief exchange: the enquirer allowing themselves to trust the question that comes to their mind, checking it for a split second, and then having the courage to risk asking it and to be open to the response, whatever it is.

Before moving into the next session I ask participants if they would like to ask or share anything from the day before, and then ask if they are ready to move on.

As I re-read the last sentence, and because I will be looking at intentions, I am now wondering what my intention was in asking that question at that point. On the content level, it made sense. It was only our second day and the previous day had been very full, with invitations to go to the edge and push some boundaries. Now, as I sit here with it, I begin to get an inkling. On the one hand, as I said at the beginning of the chapter, I wanted to 'pull the chair out from under the mind'. On the other hand, I probably had a pull-back at that moment and wanted reassurance from the group that they were still with me and on board with the course, giving my mind something to hold onto before the next deep dive. That is fine too; a little kindness is in order.

Intent and impact

I refer to the CLEAR model, that yesterday we focused on contracting, today the focus is on listening and exploring and tomorrow we will cover action and review. Of course, these activities are also happening simultaneously, and we are selecting aspects of the supervision in order to take a closer look at the practices and the principles. So onto the next experiential learning: the 'intent and impact' exercise.

The concept of 'intent and impact' comes from the book *Difficult Conversations* (Stone, Patton & Heen, 2000: 44-57) and I share some of the theory after the practice.

I ask the participants to form new triads of supervisor, supervisee and observer. Each supervision session will last seven minutes. The supervisee brings a live issue from their work and the supervisor explores it with the supervisee. The observer's task is to make a note of the interventions of the supervisor and the impact they notice on the supervisee, and from their observations, to see if they can make a guess as to the intent behind the intervention. A second task is to notice whether any questions could also be a statement – for example, 'Is that all you are going to say?' meaning 'You need to say more.'

At the end of seven minutes, the triad gives the supervisor feedback using the feedback structure: one thing I appreciated, supervisor to self; supervisee to supervisor and observer to supervisor. Then the triad has another five minutes to share the observer's observations, with the observer leading this discussion. In a way, it is like supervision on supervision: participants share the discoveries they have made by mining for more minerals and gems in the same place.

According to the authors of Difficult Conversations, *on the conscious level, only the person delivering an intervention/communication can know the intent behind it and only the recipient of the intervention/communication can know the impact. However, I have observed that, when the intervention/ communication has a different impact on the recipient than was expected, and if one or both parties can stay there at that point, rather than running for cover, one or both of them may have an opportunity to learn something new about their unconscious communications and responses. The deliverer may discover an intent behind their intervention that they weren't aware of or were unconscious of, and the recipient may discover something they are/ were unaware or unconscious of in their reaction. For example, I might say to my son: 'Have you made that phone call?' My conscious intention is to get information, but beneath I am conveying my irritation that he promised to do it and hasn't yet. He may pick up that irritation and respond similarly, by saying: 'Why do you keep asking me that? I said I'd do it.'*
I am reminded here of a quote from Bandler and Grinder's book, Structure of Magic (1989): *'Match for rapport. Mismatch for change.' In other words, if you match you have rapport, but if you mismatch and stay*

with it, you have an opportunity to deepen the relationship. Either way, it is
a win! Everything is simply data. Welcome it. We discover our unconscious
projections and transferences that date back to earlier times in our lives and
need attention, resolution or dropping, as they are obscuring our view of
what we are attempting to look at and listen to now.

Robin and I were co-facilitating a group supervision of 12 psychotherapists – 11 women and one man. The sole male participant had presented a case and the other group members were attentive. However, gradually they began to focus more on him rather than his client, and he became 'the patient' that everyone wanted to 'help'. I listened for a while and wondered about the parallel process – how he and his client had fallen into a victim/rescuer relationship. After maybe half an hour, I made an intervention that I thought would help him and the group from going around the same loop again. That was my conscious intent. However, I noticed the impact on this man. He moved almost imperceptibly back in his chair. So it occurred to me that the impact of my intervention on him might tell me about my unconscious intent. Immediately the thought came, 'It was obviously me I wanted to help more than him,' so I shared that thought with him. He leaned forward. Later, when we were reviewing the work, he said that moment was the first time he felt able to move out of his stuck role. For me, it was a very useful experience of learning something new about my intent by attending to the feedback from the impact. It also helped the work with the client in terms of the parallel process – that is, the client was pulling back from the man's offers of help.

Stone, Patton and Heen (2000) also comment that we tend to project bad intentions onto other people and more charitable intentions onto ourselves. One of the examples they give is from a work situation:

> When a co-worker criticises you in front of department colleagues, you
> see it as she is trying to put you down. When you offer suggestions to
> others in the same meeting, you see it as trying to be helpful. (pp47–48)

So we have had a lively discussion about the theory and their discoveries in the practice and by now it is 11am and time for a break and cake. Cake is an essential ingredient in the training, it seems. I have tried analysing why it is so essential but now I just accept that it is.

After the morning break

A question we are frequently asked on the Core Course is, 'What are the differences between counselling, psychotherapy, coaching, mentoring and supervision?' A more fearful way of asking much the same question is, 'How do you make sure that supervision isn't therapy?' At first, I would try to answer these questions, but then I realised that I did not know what was triggering them, and especially what they were meaning by the word 'therapy'. I did register that there might be fear behind the use of the word. So, instead of trying to answer it, I devised an exercise to listen more deeply into this question and explore it. When we do this, we find that, although the fear feels real, it is usually unfounded.

I ask the larger group to form smaller groups of six each. I then offer six roles for each member of the groups to choose from: supervisee, supervisor, manager, therapist/practitioner, love and fear. I invite the supervisee to talk to the group for five minutes about their work or client, and the rest listen from their roles. Then I ask the supervisee to position themselves a little out of the group but so they can still hear what is being said. I ask the five remaining people to share what they focused on from their role, what feelings arose and the direction they found themselves wanting to take the supervisee. When they have finished (and I allow 10 minutes for this part), the supervisee returns and shares what they appreciated from listening in.

I then call the groups back together. The group members notice how much having a certain role or mindset affects and often limits what they see and hear and how they might be able to expand that now. The supervisees often notice that being listened to for five minutes without interruption means they can hear themselves better and begin to develop their inner supervisor. The group is beginning to get a feeling for the supervisory process and relationship and to relax into it, rather than needing to rush to a premature solution and a place of 'safe certainty'. They are beginning to find a learning space between the comfort zone and the panic zone. Gilbert and Evans (2000: 82) say one of the main jobs of the supervisor is to reduce the supervisee's fear and anxiety. We finish the morning with the exercise below.

This is one of Robin's exercises, which he uses to enquire into the supervisory relationship, particularly where there is fear. He gives participants two statements and asks them to complete them in writing. The first is for their eyes only, he says, and he is not going to ask them to share it; the second he invites them to share.

- **First sentence:** 'What I would least like my supervisor to know about my work is…'
- **Second sentence:** 'I would not want them to know because…'

People share fears such as 'I wouldn't want them to think I was unprofessional or that I didn't know what I was doing or I was found out to be a fraud.' Robin asks the group members to put up their hands if anyone present hasn't been afraid of being found out to be a fraud. No one ever does. He points out to the group that these fears are universal and that we can support each other if we share our fears, rather than hiding away and feeling isolated and self-defeating, and that in doing so we are modelling what we are wanting for our clients, colleagues and fellow human beings.

And so to lunch.

Exploring core beliefs and 'stories'

Bad supervision

During the lunch break, I set up an outer and an inner circle of chairs, enough for everyone in the group, with each inner chair facing an outer chair. As people come back from lunch, I invite them to occupy the chairs – the inner circle is for the supervisors and the outer circle for the supervisees. When everyone is back, I instruct the pairs to have a two-minute supervision session, with the supervisor giving 'bad' supervision to the issue the supervisee brings. I keep time and after two minutes I tell the supervisees to move one seat to their left and for the supervision to recommence. The supervisees bring the same issue to the next supervisor, who continues to give 'bad' supervision. We do this three or four times, and then I ask them to switch roles and move the opposite way three times. The exercise generates much laughter, high energy and movement.

We then dismantle the circle, go back to our original seats and share some of the paradoxes and insights that have emerged. These often include the observation that some of the 'bad' supervision received was useful and in some cases more useful than 'good' supervision. Some people find that the impact of their being 'bad' has a different impact on the supervisee than they expected. Some feel released from the straitjacket of trying to be a 'good' supervisor and realise how much energy it has been using and how much it has been taking them out of the present and out of connection with their supervisee. Some people find it disturbing to see how available other states are, just below the surface, and begin to get curious about that. The exercise provides a light-hearted way to begin to question some of the beliefs that we consider to be true and right. 'Core beliefs' form the focus of the rest of the day.

Core beliefs and 'story'

I invite the group to explore and examine some of their core beliefs: beliefs about supervision, work, their culture, their society, their world and themselves. Beliefs are seen as self-evident, fundamental truths. It is not the beliefs themselves (we all have them) that cause problems, I am suggesting, but the strength of our attachment and our blindness to them.

Byron Katie says in her training:[1] 'All there is is man or woman standing, sitting or lying down, the rest is story.' She also says, 'If your belief works for you, keep it, but if it doesn't, inquire.' This is where supervision and the supervisory relationship come in. The supervisee often brings to supervision something that isn't working for them, for their client, or for the system or organisation they are working with. There is an attachment to the story, the belief. The mind, the voice in our head, wants to be in control – or it thinks it does. It is as if there are two of us inside our heads.

---

1. www.thework.com

Eckhart Tolle, in the foreword to his book The Power of Now *(1999), talks about a time when he was deeply depressed and he heard himself repeating, 'I cannot live with myself any longer.' Then he suddenly became aware that this was a peculiar thought: 'Am I one or two? If I cannot live with myself there must be two of me: the "I" and the "self" that "I" cannot live with. "Maybe", I thought, "only one of them is real."' He writes that he was so stunned by this strange realisation that his mind stopped. He felt drawn into what felt like a vortex of energy, fell asleep and, when he awoke, found himself to be in a state of uninterrupted bliss.*

Michael Singer, in the Untethered Soul *(2007), talks about the internal storyteller, or mind, that is talking all the time. He says: 'What you are experiencing is really a personal presentation of the world according to you, rather than the stark, unfiltered experience of what is really out there. The mental manipulation of the outer experience allows you to buffer reality as it comes in… You recreate the world within your mind because you can control your mind, whereas you can't control the world' (Singer, 2007: 12).*

He goes on to say: 'True personal growth is about transcending the part of you that is not okay and needs protection. How to do this he continues is by constantly remembering to notice that you are the one inside that notices the voice talking. That is the way out' (2007: 12).

Jill Bolte Taylor is a researcher and neuroanatomist who experienced a stroke in the left side of her brain. She wrote a book about her experience titled My Stroke of Insight *(2009). In Chapters 16–19, she explores these two voices. The 'storyteller' part of her brain had been wiped out by her stroke, and when it came back online she was amused to see how it would draw conclusions based on minimal information and expected the rest of her to believe the stories it was making up.*

The following exercises are designed to help us catch sight of the stories and, in so doing so, begin to unravel them and be unravelled. Hence the Hafiz quote (2006) at the beginning of this chapter. Helping us recognise some of our core beliefs enables us to work with a greater range of supervisees, to be less reactive and judgemental and to stay in the present.

I invite the group to fill in the page on 'Discovering Core Beliefs' in our manual, which is reproduced below.

- Women are…
- Men are…
- Children are…
- People should always…
- People should never…
- I should always…
- I should never…

- Supervision is…
- I have a right to be angry if…
- I will have fulfilled my life if…
- I can help people by…
- I can damage people by…

I invite them to add two of their own (which you, the reader, might also like to do).

Then we move on to look at two ways of questioning story/script/belief by means of a sentence completion exercise.

Sentence completion

Here are some sentences and, below them, an example of using them.

I need this belief because… *or* in order to… *or* and that means…

- without it I would be…
- the cost of this belief is…
- the value of this belief is…
- the purpose of this belief is…
- where I learnt this belief was…
- I need to explore this topic because …
- if I don't keep it, I am afraid of losing…

Example – I was supervising a manager of a drug addiction unit on the phone and she said she was very stressed because she had just heard that morning that a major funding application had been turned down. She said she was feeling so anxious she couldn't attend to the other issues that she was going to bring to supervision.

Supervisor: So you have lost your funding, and that means?

Supervisee: I won't be able to pay my staff.

Supervisor: And that means?

Supervisee: There will be no counsellors for the clients.

Supervisor: And that means?

Supervisee: Some clients will die.

Supervisor: And that means?

Supervisee: I will be called before the trustees.

Supervisor: And that means?

Supervisee: They will sack me, charge me with neglect of duty and I will have to go to court.

> **Supervisor**: And that means?
>
> **Supervisee**: I will be found guilty and end up in prison.
>
> At this point I remember thinking, 'This process isn't working and I am facing failure – just like her.' So we were right there together, meeting the feeling and feeling it. Then I heard a gasp at the other end of the phone, and a sigh of relief, and the supervisee said, 'And then I can have a rest.' The whole state dropped away from her and we carried on attending to the other issues she wanted to bring to supervision. A week later, some funding came in from another source and she carried on running the project successfully for the next three years, until she left. She said that, from then on, whenever she felt tension, she would think about landing up in prison and being able to rest, and she would relax.

The other structure I use are the worksheets of Byron Katie.[2] Her approach to enquiring into core beliefs is twofold. One is the 'Judge your Neighbour' worksheet, which she asks you to fill out. Here are some of the questions on that worksheet:

- What angers, disappoints or confuses you about X?
- What is it about them you don't like?
- How do you want them to change?

She says that judgement is what we do best and has designed the worksheet to encourage us to feel the hurt, pain, fear and anger, and honour it and write it down. You are invited to be judgemental, harsh, childish and petty; not to try to be wise, spiritual or kind, and to allow your feelings to express themselves, without any fear of consequences or any threat of punishment.

When you have done that, she invites you into the inquiry with the following four questions. For example, a supervisee might write that their client does not value the work together, and we can ask:

- Is it true?
- Can you really know it's true?
- How do you react when you believe that thought?
- Who would you be without that thought? (And Byron Katie is very clear she is not asking you to drop it.)

Frequently I will simply ask a supervisee, 'Is it true? What is the evidence?' Often they will say that maybe it isn't true but it *feels* true, and I will point out that this

---

2. The worksheets are available to download from her website at www.thework.com, with spaces between each question for you to fill in.

is different. Then I might go on and look at how they react when they have that belief (for example, that they don't value their client) and who they might be if they did not have that belief (more open and curious).

We can offer or invite some reframes (or turnarounds, in Katie's terms), such as, if the person says the client does not value the sessions, find three ways they do value them (for example, they do turn up).

> The starting point for the inquiry is always the work, and at the end the supervisor brings it back to how this inquiry will have served their work and their clients. We are trying to separate feelings and interpretations ('The client doesn't value the sessions') from facts. I am reminded of a saying of Krishnamurti, the Indian teacher: 'Observation without evaluation is the highest form of human intelligence.'
>
> On similar lines, Byron Katie says: 'I don't let go of my concepts (beliefs). I meet them through inquiry, then they let go of me.'[3]
>
> I see supervision as a process that supports inquiry, with the aim of freeing myself, the supervisee and their clients from the tyranny of story, conditioning and unexamined beliefs. This enables us to move from the personal to the more systemic. We inquire around concepts such as right/wrong and good/bad that can lead to judging and excluding people. As Bert Hellinger (1998: 211) wrote: 'If you want to work systemically, you must find a position beyond moral judgement, a position that allows you to see larger systemic phenomena and their effect on other people.' Through inquiry, we come to see that what we have judged we have made other. We can move back into relationship when we ask questions like 'Is it true?', and we see that what we have judged is also part of us.

I quote a friend who says that if we have a conflict it means someone has broken one of our rules. We have a discussion about how our beliefs and rules limit us and about the value of inquiry, using Byron Katie's questions or sentence completion.

Six-category intervention analysis exercise

If there is time after the two afternoon practice sessions, I like to do a whole-group exercise using John Heron's six-category intervention analysis (1989), which he developed at the Human Potential research project at the University of Surrey, in 1975.

This provides participants with another window on their preferred mode of intervention – the intent behind our interventions and our beliefs. I invite the group to look at the summary below and then move to the other end of the room, where I have arranged six pieces of paper on the floor, each with one of the six interventions written on it. The group members are invited to stand by

3. www.thework.com

the intervention they most prefer. The people clustered around each intervention share for five minutes what they see as its strengths. They then share those strengths with the whole group. In the final part of the exercise, I ask them to stand by the intervention they use least, and then return to their triad one last time for a seven-minute supervision with the person who hasn't supervised that afternoon, using the intervention they normally least use or least prefer.

Six categories of intervention

The six categories of intervention apply equally to one-to-one and group situations. They are as follows:

1. **Prescriptive** – give advice, be directive – for example, a) 'You need to write a report on that'; b) 'You need to stand up to your father.'

2. **Informative** – be didactic, instruct/inform – a) 'You will find similar reports in the filing cabinet in the office'; b) 'This is how our filing system works.'

3. **Confrontative** – be confronting, challenge the other person's behaviour or attitude. This is not to be confused with adversarial confrontation: confronting is positive and constructive; it helps the other person consider behaviour and attitudes of which they would otherwise be unaware – for example, 'I notice when you talk about your boss you always smile.'

4. **Cathartic** – release tension, offer abreaction – for example, 'What do you really want to say to your client?'

5. **Catalytic** – be reflective, encourage self-directed problem-solving – for example, a) 'Can you say some more about that'? b) 'How can you do that?'

6. **Supportive** – be approving/confirming/validating – for example, 'I can understand how you feel.'

Although they may not be exhaustive, the categories help us to become aware of the different interventions we use, those we are comfortable with and those we avoid. Following on from that we can, with practice, begin to widen our choices. The emphasis in the definition is on the intended effect of the intervention on the client. There is no implication that any one category is more or less significant and important than any other. Heron (1989) suggests that, when we are not conscious, our interventions can become degenerate or perverse. Degenerate he defines as using interventions in an unskilled, compulsive or unsolicited way, usually rooted in lack of awareness; perverted interventions are ones that are deliberately malicious.

The day finishes with the participants returning to their home groups for 15–20 minutes. I ask them to look at their manuals where they wrote down their learning needs on the first day, and think about what they would like to focus on the next day. The first session will be tag supervision, explained below; the second session will be on the Karpman triangle, as mentioned on the first day, and this will be followed by a free-choice session. The afternoon will be devoted to goal setting and next steps.

∾   ∾   ∾

Day 3

At 9.30am, I start the day by inviting people into a short relaxation. I ask them to close their eyes, breathe and imagine it is 4pm and they are leaving: is there anything they would regret not saying or doing or asking for before they leave? I then invite them to share these and we write them up on the flipchart. The topics today are Karpman's drama triangle; self-disclosure; working on Skype or other Voice over Internet Protocol (VoIP) apps; working in dual roles; working with difference, and how to create a working alliance. We will not have time for them all so I let the list compost while we engage in tag group supervision, described below.

Tag supervision

I set up two chairs facing each other, one for the supervisor and one for the supervisee. I say we have time for two tag supervision sessions and ask who has a live issue they'd like to discuss. Two people volunteer and we decide which one will go first. I invite them to take the supervisee's chair, turn to face the group and describe in one sentence what they are bringing, then turn back to face the empty supervisor's chair.

In tag supervision, different people come and sit in the supervisor chair. At any time any member of the group can clap themselves into the supervisor's chair to make an intervention and see the response of the supervisee. They can clap themselves out when they want, or another member of the group can clap them out when they want to supervise, or I clap them out if I see they have completed their intervention, so someone else can have an opportunity to supervise. There is time probably for around seven or eight supervisors over a 10-minute session. Here is the beginning of an example from a recent course.

> **Supervisee:** I don't know what to do with my client.
> **Supervisor 1:** Can you tell me a bit more about the context?
> **Supervisee:** I am seeing her at a young person's drop-in centre. She has come for six sessions but missed the last two and I have written to her. (Supervisor 1 claps themselves out and supervisor 2 comes in.)
> **Supervisor 2:** How did you feel about that?
> **Supervisee:** I felt very disappointed as I thought we were getting somewhere. And frustrated. (Supervisor 2 claps themselves out and supervisor 3 comes in.)
> **Supervisor 3:** I wonder if you could become your client and speak as them, so we can see it more from their point of view?

And so on for seven or eight interventions. (In the next chapter we give a more detailed account of a session.)

To finish, I ask the supervisors to say what they appreciated about their intervention and then the supervisee shares what they appreciated. The supervisee usually says all of it was useful and then picks out one or two that were particularly so, and also remarks how joined up it felt, even though there were so many different supervisors. We then have another supervision session with a different supervisee taking the chair. After the two sessions, the whole group looks at what was learnt from having the opportunity to engage with the tag supervision sessions. One of the learnings, besides the interventions themselves, is the value of simply holding a client in mind. This is a core concept in supervision. The supervisor holds the supervisee in mind, who in turn holds the client in mind.

The Karpman triangle and the beneficial triangle

The next 40 minutes are spent exploring the Karpman triangle, beginning with the drama triangle (Karpman, 1968) and the beneficial triangle. Karpman proposes that the purpose of any game is the pay-off. On the first day of the course, we looked at the 'games we play' when trying to manage ourselves in any relationship, including the supervisory relationship. We look at and share what the pay-offs are for each of us when we find ourselves in one or more of the roles of victim, persecutor or rescuer. Mostly, for the persecutor, the pay-off is that they feel in the right; for the victim, it's that they feel blameless, and for the rescuer, it's the feeling that they are good. These pay-offs resonate with most of the group members.

'I'm right' also reminds us of the question, 'Would you rather be right or happy?' It is worth exploring this simple question to find out if being both right and happy are possible. It isn't, is the general conclusion, because being right takes us back inside our own heads, into closed looped thinking, so there is no chance of looking outwards to the world and engaging and receiving anything from it. It is very lonely and barren inside our heads and all we have for nourishment is that we are right, and even that isn't true.

One member quotes some graffiti he has seen: 'So if I give all the blame to you, I won't feel so bad about myself.' One of the purposes of being a victim

Figure 3.1: Drama triangle (Karpman, 1968) and beneficial triangle

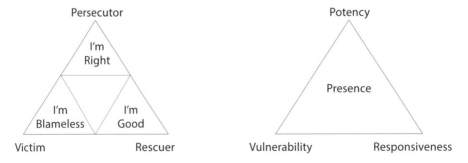

or blaming another is to feel less bad about yourself. Another group member says she realises that she plays out the whole drama triangle inside her head. She berates herself; she feels a victim and then she tries to rescue herself from this internal nightmare.

I then ask everyone to complete the sentence: 'I need to be right because…' Here is one person's answer:

> I need to be right because… I need to be heard.
> I need to be heard because… I need to be seen.

I ask what the person needs in order to be seen and by whom. He pauses, and then says: 'I need to be seen as a bit good and not just bad… by my family.'

So, for him, being right is an attempt to wipe out the fear of being bad. It also usually comes from a young place where we experienced trauma or felt devastated because we had displeased our parents, on whom our survival depended, or that is how it felt to us. We look at how we develop defences to manage the pain or hurt and how they can become demon protectors (Kalsched, 1996) and prevent anything getting in, so limiting access to life.

The drama triangle is very helpful in understanding how we humans get stuck in relationships. The beneficial triangle points to a possible way out. I cannot find who used the term first, but it has been used in therapy and counselling circles for many years.

The strength of it is in the words at each point of the triangle: vulnerability, potency and responsiveness. Add 'presence' and that is what we are aiming for in supervision and beyond. It is also what we are defending against because most of us find vulnerability difficult, even though I believe, along with Brene Brown (2015), that is our true nature.

> *As I write this, I am aware of being in the drama triangle right now. I feel a victim, I am reacting by being persecutory both internally and externally, and simultaneously I am trying to rescue myself. My belly is tight, my thoughts are jumping from place to place and my breathing is shallow. So can I, by means of the beneficial triangle, pause and stay with vulnerability, potency and responsiveness? I notice I am beginning to slow myself down and my belly begins to soften. I notice my shoulders drop a little and my mind feels a little less scrambled. I notice I feel embarrassment, the edge of shame at being in this place now and I am in a judgement as to whether this is useful or, even more edgy, acceptable to you, the reader, or whoever else I am projecting onto. I am now free enough to move back into the task, which in this case is the task of writing.*

Several people in the group share their stories and those of their clients and what helped them. A major step is in recognising we are in the triangle.

It is time for a break.

Self-disclosure

After the break we decide to explore self disclosure and working online. We brainstorm some rules of thumb for self-disclosure and come up with:

- Do it if it contributes to the connection.
- It depends very much on the context.
- It can't be generalised and should be navigated individually, for each relationship.
- It probably involves some risk.
- We can only find out by risking it and seeing the impact.

People share experiences of when they have disclosed and their own supervisor has made a self-disclosure. Sometimes they felt joined by their supervisor and this helped them to feel they belonged to the human race, and sometimes they felt the session became all about their supervisor.

I have a simple example from my own practice: I had to change a session and began to tell the supervisee why I needed to change the date, and she said, 'I don't need to know the reason. I will check my diary and see if I can change.' She could, and it took less than a minute; there was no need for explanations – they were my need, not hers.

We also touch on what to do when we have a hospital appointment or are receiving treatment for a potentially terminal illness. Participants agree that they need to address it client by client and it is helpful to explore it in their own supervision. People also describe experiences when they have revealed something about themselves they had not intended to and it had apparently not been helpful, but exploring this in supervision had led to new understandings about the relationship.

Skype and other VoIP apps

We then look at the use of telephone, Skype and other VoIP apps. Quite a few of the members of the group say they use the telephone or other such devices as part of their practice. It is useful to see what people project onto the devices and also what people's experiences are, both in the giving and receiving. Some (including me) have found to our surprise we can do body work just as well, or sometimes even better, on Skype. We have extended what we had imagined was possible, especially as we became more practised at using it. I have found it is important to have a clear contract. It doesn't work if someone rings up at the last minute to say they can't make the session and can they have it on Skype – it interrupts the relationship and bypasses important processes and material. With a clear contract, however, it works well and sometimes makes possible work that would not have been possible any other way.

Finally, before lunch, the group goes back into new triads for a last supervision session, with a longer session of 20 minutes in each role, including feedback.

Each triad manages its own time. I suggest that the supervisor asks the observer to give them feedback on something specific, such as non-verbal behaviour, body language, intent and impact, interventions, the focus of the supervision, who is leading and who is following, implicit and explicit contracting, or whatever the supervisor would like. After these they go straight to lunch.

Final afternoon

After lunch we feed back from these supervision sessions. They share that the sessions were useful as they felt themselves integrating their learning and are now feeling excited rather than scared at the prospect of supervising. They also notice that they feel they have grown as supervisees and can see themselves making better use of their own supervision.

> *This is the point on the course when the participants are looking forward to the next steps in the training and the next steps of going back to work. However, it is also a point when people's anxieties seem to return, having been dissipated by the fun, joy and creativity of experimenting and practising, so there are always quite a lot of questions and requests for clarification that only go some way to reassuring them. I think it is, in some part, our defence against feeling loss. As a trainer said to me many years ago, early on in my career, 'Loss is loss. It doesn't matter if it is your favourite pen or a close friend or relative; we feel the impact.'*

Several people share how much they are going to miss the closeness and intimacy they have felt in the group. This leads on to a short but poignant exchange of how we deal with endings by such strategies as becoming very busy so as not to feel, zoning out, finding a way to leave early, finding distractions or going into future planning. I am glad that there has been space for these feelings to emerge.

We now take time to go into their questions in relation to the training and certificate. We also discuss fears around stepping up as a supervisor. We have participants at all stages of their work life, so some will have already been supervising for some time and others will be only beginning to supervise. Some will be asked to supervise at their place of work but others will be seeking supervisees and will want to know how to set this up. In effect, they will be looking at the business side of running a practice. We invite them onto our list of trainee supervisors on the CSTD website as, over the years, small organisations and charities have approached us looking for low-cost or expenses-only supervisors.

I now invite the group members to take 10 minutes on their own in which to collect their postcards, look at their learning log and what they wrote on the first morning and, if they want to, write about some key moments on the course. I then invite them to imagine finishing with this group and saying goodbye and going home. I pause and ask them to imagine that they are going back into work on the

Monday morning and to think of one thing they would like to do, be, introduce or be supported in at work and write that down. Finally, I ask them to return to their home groups one last time and spend half an hour together focusing on what their next steps are and completing, as a group, with appreciations.

We then complete as a whole group, sharing what the course has meant to us. I present them individually with their certificates and the rest of the group applauds. We round off this small ceremony by taking a group photograph, which we post in the gallery on our website.

In the core course, as in all the subsequent courses, I am inviting the trainees to move into being present with what is and to slow down. The challenge is to give up the attachment to fixing the supervisee and the clients being brought to supervision, as if they are all separate and problems to be solved, managed or defended against. If any action is needed, it will emerge from the contemplation of what is and the relationship. The offer to the trainees is to embrace their judgements, fears, core beliefs and conditioning and, from that place, to trust the present moment.

Summary of exercises

1. **Paired exercise: who you are, how you got here and what did you leave behind?** (p41)
   Purpose: to give permission to bring all of oneself and to become more present.

2. **Postcard exercise: choosing postcards for self and for supervision** (p43)
   Purpose: using a different part of the brain from the verbal.

3. **Sparkling moment exercise** (p44)
   Purpose: to focus on people's strength and resilience, to build rapport, to present a strengths-based way of working for both work and life.

4. **Learning log and feedback sheets** (p45)
   Purpose: a written record of the participants' strengths, resources, learning needs and sabotages.

5. **CLEAR model** (p47)
   Purpose: offering a framework for supervision.

6. **Contracting exercise** (p48)
   Purpose: to see how much of contracting is implicit as well as explicit.

7. **Hopes and fears exercise** (p48)
   Purpose: to show how these can affect the contracting.

8. **Helping roles exercise** (p49)
   Purpose: to see how these roles are operating under the surface and are affecting the supervisory relationship.

9. **Feedback structure** (p52)
    Purpose: to ensure the supervisor gets feedback to help their learning.

10. **What your name means to you** (p54)
    Purpose: to deepen connection between people and to connect with the legacy of our ancestors.

11. **Open and closed questions** (p55)
    Purpose: to raise awareness of how the type of question we ask can influence the session and the relationship.

12. **Intent and impact** (p56)
    Purpose: to understand more about conversations and how we connect and disconnect moment to moment.

13. **Listening from different perspectives** (p57)
    Purpose: to explore the frequently asked question about the differences between supervision, therapy and coaching.

14. **Bad supervision** (p59)
    Purpose: to have fun and also to show how much we restrict ourselves by trying 'to get it right'.

15. **Sentence completion** (p60)
    Purpose: to demonstrate how quickly it is possible to drop to a deeper level.

16. **Core beliefs inquiry** (p61)
    Purpose: to show how much these can run our lives without our realising.

17. ***The Work* of Byron Katie** (p62)
    Purpose: to elicit core beliefs.

18. **Six-category intervention analysis exercise** (p63)
    Purpose: to explore different styles of intervention and their relevance at different times.

19. **Tag supervision** (p65)
    Purpose: to provide practice and show that there are many different ways of intervening around the same issue.

20. **Drama triangle** (p66)
    Purpose: to illustrate a dynamic that operates in much of our lives.

21. **Beneficial triangle** (p66)
    Purpose: to provide a concept and means to move out of the drama triangle.

22. **Self-disclosure** (p68)
    Purpose: to explore how self-disclosure can be used.

Foodnotes

Below are the cake recipes I often bake for the Core Course. I would like to suggest that you bake them, but also go beyond them, experiment, make them your own – in short, get into relationship with them. And, of course, this approach is not limited to baking cakes: here are a couple of quotes that illustrate this from Nicole Daedone (2011: 22–23), who learned to cook from her grandmother.

> My grandmother was teaching me the most important lesson of cooking, but also of living: anything you really get into relationship with will reveal its secrets to you. All you have to do is to stand in the kitchen with an open mind and heart, recognizing the honour of cooking food for your family. The recipe will come.

> You open yourself and the answers come through you. You find you know things you never knew before. You discover that a masterpiece doesn't actually require you to master anything at all. It simply requires you to feel, to listen, and to trust yourself.

Carrot cake

From *The Boxing Clever Cook Book* (Jones & Wilmot, 2002)

My sister, Joy, gave me this recipe and it is perfect for the start of the training, as it is delicious, generous and nourishing and provides a good foundation for the hungry work of learning. (Just choose one cup and use it for all the measures.)

> 1½ cups sugar
> 1½ cups sunflower oil
> 4 large eggs
> 2 cups self-raising flour
> 2 tsp bicarbonate of soda
> 2 tsp cinnamon
> 1 tsp salt
> 3 cups carrots, grated
> ½ cup chopped mixed nuts
> 1 tsp vanilla essence
> Topping: 200g crème fraiche and 1 tbsp orange juice

1. Preheat oven to 180°C/350°F/Gas mark 4).
2. Mix together sugar and oil.
3. Add eggs, beat well.
4. Add sifted dried ingredients and mix in.
5. Add carrots, nuts and vanilla essence.
6. Line a large roasting tin 30cm (11") square with foil and pour in mixture.

7.   Bake for about 50 minutes until firm and golden brown.

8.   For the topping, flavour the crème fraiche with orange juice and pour over the cooled cake.

Shortbread

I like this one because it is so easy and is always appreciated. Sometimes in cooking, as in supervision, simple is effective.

> 75g/3oz salted butter
> 40–50g/1–2 oz caster sugar
> 75g/3oz plain flour
> 25g/1oz cornflour

1.   Cream butter with half the sugar.

2.   Work in the flour and cornflour and then the remaining sugar.

3.   Knead the dough and press into a tray or cut into shapes, or whatever takes your fancy, at whatever thickness you like.

4.   Cook until light brown on top: either slowly at 300–325°F/150–170°C/Gas mark 2 or quickly at 350°F/180°C/Gas mark 4. The timing depends on your oven so it's best to keep an eye on it the first time you bake it. I often know it is ready by the smell.

5.   If you have left it in the round, cut into slices immediately, while it is just out of the oven, and leave it to cool before taking the slices out of the tin.

References

Bandler R, Grinder J (1989). *The Structure of Magic I: a book about language and therapy*. Palo Alto, CA: Science and Behavior Books.

Berne E (1964). *Games People Play*. New York, NY: Grove Press.

Bibby T (2010). *Education – an 'Impossible Profession'? psychoanalytic explorations of learning and classrooms*. London: Routledge.

Bolte Taylor J (2009). *My Stroke of Insight: a brain scientist's personal journey*. London: Hodder & Stoughton.

Brown B (2015). *Daring Greatly*. London: Penguin.

Cooperrider DL, Srivastva S (1987). Appreciative inquiry in organizational life. In: Woodman RW, Pasmore WA (eds). *Research in Organizational Change and Development, vol 1*. Stamford, CT: JAI Press (pp129–169).

Cooperrider DL, Whitney D (2005). *Appreciative Inquiry: a positive revolution in change*. San Francisco, CA: Berrett Koehler Publishers Inc.

Daedone N (2011) *Slow Sex*. New York, NY: Hachette.

Donnellan D (2005). *The Actor and the Target*. London: Nick Hern Books.

Gilbert M, Evans K (2000). *Psychotherapy Supervision: an integrative rational approach to psychotherapy supervision*. Buckingham: Open University Press.

Hafiz (2006). *I Heard God Laughing: poems of hope and joy*. (D Ladinsky, trans.) London: Penguin Books.

Hawkins P, Shohet R (2012). *Supervision in the Helping Professions* (4th ed). Maidenhead: Open University Press.

Hawthorne L (1975). Games supervisors play. *Social Work* May: 179–183

Hellinger B (1998). *Love's Hidden Symmetry: what makes love work in relationships*. Phoenix, AZ: Zeig, Tucker & Theisen Inc.

Heron J (1989). *Six Category Intervention Analysis* (3rd ed). Human Potential Resource Group, University of Surrey. Guildford: University of Surrey.

Horn F (1981). *I Want One Thing*. Camarillo, CA: Devorss & Co.

Houston G (1995). *Supervision and Counselling*. London. Rochester Foundation.

Houston G (1985). Group Supervision of Groupwork. *Self and Society* 13(2): 64–66.

Jones J, Wilmot J (2002). *The Boxing Clever Cook Book: twelve recipe books in one*. Findhorn: J&J Publishing.

Kadushin A (1976). *Supervision in Social Work*. New York, NY: Colombia University Press.

Kalsched D (1996). *The Inner World of Trauma: archetypal defenses of the personal spirit*. Hove: Routledge.

Karpman S (1968). Fairy tales and script drama analysis. *Transactional Analysis Bulletin* 26(7): 39–43.

Katie B (2019). 'Judge Your Neighbour' worksheet. [Online.] In: Katie B. *The Work of Byron Katie*. Byron Katie International. http://thework.com/wp-content/uploads/2019/02/jyn_en_mod_6feb2019_r4_form1.pdf (accessed 30 September 2019).

Katie B (2002). *Loving What Is*. New York, NY: Harmony Books.

Liedloff J (1975/2004). *The Continuum Concept: in search of happiness lost*. London: Penguin Books.

Rumi (2004). *Selected Poems*. London: Penguin Classics.

Ryan S (2004). *Vital Practice – stories from the healing arts: the homeopathic and supervisory way*. Portland: Sea Change Publications.

Shohet R (ed) (2011). *Supervision as Transformation*. London: Jessica Kingsley.

Singer MA (2007). *The Untethered Soul: the journey beyond yourself*. Oakland, CA: New Harbinger Publications.

Stone D, Patten B, Heen S (2000). *Difficult Conversations: how to discuss what matters most*. London: Penguin Books.

Tolle E (1999). *The Power of Now*. Novato, CA: New World Library.

Whyte D (2002). *Crossing the Unknown Sea: work as a pilgrimage of identity*. New York, NY: Riverhead Books.

Zander B (2012). *Work (how to give an 'A')*. YouTube; 26 February. www.youtube.com/watch?v=qTKEBygQic0 (accessed 30 September 2019).

4

The seven-eyed model of supervision

Joan and I have been teaching the Seven-Eyed Model of Supervision for more than 30 years, and we are continually devising new ways of presenting it and bringing it alive. I think part of its strength is that it provides a map, a framework, with which to view the landscape of supervision. One of the rewards of teaching it is seeing how the map enables people to navigate their supervision practice with increasing confidence.

It is the most theoretical of our courses. However, we think the Seven-Eyed Model can be applied to any profession to increase practitioners' creativity and joy in their work. For example, earlier (p10) we mentioned how a colleague, Joseph Wilmot, was able to use it with IT workers, by regarding IT as the client who needed to be integrated into the organisation.

The model was originally developed by Peter Hawkins in 1985 and is described in *Supervision in the Helping Professions* (Hawkins & Shohet, 2012) where there is a more theoretical exposition. This chapter describes our teaching of it. It is written up in the style of a transcript, drawing on several different courses, as all follow a broadly similar structure. The transcripts are anonymised creations drawn from our experiences of many courses.

Like Joan on the Core Course, I arrive early to set out the room. As this is the second course in our certificate programme, Joan will have already met everyone. I have not asked her for any feedback on the participants as I like to come fresh to the group. The group won't be identical to those who attended the preceding Core Course, as people can take as long as they want to do the certificate. Some may have done the Core Course as long as two years ago, although there will be a number who attended the course that ran a few months previously.

I have the list of participants and I welcome them as they come in, and ask their names. Everyone is here by 10am – the culture of punctuality has been set in the previous course. We learnt this in our therapeutic community work. If we were unclear or sloppy around our boundaries, the residents would pick this up and feel insecure and act out.

Even though I have done this course dozens of times, I notice a flutter of anxiety at the beginning. I know this will probably mirror the participants' own anxiety, and I often think how brave people are to come on courses and face the potential, or very real, difficulties of learning. I find it much easier to be a facilitator, where I can see not knowing as interesting, than being a member, where I feel the potential for shame. For many, the reverse is true: leading creates more anxiety than being a member.

∾   ∾   ∾

Day 1

I welcome people to the course, making eye contact with each person. I suggest we go straight into the Sparkling Moment exercise, which most people will already have done on the Core Course (see p44). Even if they have done it before, I tell them it is never the same, and give them the Heraclitus quote that you can't step into the same river twice.

I notice a slightly defensive tone here, and, as I reflect now, remember another course when someone said they had done an exercise before and didn't want to do it again. Clearly, this has lodged within me. Extraordinary how much baggage we (I) carry. It's not a big deal but it's interesting to note how hard it is to be fully present 'without memory, desire, understanding' (Bion, 1970: 43).

I have found Sparkling Moment a good way to start a group, whatever the size. Everyone has a chance to introduce themselves to at least one person. I know Joan has written it up in her description of the Core Course, and I will repeat the essence of the exercise here.

Sparkling moment

Partner up, one A, one B. Have a pen and paper handy.

Describe a recent sparkling moment at work. Define sparkling in whatever way you like.

The partner can just listen; they will not have to repeat the story to the group. Switch.

See your partner telling their story in your mind's eye. Hear them.

Write down two qualities about the other person that you have intuited from the story.

Share the qualities with your partner and make sure you really receive what they tell you.

I am always a little cautious about asking readers to do exercises. I often skip them when I'm reading a book like this. For me, they interrupt the flow of my

reading, but you might like to think of a sparkling moment yourself, about
work. It will only take a few seconds, so you might like to try it before you
read on. Maybe one has already popped into your head.

> *Sparkling Moment is one of my favourite exercises. I almost always use it*
> *at the start of any training. It helps to create safety and is often very moving,*
> *as the feedback shows when we return to the larger group. People report*
> *feeling seen and are pleasantly surprised at how much can be learnt about*
> *another person in such a short time. These days, I write out its different*
> *stages on the flipchart as we have found that precise instructions are really*
> *important. For example, I have on occasion forgotten to mention that people*
> *will not have to retell their partner's stories to the whole group and found*
> *out that this was a source of anxiety to many participants and stopped them*
> *engaging fully with the delight of it.*

I call them back after about six or seven minutes and tell them about the
origins of the exercise, which comes from Appreciative Inquiry (Cooperrider
& Whitney, 2005), which Joan mentioned in Chapter 3 (p44). I reiterate that
Appreciative Inquiry is about looking at what works well in a system, whether
that is an organisation, a team, a family, a couple, or even an individual. In other
words, it is a strength-based way of looking at the world, seeing it as a mystery to
be embraced rather than a problem to be solved. I quote Einstein, who is widely
reported to have said that the most important question facing humanity is, 'Is the
universe friendly?'

> *Once we start exploring this idea of our attitude to the universe – whether*
> *we see it as friendly or non-friendly – we see how much it can shape our*
> *approach to everything, including supervision. A belief in an unfriendly*
> *universe will naturally move us to fear; a belief in a friendly world is more*
> *likely to move us to a loving approach, even if we inevitably face problems*
> *(for more on this, see Chapter 8 and the workshop on love and fear).*

I ask them what they appreciated about themselves, their partner or the exercise.
There is much positive feedback, especially towards partners: how they listened,
how they felt their partners had met and understood them, and an appreciation of
the exercise itself. I say that I use it in teams where there may be conflict or people
are seeing each other in very limited ways, which can happen when we are with
others on a daily basis. People have their set roles, which are difficult to change.
This exercise reminds everyone about the strengths in the system, whether couple,
family, team or organisation, and it can help break up some fixed images.

Appreciative Inquiry

I then go on to say more about Appreciative Inquiry, re-quoting that it invites
us to see the world as a mystery to be embraced rather than a problem to be

solved. This obviously applies to people as well, as we can get into seeing them as problems. And, because our work is interactive, if we see them in this way, they are more likely to behave like that. I say that, in our work, I would suggest relationship is primary and we do not see people as problems to be fixed. This idea of cure, fixing, has had profound implications for our work, I suggest, and may have been influenced by the medical model. But medical practitioners are now recognising increasingly the value of relationship in healing.

> *Now, as I write, I think of Martin Buber's I/Thou and I/It dynamic (Buber, 1923/2000). I/It emphasises separation and sees you as other, and therefore someone to be controlled. At some level, I think separation is bound to create fear. I/Thou recognises interconnectedness and relationship and our importance to each other.*

I share how I first began using Appreciative Inquiry in a comprehensive secondary school in the East End of London. I tell how I started with a few staff and a couple of students and asked them what their goals might be. A teacher said, 'To stop the vandalism.'

Here I pause and ask the group, 'What pictures come to mind when you think of vandalism?' They reply variously: 'Broken windows, graffiti.' I ask, 'And stopping the vandalism?' They reply, 'Closed circuit television, punishment.'

I ask them to hold those pictures in their minds and suggest reframing the goal into helping to create a beautiful school environment. What do they see now? The group reports that the pictures in their minds are completely different. They are now seeing pictures of fountains, soothing music, quiet areas. If we redefine the goal, the problem of vandalism would be tackled in a very different way.

I continue with the story of the school. 'The following week, the staff in the school said another goal was to reduce the truancy. Again, the pictures in their minds were negative. Letters to parents, punishments etc. I suggested a reframe of making the school a place where pupils wanted to come. And with those two reframes, both staff and students worked towards creating a beautiful environment where people wanted to come. Of course, there was a lot of hard work – meetings, talking to staff who were new to the idea and needed time to assimilate it, fitting in with people's busy schedules – but the groundwork was set with the reframing.'

I tell this story because it shows how quickly we get caught into problem thinking and negative imaging, and how we move towards the images we have made in our minds. It also sets the scene for talking about how we approach supervision. I say they can find out more about Appreciative Inquiry on the internet. I can spend up to half an hour on this exercise as I think it sets the tone of our work – the questioning of the current zeitgeist of looking for faults, which is part of our wider blame culture, and reminds us (me included) how valuable it can be to focus on what is working well.

Introductions, needs, sabotages

Next, I suggest we go around the group with each saying their name and something they would like the group to know about them.

It is interesting what people choose to share here. They share the experience of becoming a grandparent, excitement at being in London, getting a new cat, going freelance. Everyone is free to share at whatever depth they want.

I then ask them to turn to the page about needs and sabotages in the course manual. (We send out a manual for each course electronically beforehand and, as Joan has already explained in the Core Course, give out a hard copy at the beginning of each course.) We do this exercise on every course as people's needs and sabotages change over time and in different contexts.

I give them a few minutes to fill that in on their own. I then ask them to partner with the person with whom they did the Sparkling Moment exercise and form a foursome with another pair. This foursome will be their home group. I explain that the home group is where they can check in to review how they are doing each day.

They spend quarter of an hour in their home groups. I don't have a rule about confidentiality. Instead I use what we call a 'good will contract' (as already explained by Joan on p54). I ask that we assume we are here to support each other's learning, to build a learning community, and so we need to feel free to expose our vulnerabilities. That means trusting people to be openhearted about themselves and each other on the course, and to continue it afterwards. It stresses learning, community and vulnerability.

I pay particular attention to the sabotages and, as Joan explains in the Core Course chapter, ask group members to write them on the flip chart. They include 'being critical', 'switching off', 'feeling I know less than everyone else' and 'feeling inadequate'. I suggest to people that these feelings belong to all of us, but if we catch the sabotages early enough, we can use them as an opportunity for growth.

This is core to our teaching and for any groupwork. If someone shares something that is potentially vulnerable, like feeling they know less than everyone else, I turn to the group and say, 'Is there anyone who has *not* had this feeling before?' Not a hand goes up. So, straight away the feeling/thought is normalised. I describe later in the book (Chapter 8, p179) how I came to this way of working but I want to stress now that the wording is very important. For example, I might ask: 'Is there anyone who has *not* felt inadequate?' If I were to ask how many people have felt inadequate, they might hesitate about confessing to this.

I suggest it is time for a break and point out the practicalities like loos and where kitchen is. I ask for a volunteer to be biscuit and cake monitor. I stay in the training room. I like to have time to reflect on the morning.

The seven modes: an overview

When they come back from their break, I say we will move on to an overview of the seven modes, or foci, of supervision. I tell the story of how this concept of seven modes originated with research by Peter Hawkins in the 1980s and how Peter, Joan and I developed it subsequently.

> *It may help you, the reader, to have a client/coachee in your mind as you read this section, so that, as well as understanding the theory, you could be giving yourself some supervision.*
>
> *At this point in the chapter, I will start using the style of a literal transcription. As previously explained, these are not verbatim transcripts from any one course, but the exchanges are typical and illustrative of those we have experienced over the past many years.*

Robin: A supervisee brings a client to supervision. *(Turning to group)* Where do you focus?

Participant 1 (P1): Well, obviously, on trying to find out as much as possible about the client.

P2: Yes, but I also try to use what is happening in the here and now, between supervisee and supervisor.

P3: I haven't got a set answer, as it will vary, but I try to find out what the outside factors are that might be influencing the case and may have been neglected. I guess this comes from working with children, where there are always lots of other people involved.

P4: I think there are always countertransference issues, otherwise there wouldn't have been a problem.

P5: All of those, but I think it is important that the supervisee finishes with some idea of what he or she is going to do.

Robin: Between you, you have come up with most of the seven modes.

I point to three participants sitting on my right.

Robin: Let's take you, Susan, as supervisor; you, Mary, as supervisee, and you, John, as client.

> *I have already drawn a diagram on the flipchart (see figure 4.1), and I find using people in the group to role play can have a more immediate effect. To explain the map below more fully, there are two overlapping circles or matrices: client/supervisee and supervisee/supervisor. The supervisee is involved in both circles, which is why they are overlapping. The outer circle involves the different contexts that supervisor, supervisee and client might partake in – the idea behind the stakeholder and ghost exercise that I will go on to describe shortly. This could be the work context of either supervisor or supervisee or both, or the family context of any of client, supervisor, supervisee, other professionals and so on.*

Figure 4.1: Map of the Seven Modes (Hawkins & Shohet, 2012: 87)

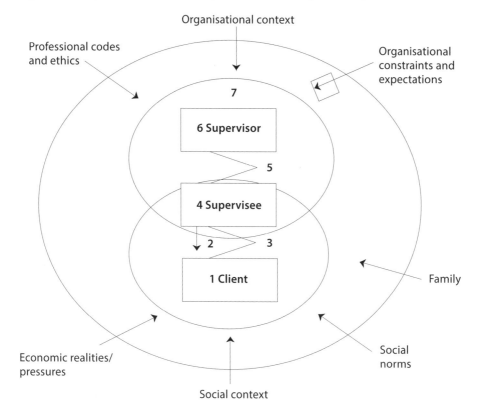

Robin: So, Mary, as supervisee, you say, 'I want to talk about my client, John.' In mode 1, Susan, your supervisor, tries to find out as much as she can about your client, John – or, more importantly, she helps you to see John with fresh eyes. Very often we get a diagnosis and we don't see past that. It colours our view of the client. We will go into that more later on.

In mode 2, we try to find out about the interventions that the supervisee, Mary, might have made or didn't make but could have, or might make in the future. Just as in mode 1, where we want to help the supervisee see John with new eyes, in this mode we want to expand the range of possibilities that Mary could contemplate.

Mode 3 focuses on the client/supervisee relationship. In mode 3, we are looking at the relationship between Mary, the supervisee, and John, the client.

Mode 4 concerns the countertransference of the supervisee – in other words, what is happening to Mary when she sees John. What goes on inside her, not only during the session but perhaps before or after? My opinion is that, if we are stuck with a client for any reason, then it has to involve countertransference because another person might not be stuck or would be stuck in a different way. In fact, countertransference is happening before the client walks into the room, in our choice of becoming a therapist, coach or whatever.

I have written about this in Supervision in the Helping Professions *(Hawkins & Shohet 2012: 8–14). I don't enlarge on this here, with the group, as I want to continue to explain the modes, but I think the reasons we come into this work hugely affect the way we work. One of the best books on this for me is* How Can I Help? *by Ram Dass and Paul Gorman (1985), which was written a long time ago but is still relevant.*

In mode 5, we are looking at the relationship between Mary as supervisee and Susan as supervisor. This can mirror the relationship between John and Mary. So, for example, if Susan is frustrated with Mary, this could mirror Mary being frustrated with John. This is called parallel process. But, of course, the relationship between supervisor and supervisee exists in its own right, as well as being a mirror.

In mode 6, Susan is using what is going on with her in the moment. She will use body sensations, images and feelings and feed them back. It is a skill to be able to both listen to the content that the supervisee brings and pay attention to oneself.

And finally, in mode 7, we are looking at the wider context. John, Mary and Susan are all part of interlocking systems that could include John's wife, Susan's supervisor, their family systems, any outside agencies, and so on.

Even if it is a lot to take in all at once, I like to give an overview. I am not expecting people to understand everything now – even after all these years, I continue to see new aspects of the model – but I am hoping the next exercise will help to give a clearer picture.

Combining the seven modes: the seven-way stretch

I ask for a volunteer who is willing to let me be their supervisor for eight minutes, so I can demonstrate how I use all seven modes. I ask the rest of the group to watch me supervise and see if they can spot all the different modes in action. Jane volunteers.

Before I describe the session with Jane, I would like to address you, the reader. Our main aim here is to describe our courses. The aim behind that, the next layer of the proverbial onion, so to speak, is to show how supervision can operate at so many levels, and the seven-eyed model demonstrates that really well, in our opinion. To get the most from the following description, I ask you to read it slowly and critically. There are so

many ways the session could have gone, and my choice of interventions
shows, perhaps, both my strengths and my shortcomings.
     The next layer of the onion, for me, is to show the enormous potential
of supervision to keep us creative and fresh in our work. And the core for
me is that supervision is about spiritual practice: two or more (in the case of
group supervision) people are able to stand back and reflect together in the
service of something more than them. We empty ourselves so we can allow
ourselves to be filled by what needs to happen. I talk more about this in
Chapter 5 on group supervision and in Chapter 8, the workshop on love and
fear in supervision.

So back to Jane. She says she'd like to talk about a session with a client she saw the previous day – what happened is bothering her.

Robin: I notice that, when you said that, I felt as if I had been kicked in the stomach.

> *This is mode 6, sharing my reaction in the here and now. It comes easily*
> *to me and I want to show how available it is. I could have gone for mode*
> *4 and looked at the client's impact on Jane or found out a bit more about*
> *their relationship (mode 3). Here I am demonstrating also that there is no*
> *particular order to the modes.*

Jane: Yes. My client verbally attacked me – it seemed like out of the blue.

Robin: My breathing has gone very shallow. I almost feel as if I am in survival mode.

> *This is another mode 6. It is often my default position, but it indicates here*
> *that I am tuning into the supervisee, and perhaps the client, and we are*
> *building a rapport. I did momentarily think of asking Jane how she knew it*
> *was an attack – perhaps by asking her to become her client – but I choose*
> *another mode 6, partly to show the group how available our feelings and*
> *reactions can be.*

Jane: Yes. Inwardly I froze, although I did manage to ask her to say more about what was bothering her so much.

Robin: Can I ask you to go back to the moment when you felt attacked, even if it is uncomfortable. (*We pause.*) Notice what is happening in your body, any thoughts, images. My guess is that what seemed like an attack out of the blue might have happened to you before. (*Jane nods.*) I don't need to know the details. I am very interested in those stuck moments, as we often see present situations through a past lens. Does another feeling of being attacked out of the blue and perhaps feeling powerless come to mind *(mode 4)*?

Jane: Yes *(tearfully)*.

I am wondering if I should have gone down this route and whether I should say so. I think what a bad role model I could potentially have given the group – I have gone in quite deep quite quickly in just three interventions. I am about to beat myself up, and then it clicks – this is parallel process (mode 5).

Robin: I am wondering if there is a fear of getting it wrong in your relationship with this client. I had this worry that I had gone in too quickly with you, that I had got it wrong, and I wonder if that is how you feel in relation to your client – a parallel process. In other words, am I feeling towards you how you feel towards your client?

Jane: You are right. The previous session she had opened up, so we had gone quite deep, and so this came out of the blue and I felt responsible, that I had got something wrong.

We are in modes 4, 5 and 6 territory. In a longer session that is not about teaching the modes, we might have stayed here. It is a lovely example of where the personal and the professional meet and can inform each other. In a way, it was a safe bet to assume there would be instances of the supervisee feeling attacked out of the blue – we all have them, and I wanted to bring it into consciousness without dwelling on it. Instances like this can be used as a source of information to tell us more about the supervisee and their relationship to their client. But, as this is a demonstration of the seven modes, I need to move us on to pay more attention to the other modes.

Robin: Can you give me an image for you and your client – what would you be if you were both animals *(mode 3)*?

Jane: I see her as a cat and me as a frightened mouse – a bit obvious really.

Robin: Not at all. The main thing is that you see it clearly. Now I want you to go back to the session before the session in which you felt attacked and see if you have a different image.

Jane: Gosh, I had an image of her being a baby and me holding her. But actually I wasn't relaxed; even then, I had a feeling that I wasn't going to get it right. I knew something was wrong even then, didn't I? So, the attack was not so much out of the blue.

Robin: So it might seem from what you have just said. I am now going to ask if you are willing to go out of the room and come in as your client.

I go for a mode 1 in asking Jane to leave the room and walk back in as the client. I stress that she just needs to be willing to do it – it isn't about getting it right or speaking with their client's accent. It is usually obvious when they are inhabiting their client's body or are still themselves. For example, if they come in with some statement like, 'I am not sure if this is quite right', it shows they are still being themselves (although the client could have a need to get it right too). If it happens that they are still themselves, I ask them to go out and come in again until they are becoming more like the client than themselves. I then ask them to notice how they feel in their bodies, what feelings they might have, how they feel towards the world and anything else they notice when they become their client. It can have quite an impact to invite them to enter their client's world physically instead of presenting them objectively.

In one instance, a supervisee, who previously had been stuck, not knowing what to do with her client, sat down as the client and then sat down as herself and said, 'I know what to do now.' Simply becoming her client and entering his world was enough to move her on.

Sometimes I interview the practitioner as their client, and I do that here to build on mode 3. Let's call the client Judith. I ask Jane to come into the room as Judith. I pay attention to how Jane-as-Judith walks into the room – her walk, her breathing and so on – and in this instance decide not to comment. Instead, I ask questions. I start with factual questions to warm Jane up to her role as Judith.

Robin (to Jane as Judith): Judith, how long have you been seeing Jane?

Jane (as Judith): Four months.

Robin: And how often do you see her?

Jane (as Judith): Once a week.

Robin: How did you hear about her?

Jane (as Judith): She was recommended by a friend.

I make a note of this, as it belongs to mode 7. How people arrive at the therapist's doorstep can affect their expectations and the therapy itself.

Robin: How have the sessions been for you?

Jane (as Judith): Well, good until yesterday. She listens well and seems to understand me.

Robin: So what happened yesterday?

Jane (as Judith): Well, I just felt furious.

Robin: Do you know why?

Jane (as Judith): Of course I do. Right at the end of the session, Jane said she was taking an extra two weeks off after Easter to go to her daughter's wedding in Australia.

Jane (coming out of role): How can I have been so stupid not to have seen that?

Robin (to Jane out of role): Now you have had this insight, what interventions might you make (*moving to mode 2*)?

Jane (as herself): If she comes back. She stormed out.

Robin: I guess she might have been giving you an experience of how she felt abandoned by you. She was doing to you what she felt you had done to her.

This is mode 3 – looking at the relationship between client and supervisee.

Robin: So, what interventions might you make? No, let's start with what you did (*mode 2*).

Jane: Well, she said, 'This therapy is a complete waste of money. I feel worse than when I started.'

Robin: And what did you do?

Jane: I said I was sorry to hear that.

Robin: And what happened next?

Jane: She said something like 'Not half as sorry as I am for wasting all that time,' and then she stormed out.

Robin: OK, so what could you have done instead (*this is mode 2, looking at interventions*)?

Jane: I could have said, 'Tell me more.'

Robin: And what else?

Jane: I could have just sat silently and waited.

Robin: And what else? Go for a wild option – she isn't here now.

We are often stuck because we have got into a box of thinking there are correct ways of being and doing. By exploring the wild option, we are accessing our creative potential.

Jane: I could have said, 'You are so ungrateful.'

Robin: I think there could be something to explore around gratitude. 'She should be grateful to me because...'

Jane: I fitted in an extra session for her.

Robin: And I did that because…

Jane: I felt guilty.

> *We are learning a lot about the relationship – mode 3, but also modes 1 (client) and 4 (countertransference).*

Robin: So we have now covered six modes and there is just mode 7. Is there someone in the system we need to pay attention to?

Jane: Well, obviously her family. She has a teenage daughter – oh dear. I just realised – I said I was going to my daughter's wedding and my client's daughter is anorexic. I can't believe I have been so blind. My daughter, her daughter, my life – I can afford to go to Australia. If I had been her, I would have wanted to kill me.

Robin: You seem to be making your own connections around you and your client. I would like to finish with our relationship (*mode 5*). I confess that I thought I had gone in too deeply too quickly until I realised it could be a parallel process.

Jane: Yes, I did feel exposed at the beginning, but when you brought it back to me and my client, I felt easier.

Robin: Thank you, and let's finish here.

I ask them for feedback, following the structure of appreciations and difficulties, as Joan has already outlined in the Core Course (p52).

1. *Supervisor to self.* One thing I appreciated about what I did, one thing I might have done differently, or found difficult (choose the wording that feels right).

Robin: What I appreciated was catching the parallel process early. What I found difficult was thinking I'd used mode 4 too early when I asked if there was something in Jane's past.

2. *Supervisee to supervisor.* One thing I appreciated about what you did, one thing I found difficult.

Jane: What I appreciated are the insights that you helped me discover in just a few minutes. What I found difficult was feeling very exposed in front of everyone.

3. *Observer(s) to supervisor.* In this case the observers are the other group members, but it is usually one person, as we practise in triads.

One of the observers appreciated how seamless and natural it felt – it didn't look as if I was trying to fit in all the modes. Someone else said that what they found difficult at first was that it seemed more like therapy but by the end they could see it was relevant to supervision.

We go through all the interventions I made, looking at which mode I was using and when. I return to the question of supervision and therapy triggered by the use of mode 4 (what is going on for the supervisee). I could repeat that the work is to help the supervisee be more present with their client, so we can go into a supervisee's history if it helps unblock them. Instead, I ask the group member who made the comment what made it OK for her by the end. She says she is always very hesitant about going into personal stuff with her supervisees, but she saw that I simply asked if this feeling of powerlessness reminded Jane of something that had happened before and she did not need to know where or how, or even go into it. Simply acknowledging it was enough.

I explain that I want to look at how, with some clients, we really seem much clumsier and more insensitive than we normally are, and with others we seem to be working brilliantly. I ask Jane if I can refer to her session and she agrees.

I tell Jane I know she thinks she missed a lot (and she did), but the way she reflected indicates that she wouldn't normally do this.

Everything is data

I say to the group (referring to Core Principle 8 on p21): 'I want to introduce the idea that everything that happens, whether apparently good or bad, is data. I ask you not to identify with either position. I invite you to be curious. If we are beating ourselves up, or feeling inadequate or whatever, and we identify with the feeling, our attention is on us. If we see these feelings as data, then we are simply a witness and can use what is happening in the here and now. For me, it happened when I started to beat myself up for going in too deeply too quickly. Then I used the idea that this is data, and that took us to parallel process.'

Robin (to Jane): So you might have been insensitive, but perhaps she drew that behaviour out of you?

Jane: It's true. I asked myself why I gave those details. I didn't with other clients. It is very strange. You know, I wanted something from her – her approval.

Robin: Yes, some of it is your countertransference, but perhaps she also evoked that insensitivity out of you. I could speculate about her, but this is not the place as we are focusing on feedback on the modes, not the client.

It is time for lunch. We usually take an hour. We are blessed with a lovely venue in Little Venice, London, and there are plenty of places providing food nearby.

Mode 7

After we have reconvened, I explain that I am going to go through the modes one by one. I start with mode 7 because it reminds us how many people are in the room when we are supervising. Donald Winnicott (1947/1964: 85-92) famously said, 'There is no such thing as a baby.' What he meant was that a baby cannot exist in isolation; it only exists because of/in relationship with the people and the environment around it. This is true of all of us as adults.

The next exercise is to introduce them to the idea of seeing things from a wider perspective, which can help us to start to think more systemically. I call the exercise 'Stakeholders and Ghosts'. A stakeholder is someone who has some investment in the supervisory relationship. I ask them to think about a supervisory relationship in which they have been involved, whether as supervisor or supervisee, and ask them to call out the different stakeholders. The list usually includes some of these:

- My boss
- The client
- My board of trustees
- My wife
- The client's family
- Social services
- The organisation.

A ghost is someone from the past who is still present in some way, and again I ask them to name some. They might come up with:

- Previous supervisors
- My 'be-perfect driver' (my mother)
- An old schoolteacher.

This is something you can try for yourself if you wish. Take any relationship that you might be struggling with and see who else is in the room. I have found that what seems like an interpersonal conflict between you and someone in your here and now nearly always involves stakeholders and ghosts.

I ask the group to each draw two circles a few inches apart on a piece of paper, one for the supervisor and one for the supervisee; they can take either role. Then I ask them to map out on the paper how the stakeholders and ghosts come into their session, with differing weights of line to connect them. So, for example, they might draw a thick line for a strong connection between the two people, and a broken line if the connection is weak or intermittent. I give them a few minutes.

I then ask them to choose a stakeholder or ghost that is really coming into the room and whose presence they might not have sufficiently taken into account. Then I tell them to pair up and share with their partner how this person or organisation affects the supervisory relationship, why they might not have taken this into account and what, if anything, now they know this, they might change.

We then share in the group what they appreciated about themselves, their partner or the exercise. We talk about how many people came into the room when they did this exercise. I say I am not surprised, and that is why it is good to start with mode 7. Often just seeing the whole system in the room can of itself be a form of supervision, as it can help reduce anxiety when people see the bigger picture.

I read out a quote from *Supervising Psychotherapy* (Stewart, 2002: 116) that I think is relevant to the anxiety that is carried in any organisation:

> Organisations providing counselling and psychotherapy, by the very nature of their task, contain a great amount of anxiety. They are subject to external pressures to do with referrals and funding, they have to manage internal organisational pressures through maintaining effective structures, and they are subject to unremitting demands to meet the needs of the patients. In organisations offering training, the anxiety of those seeking qualifications will add to the intensity of the projection to which the organisation is subjected.

Mode 1

We then go on to mode 1. I remind them that in mode 1 we are finding out more about the client. I point out to them how, in the demonstration, I asked Jane, as my supervisee, to come in as the client. I now ask them to bring a client to mind and think back to a recent session. I tell them they can, if they wish, close their eyes.

Robin: I want you to see this in your mind's eye – how did the session begin? Let yourself run the video in your head, and when you have a clear picture, open your eyes and we will hear a few.

Participant 1 (P1): I went down to answer the doorbell and saw that she looked quite hostile.

P2: My client was late. The receptionist buzzed up to tell me he had arrived and I went down to fetch him. I saw through the glass doors that he was pacing up and down. I imagined something had happened as he had never been late before.

P3: My client came in, flopped on to the chair, and said, 'It's been a hard week.'

Robin: If we take the first one, the client was described as hostile. I would want to know how you knew that. I am not saying she was or wasn't hostile but what are your data?

P1: You know when someone is hostile. You feel it. She glared at me. OK, she stared at me without blinking, and I think her lips were pursed.

Robin: Mode 1 is also about being more observant, sticking to data rather than interpretations, so I wanted to unpack the word 'hostile', what was actually observed. Hostile is an interpretation. So here you *see* her looking at you without blinking, you *imagine* she is hostile, and you *feel...?*

P1: Wary.

At this point I ask everyone to stand up (*it's always good to include opportunities to move around a bit*), form pairs and in turn say first what they see, then what they imagine, then what they 'feel'. I demonstrate with one person.

Robin: I *see* your forehead is creased. I *imagine* you are frowning and that you haven't understood something. I *feel* insecure, that I haven't explained myself well.

When they have done a couple of rounds with each other, I ask them how it was. One person reports that it was difficult. He says he saw his partner looking annoyed, he imagined she did not like the exercise, and he felt as if she did not want to be doing it with him and felt rejected.

Robin: How do you know she was annoyed?

P4: She... she was frowning and did not look at me or smile.

Robin: And you imagined she was annoyed and a whole story developed about how she did not want to do the exercise and, even more, did not want to do it with you?

P5 (his partner in the exercise): I was just trying to focus on what was going on inside me. I often frown when I concentrate hard.

P4: We debriefed it after and had a good laugh. But I am shocked at how quickly I jumped to conclusions. Do you think clients do that with every gesture we make?

I say that I think what went on here, in this example and in my demonstration, is probably true for all of us. It's just that this exercise slows the process down so we can see it and can reconnect, as our imaginings separate us.

I then tell a story of how I was asked to do four sessions of humanistic psychology with a group of analysts that I saw as very resistant. (*How did I know they were resistant? Well, they kept asking me questions – but perhaps they just had inquiring minds.*) Anyway, the person I interpreted as most hostile came back the following week and said he had got what I was talking about. He had been up in the loft and he saw his four-year-old daughter starting to climb the ladder. He was just about to shout 'Be careful!' when this 'bloody exercise' (his words) came into his head and he found himself saying to himself, 'I see my daughter climbing the ladder. I imagine she is going to fall. I feel scared.' Instead of acting on this feeling, he watched her climbing with great skill and care, and all was fine. He acknowledges that, if he had shouted out, he would have passed on his fear to her.

I add that I notice that people who work with children are often more observant because they have to notice everything the child does, as so much is non-verbal. Mode 1 is natural for them.

I return to the second participant, who said his client was pacing and he imagined something had happened.

Robin: How did you feel?

P2: I noticed how scared I felt. I had always seen him as angry and I was scared. So, when I saw him pacing, I imagined he was angry and I felt scared. However, I could say, 'I see him pacing and I imagine he is agitated and I feel compassion.' In fact, that is what happened in the session.

At this point I tell them a few stories relating to mode 1. I tell them about a participant in one training session who said, 'My client came in displaying attachment behaviour.' This meant nothing to me and some of the group laughed, but she was bewildered as to why. She had confused a diagnosis with an observation and her client was well on the way to being put into a box.

The second story is from Bruno Bettelheim's book *The Art of the Obvious* (1993: 105-107). A student in Bettelheim's supervision group began: 'I want to present a young boy who is trying to destroy the environment.' Bettelheim rather scathingly replies: 'A young boy has a hard job destroying the environment single-handedly. What exactly was he doing?' The student replies, 'Trying to pull down the curtains,' and Bettelheim says, 'That is not exactly destroying the environment.' And then the telling statement: 'If I didn't know better, I might think you were trying to turn me against this child.' Bettelheim susses out straight away that this child was being presented in a way that was inviting the supervisor to prejudge the child as 'difficult'.

This happened to me in a lecture where a member of the audience was saying how terrible her organisation was, how arrogant her employers were and how they would not listen to her suggestions. There were sympathetic noises from the rest of the audience until I quoted Bettelheim, and the audience member acknowledged she was trying to get us all on her side.

I suggest it is time to practise and ask them to go into threes: supervisor, supervisee and observer. This is an important point, when they go off to work on their own. I remind them that they are here to learn, and they are not here to fix their supervisee's client. In fact, if good supervision happens, as it always does, this is a bonus. The sessions are for the supervisor to practise and learn. I remind them that their saboteurs, which they shared on the first day, could come into play. I also say they will not believe me when I say there are no mistakes and, even if there were, that is how we learn.

I ask the person in the role of supervisor to concentrate on the beginning of the session and help the supervisee stick to observations, not interpretations. I suggest they take the supervisee back as far as possible – for example, to the opening of the door, the ring of the doorbell, the going to get the client, or however the session started – and I remind them to ask the supervisee to be their client coming in and see how that feels too.

I suggest they do two or three sessions of this (depending on how much time we have), with different people being the supervisor, and to include the feedback at the end of each session.

> I think the ability to observe and separate observation from judgement is a really important life skill. Even praise is a form of evaluation.

When they have done this, I ask for feedback. Typically, participants say it revealed a lot of information in a short time – there was no need for a long case description. One person says they found it difficult to just stick to mode 1. I say it is like learning musical scales – in a way unnatural but still important.

Another useful technique that can yield a lot of information quickly is for the supervisor to ask the supervisee to say three things about the client that they would really like me/us to know. Supervisees are often quite surprised by what they choose to share.

> What I am wanting to do here, in mode 1, is to help the supervisee see this person with fresh eyes, not as a diagnosis. In the Richmond Fellowship therapeutic community, when we interviewed a new resident, we never looked at their notes first. We wanted to see the person without prejudice or judgement – ours or anyone else's. Then, when we later looked at their notes, it was useful to see another perspective. There is so much we can pick up if we are present with the person, with our thoughts unclouded by other people's interpretations.
>
> For people who are quite intuitive (like me), focusing on detail is a good counterpoint. But, as with any strength, we can overuse it.

I suggest we take a short break, after which I will ask them to go into their home groups and review how the day has been, before we finish as a large group.

> I make time for the home groups as participants have been given a lot to absorb and it gives them some time for processing. I also like to finish in the large group. If we have run out of time, I just ask each person to say one word about the day. If there is more time, I ask for any questions or sharings.

I don't have a fixed timetable but know roughly where I would like to get to by the end of the day.

Day 2

I welcome the participants back and ask if they have brought any issues from the day before that they would like to share, or questions they would like to ask. A typical question might be, 'What is the use of the seven modes? Do you really need to know them to be a good supervisor?'

I think there might be a statement and a feeling behind this question, as there often is in a question, but at this point in the training I choose to answer it on a content level.

I explain my point that the seven modes are a bit like a map – they help you locate certain things more easily. But, even with a map, you can lose your way, so it doesn't solve all problems. In the same way, knowing the best routes up a mountain is really important but it does not replace your skill as a climber. The seven modes also provide a context for the exercises we are learning together.

Mode 2

I ask if they are ready to move on to mode 2. I remind them it is about looking at the interventions of the supervisee. I ask them to take the same client as for mode 1 and, if they are willing, to close their eyes. I want them to go to a recent session, to a place where they felt stuck, and see in their mind's eye what is happening. It could be, for example, wondering whether to interrupt a client or let them carry on talking, or feeling out of their depth and not knowing what to do. I ask them to recall what their client said or did and what they did, and invite them, when they are ready, to open their eyes and share, if they want to. From these, I choose Premila to work with.

Premila: This is a client I have been seeing twice weekly for three months.

Robin: I just want the stuck moment. This is important. For this mode initially, we do not need to know anything about the client – just the stuck moment.

Premila: Oh, OK. He said that his wife had said they couldn't afford for him to keep coming.

Robin: And you said?

Premila: I asked him what that meant in terms of us working together. And then he said, 'So this will be our last session.' I said that this was sudden and it might be better if we had a couple of sessions to finish. He said no, and I felt lost. In fact, I felt lost throughout the three interchanges.

Robin: We could take any of the three moments when you felt stuck. Let's go with the first. You said, 'What does that mean in terms of us working together?' Let's brainstorm other options.

I ask Premila to brainstorm 10 other options for what she might have said.

> *This stretches her and invites her outside the box. I could ask the group to add to the list if she is stuck but it's important not to be rescuing. A useful prompt is to ask the person to think of someone she admires and say what they might do.*

I ask her for a wild one and say it does not need even to be legal or physically possible at this point. When she has her 10, I ask her to choose one she feels energy for that she would like to try out in a short role play.

We do a role play that starts with my being the supervisee and trying out a version of her chosen intervention.

Robin (as Premila, speaking to her client): What the hell are you up to? What made you bring your wife into it?

Premila says that, when she took the role of the client, she was surprised to realise she found it much more acceptable to hear a challenge than she feared, and in fact, as the client, she was relieved to be challenged.

> *This often happens. I think, as a profession, we can pussyfoot around our clients, under the guise of unconditional positive regard. I know some might disagree with this, but my experience is that there is often relief when a game has been named.*

Robin (de-roling): Is he coming back?

Premila: We agreed on one more session.

We finish with my saying I think that just allowing herself to know how she felt about the client's statement and decision would release something in Premila to become more present with her client. However, to anchor the work, I ask her to play herself and I will play her client. She tries another intervention.

Premila (as herself to Robin playing the client): You took me by surprise last week, and I am glad we have this session. I have a confession – I felt critical that you were doing what your wife wanted and I know this is something we have talked about a lot. I don't know what you truly want. I was also disappointed and wonder if you have been disappointed in our work together?

Robin (as client): Yes, I picked that up in the last session from how you responded. (*I think clients are very accurate about what is going on for us.*)

I ask if it is OK to leave it there and Premila says that she feels quite freed up by the exercise.

Finally, I invite Premila to imagine her (actual) next session with the client and how she might bring this intervention into practice.

> *In one way, the exploration we have just done in supervision will have affected how Premila is in her final session with this client anyway, because she is different. But if she wants to bring the intervention we have role-played into the session more actively, how might she do that? If she doesn't feel ready, and I say this to the group as well, I suggest she imagines doing it while she is in the session. It is uncanny how simply contemplating the possibility of the new option can often evoke changes in the client.*

I then explain the purpose of the exercise, which is to show how we keep ourselves stuck by not allowing ourselves to have so-called unprofessional thoughts, let alone say them. It's like an internal thought-police force, which can happen in training when people swallow ideas in order to conform. I say I hope this will not happen here, but that it certainly will. We are also told not to judge, which I don't think is possible. I tell them they should use their judgemental thoughts, but they can't do that until they see them as interesting data, because they are too busy judging themselves for being judgemental. They are not fully present. But if they are seeing their judgements as data, then they can use them. I tell them that, when I feel judgemental, I can usually trace it back to a fear. This makes judgement a very good signal that we need to explore why fear might have entered the room. If I judge my judgement, it may mean that I am frightened of that part of myself; I am preoccupied with dealing with myself in some way, as opposed to welcoming the trigger as data.

> *I have made a lot of different points here, but they all boil down to identifying some of the factors that stop us being present so we can be freed to be creative in our interventions.*

I now move the group on into a practice session. I ask them to form the same groups of three as they did for our exploration of mode 1. I write up the steps on the flipchart:

1. The supervisor invites the supervisee to share their 'stuck moment' or either/or -ism.
2. The supervisee brainstorms 10 ways of responding, including at least one wild one.

3. The supervisor invites the supervisee to choose one to roleplay.
4. The supervisor takes the role of the supervisee and uses that intervention, while the supervisee becomes the client.
5. The supervisor (back in role as supervisor) asks the supervisee-as-client what impact the intervention had.
6. The pair switches role so the supervisee is now back as themselves and the supervisor is the client. (I remind them it's important to let the supervisee find their own words.)
7. The supervisee imagines the next session and how they might take this forward.

I remind them to start with the stuck moment only and not get a case description, and that mode 2 is not about fixing or getting the 'right' intervention; it's about looking at how they might be holding themselves back and about playing a bit. We then do a group feedback in the usual way, highlighting the appreciations and difficulties.

The supervisees mostly experience the exercise as very freeing. I think much of the value is the permission it gives them to dare to think of wild options. In my experience, we are very often stuck because we hold back our aggressive thoughts. These come out in the wild options, and the freedom to express them can free us up.

We then have a coffee and cake break.

Mode 3

Following the break, we move on to mode 3, looking at the relationship between client and supervisee. I remind them that, in the seven-way stretch, I used animals as a metaphor to look at the client/supervisee relationship. I ask them now to stay with the same client they had in mind when we were practising modes 1 and 2 and to close their eyes and answer inwardly the following question:

- If you and your client were on a desert island together, what would be happening?

I invite them to share their responses. Answers typically might be:

- We would be on opposite sides of the island.
- We would be building a shelter together.
- She would be chasing me, and I would be trying to get away.
- We would be making love.

The beauty of a desert island question is that it can tell us a lot about the dynamics going on under the surface. Let's take the one about building a shelter, which comes from a young woman whose client was a young man. She says he was building the shelter for them both and she realised he had a whole range of skills that had not been acknowledged in their work together.

In the case of the one about chasing, I suggest they would have to stop sometime and then what would happen? The participant says: 'Well, this is an older woman and my mother came into my head. Embarrassing. Now I know what I could do; I could sit down and say, "Let's have a sparkling moment".'

There is laughter in the group. I know he is taking the mickey and I quite like it. He has owned that it is mother stuff, so I take it in good humour and reply in kind by thanking him for his honesty and saying: 'I see resonances in the group – or rather, I see nods, I imagine resonances, and I feel amused, as I could imagine my mother is often in the room, too.'

I turn to the response about the participant and their client being at opposite ends of the island. I ask, as a continuation, what might be happening 36 hours later? Would they would move together, and if so, how and why, or would they stay separate?

I refer to the making love scenario. I do what I often do when someone has shared something that could potentially make them feel vulnerable, I ask: 'Is there anyone here who has *not*, however fleetingly, had a sexual feeling towards a client?' No hands go up and I am glad it has been normalised and not left with one person. I say there are other metaphors and ask for suggestions. Someone suggests going on a journey together. I say that this can uncover a lot of information quickly and, in fact, I once used it with a team leader who had just come into post and she said, 'Oh my goodness, the bus hasn't been serviced – it's not safe, and we don't have a driver and, what's worse, we don't even know where we are going.'

One person comes up with the image of a dance together and I ask, 'What kind of a dance? Who leads?' Another suggests preparing a meal together. I ask, 'Who chooses the menu and buys the food?' Another reports she is already visualising the animal one. I think of her as a fox, watchful, prowling. She is not sure what she is – perhaps a monkey, watching from above.

I ask them to choose a new group of three and have three sessions, with each one playing each of the roles – supervisor, supervisee and observer – where they use whatever imagery they like to get a picture of the relationship between supervisee and client.

When they return (I give them seven minutes per person for the exercise, plus three minutes for feedback), I ask how it was. One says: 'Fascinating. My supervisor asked me to tell the story of my relationship with my organisation as if it were a fairy story and I came up with Red Riding Hood. I haven't been careful enough and, if I am not more attentive, I am going to get gobbled up.'

I mention another way of getting a picture of the relationship. In mode 1, we asked the supervisee to come in as their client, and we interviewed them. You can get a picture of the relationship from the client's point of view. For example, you ask the supervisee playing their client, 'What do you think of your therapist/coach/whoever? What do you like about them?' You are asking the supervisee to take their client's perspective on the relationship.

> *At this point we are halfway through the course. There is a buzz in the room; people realise that supervision does not have to be deadly serious and that playing with options can give powerful insights.*
>
> *As I write, I think of you, the reader. Have these modes and interactions come alive for you? Our belief is that this course is far more than just about the modes and, as we have said, supervision can be useful in any field of work or relationship. So you could bring an issue with your husband/wife, boss, best friend, and I could ask you to be them (mode 1), to say where you got stuck and what you would like to say to them (mode 2), to think of an image for your relationship (mode 3), to identify what feelings this person evokes in you (mode 4), or to say if there is anyone else who might be affecting your relationship – either someone from the past or someone who currently has some influence over one of you (mode 7).*

We break for lunch.

Straight after lunch, I lead a simple game. I ask them to count randomly to 20 as a group, each person saying the next number. If two people say the next number at the same time, they have to start again. As always happens, people start by saying the next number quickly, to get it in before anyone else does, and inevitably two people call a number together. I suggest they slow right down, wait, feel the silence and, if they are moved, say a number. It has happened so many times that I know it isn't a coincidence; if everyone does this, the very next time, or the one after, the group gets to 20 with no problem. We discuss how slower is faster and vice versa.

Mode 4

We move into mode 4. In this mode we are looking at the countertransference – put simply, when the client with whom you are working elicits feelings in you. There was a time in the history of psychoanalysis when it was thought of as an obstacle to therapy because it compromised the supposed neutrality of the analyst, but increasingly it is seen as a resource to be used, which is how we see it.

In fact, we say that countertransference cannot not 'happen'. It is there in why we chose to do the work we do; it is there in why we get stuck; it is there in how we find some clients easier than others. We could even go so far as to say there is no client: when a supervisee presents a client, we only have their version, as we saw in mode 1. That may sound extreme, but I ask the group to just hold it in mind, as a partial truth that could be useful.

So, accepting that countertransference might be continually present, I ask them what alerts them to the fact they might have more countertransference onto a particular client.

We brainstorm a few 'clues' – for example:

- dreaming about them
- wishing you had met them in other circumstances
- dreading a session
- looking forward to a session
- not bringing them to supervision
- overrunning
- strong feelings
- behaving in a way that is atypical

I thank them and suggest an exercise that Peter Hawkins and I devised when we were co-writing *Supervision in the Helping Professions* (2012). I was talking about a student I was teaching – let's call her Freyda. I was having a lot of problems with her – I knew she was badmouthing me to other students, and I was angry with her, but I also felt quite paralysed as I did not know how to confront her. Peter then suggested I tell him about another student. I talked about how much I liked Maggie and enjoyed our supervision together. He then suggested I talk about Freyda in the same tone of voice as I had talked about Maggie. I could not do it, and it helped me to see how much I was attached to thinking of Freyda in a certain way.

I ask them to form their usual triads of supervisor, supervisee and observer.

1. The supervisee talks about client A (5 mins).
2. The supervisee talks about client B (5 mins).
3. The observer makes a note of any differences in body language, tone of voice, facial expressions.
4. The supervisee goes out of the room and supervisor and observer share observations (5 mins).
5. The supervisee comes back into the room and the supervisor uses the observations about the differences between A and B to supervise on client A (5 mins).
6. Feedback in their triads in usual way and then discussion in their triads (10 mins).

In the feedback, participants often report how interesting it is to see how, even when they know the purpose of the exercise, they cannot *not* be different with each client they present. The supervisor and the observer pick up clear differences in the supervisee's tone of voice and body language as they talk about the different clients.

Besides showing how easily you can pick up how a person feels about someone by listening to their tone of voice and watching their body language closely as they talk about that person, I think this exercise has spiritual connotations. If we talk about someone we love, we expand, and if we blame or criticise, our bodies contract in subtle (or not so subtle) ways. There is also another way – paying attention to how we actually feel, and we will come on to that in mode 6.

I refer them to John Rowan's definition, in *The Reality Game* (1983: 110–111), of the different types of countertransference, which I think are very useful:

a) defensive countertransference, where the client triggers the supervisee's unresolved issues.

b) aim attachment countertransference, where the supervisee wants the client to change to show how well the supervisee is working, when there are needs for success, recognition or power.

c) transferential countertransference, where the supervisee sees the client as someone from their past like a parental figure.

d) reactive countertransference, when the supervisee responds to something the client has said instead of helping the client understand where their statement has come from (for example, a client says the therapist has a dirty toilet and she becomes defensive rather than looking at what that means to the client).

e) induced countertransference, when the supervisee starts to behave out of character, conforming with the client's usually unconscious expectations. (*I say more about this later when I talk about projective identification.*)

f) identification countertransference, where the supervisee overidentifies with the client (for example, taking their side if the client's partner has had an affair).

g) displaced countertransference, when a client triggers something that is happening in the supervisee's personal life at that time (for example, if the supervisee has had a row with his wife and is then abrupt with his female client).

I have devised two of my own:

h) Nosey Parker countertransference, where the supervisee wants to find out how the client's life is going for their own reasons (for example, asking where they bought their trousers, or asking how things are going with their partner when the client has not brought up the topic).

As I write this, I have just read about different forms of stealing, in a chapter on ethics in Supervising Psychotherapy *(Martin, 2002: 121-123). This has prompted me now to consider Nosey Parker countertransference as a possible ethical issue that could seem relatively harmless (asking about the husband might be intended as caring but why the need to ask?), but could also demonstrate a narcissistic tendency in the practitioner. I know I and others have been guilty of it, and I mention it not to point the finger but only because I have not seen the issue framed in this way.*

And the second:

i)   cultural countertransference, which John Rowan does not mention, and which has a huge impact on the relationship.

Jeff and Sue Allen describe a very good example of a cultural blind spot in their book How Love Works *(2012: 226), in a story about Malidoma Some, a Western-educated author and workshop leader from the Dagara Tribe of West Africa referred to earlier on p41. When he tried to explain the notion of suing to the elders in his tribe, they were completely bewildered, asking, 'How do these people ever learn?' I think this is telling us that when we sue for compensation, we go out of relationship and the joint learning gets lost. Any learning that we gain is all about strategies of winning.*

Even as I write, I think of another:

j)   envy countertransference, where I cannot enjoy my client's good fortune.

The list could go on and on. An interesting exercise here might be to think of a client you have difficulty with and identify the type of countertransference. As Rowan writes (1983: 109), we can't use it until we are aware of it. One of the cornerstones of our work is to raise awareness, and knowing the different types of countertransference can help with that.

I share some questions that can be useful when thinking around mode 4. I ask them to think of their client as I ask these questions:

- What would you least like me to know about you and your client?
- How do you want them to change?
- What have you not been able to say to them?
- Who do they remind you of?

The last question is an exercise that comes from co-counselling, called an identity check. Joan often uses this in her teaching on mode 4. This can be done in pairs. The theoretical basis for this exercise is that very often someone with whom we have a difficulty is reminding us of someone in the past, and often we are unaware of this. The identity check can be used for any relationship, not just supervisory ones.

Identity check exercise

1. Who does X remind you of? Repeat this question until both parties feel they have arrived at the 'right' person.

2. In what ways is X like this person?

3. What do you want to say to this person? (It is useful if they address this to a cushion or chair representing this person, and they swap roles – ie. become the other person. This is usually a clearing experience so they can return to X with less or no baggage from the past relationship.)

4. Move back to X by asking the supervisee to list three ways in which X is different from this person. If the previous stages have been completed satisfactorily, then the supervisee will be able to be more present with their client.

I ask what the group members have got from the practice sessions and several people respond by saying how powerful the questions are. I introduce an expression I like – 'homeopathic supervision', in which you make the minimum intervention possible for maximum effect.

We break for tea at this point, before moving on to mode 5.

Mode 5

Mode 5 is about the relationship and, therefore, centrally about parallel process. (You can find an article on parallel process in the Resources section, on p211.)

I explain that parallel process occurs when the relationship between client and supervisee is mirrored in the relationship between supervisor and supervisee. So, for example, if the client is passive aggressive or withholding, when the supervisee comes to present them, they will do so in a way that could leave the supervisor feeling frustrated. If that is not normally how this supervisee presents, then perhaps the supervisee is showing their supervisor how it feels to be working with the client.

In the previous exercise contrasting clients A and B, we have seen how, when we talk about a client, we unconsciously become some aspects of them, so this is not surprising.

Although it is more usual for the parallel process to move from client to supervisee to supervisor, it can go the other way round: ie. from supervisor to supervisee to client. So, if the supervisor is anxious and deals with it by telling the supervisee what to do, that can get reflected in the supervisee being quite prescriptive with their client. I also see this reverse parallel process happening when, say, an organisation is worried about its reputation, so it puts pressure on its practitioners not to take risks. The supervisor then 'punishes' the supervisee by being critical of them: for example, if they haven't followed a certain protocol, even though the supervisor might not believe in it themselves. And this 'punishment' can get transmitted to the client. That is partly why I start the course with mode 7, to see what external influences there are in the room.

Positive parallel process can also happen. So, when a supervisee brings a client to supervision, because they have held that client in mind in the space between sessions, the client is different in the next session. It is as if the positive feelings evoked from the supervision are felt by the client. Of course, the supervisee's perception of their client is different, which is one of the main aims of supervision, but supervisees report that the client has come in differently, and it is not just their perception.

Projective identification

I then introduce the concept of projective identification, which we mentioned briefly in the core propositions and principles in Chapter 2 (p24). I explain it as a bridge between reflection and acting – a form of mindfulness, if you like. I ask, how many people have heard of projective identification? (*Usually several hands go up.*)

It is quite a mouthful for something that is happening all the time. I explain it by asking if any participants have noticed that sometimes they can feel inadequate in a particular person's presence? (*There are nods from group.*) Our natural tendency is to think it is to do with us – perhaps we are inadequate. But if we generally feel OK, and it is always with this particular person that we feel inadequate, then perhaps it is not just us. What could be happening is that the person themself feels inadequate and is getting us to feel what they cannot feel themself. We are all familiar with the idea that a bully is a coward. They have a fear that they will not or cannot acknowledge, and they similarly get others to feel their fear.

I explain to the group that this is a very early form of communication. A baby does not have words. When a baby cries, it is almost impossible not to attend to them. The baby is getting you to feel their distress, so you will act. This is not a deliberate act; it is almost an innate biological survival technique. As we get older, most of us acquire words to articulate what we want and how we feel, but this form of non-verbal communication is still happening all the time. We become conditioned to listen to words and stories and lose touch with this vital form of communication.

I take envy as an example. I know someone who is very successful and arouses envy in other people. A few of us who know him have discussed this. I find myself wanting a posh car like his when, in reality, I am not interested in having one. This person, now successful, had a very deprived childhood and has compensated brilliantly, but his own feelings of inadequacy and needing to prove he is successful are still there and we pick them up. So, rather than beating myself up for having envious feelings (which I can do), I use my feelings as data – I get curious. Are my envious feelings just mine or can they tell me something about the other person? Of course, they are always ours as well, or we could not pick them up, and the concept of projective identification enables us to both know about our own state and to connect to the other.

I say a little bit more. If something unbearable happens to us, something that we cannot handle, then to survive we have to split it off from our consciousness, and then split off from knowing we have split off. Projective identification happens when I put this split off bit into you. I do this both in order that you will feel what it is like to be me, but also in the hope that you will manage it inside you and help me to do the same. I hope you will be able to bear it and, in bearing it, return it to me in a way that I can finally embrace. That is why it is so important that we are able to feel dreadful sometimes in sessions and can use these feelings in the service of the client rather than either disassociate or be overwhelmed by them.

> *Some people might object to the language of putting things into each other and I can understand that. I do not mind how the concepts are explained. My experience is that we pick up things in each other and this can induce us to behave in ways that are uncharacteristic. This is especially true in groups.*

Projective identification is also a very practical tool. I was once describing it to a group and saying how someone who scares you is probably very frightened themselves, and there was a loud gasp from one participant. She said she worked in a residential establishment with a girl with learning difficulties who was quite violent, and the staff were frightened of her. Every morning, four people would go to wake this girl up: one to go into her room and three to wait outside in case there was trouble. The woman saw how terrifying this must be to the girl and said, 'No wonder she is violent. I never even thought of the possibility that she might be scared. That makes perfect sense. I will approach her quite differently now.'

The following week she came back beaming. She had approached the girl with this new perception, very slowly and gently and with no fear. The young person sensed this and was immediately very responsive. Within hours, this hitherto violent child had her head on this staff member's lap and was utterly peaceful. The other staff were amazed. They were not ready to let down their guard or change their opinion of the girl yet. It was almost as if they had an investment in her being the way she was, but that is another story.

I now relate this to supervision by explaining that what our clients cannot feel, they will put into us. And what we cannot feel, absorb or digest, we will put into our supervisor. That is why the supervisor needs to know themself and can be in the moment. We have returned to parallel process. The relationship between client and practitioner is mirrored in the practitioner/supervisor relationship. We use the data – in this case, our feelings and body sensations – to work out what might be happening with the client.

In fact, at this point, I sometimes say there is no client. The client is not in the room, so we only have the practitioner's account. So, in one sense, the data we pick up through the non-verbal channel can be a better version, or at least additional information. This is why I don't go with long case histories. The practitioner is telling us what they already know and can be subtly trying to influence us to think in a certain way. You may remember the example I gave earlier from Bettelheim's book (1993: 105), where he says, 'If I did not know better, I would think you were trying to turn me against this boy.' In other words, pay attention to how the supervisee's so-called descriptions may be very selective and contain within them judgements and subtle, or not so subtle, attempts to influence you.

For me, projective identification and parallel process go to the heart of supervision. I guess we choose what suits our temperament. I am quite inward-looking, so I gravitate towards looking at what is going on inside me. And this relates to our topic – any uncomfortable feeling we have can be used as a starting point of inquiry in quite a practical way, as in the example of the young girl who seemed aggressive but was really frightened. And, through understanding projective identification, quite often we will find fear behind the uncomfortable feelings. The more we can bring feelings into our consciousness, the more chance we have to help the client make sense of what is going on with them.

Mode 5 mirrors mode 3 in some ways. If you remember, mode 3 is looking at the supervisee/client relationship. So you could, for example, ask your supervisee for an image of their relationship with you, or simply ask, 'How are we doing together right now?'

To make use of parallel process, you need to check what might relate specifically to you and your supervisee. To take the earlier example, if you are generally frustrated with your supervisee, then you will need to go there first rather than starting with the parallel process.

Commenting on the relationship is not so usual in everyday life, so this may take a bit of practice.

Mode 6

Mode 6 is when the supervisor notices what is going on with them and feeds it back to the client. It can be a body sensation, a feeling, an image, a noticing where their attention is. I use this mode a lot in group supervision where different members feed back their responses to what is being presented.

Modes 5 and 6 are separate but we can use mode 6 where the supervisor is sharing what is going on with them as a way to get to mode 5. For example:

I notice I am frustrated as I listen to you (mode 6).
Is this how you feel with your client (mode 5, parallel process)?

I ask for a volunteer to demonstrate using modes 5 and 6. One participant, Pete, describes a coaching client. They have just finished a course of sessions, and in the last one the coachee is what Pete considers excessively complimentary about him, saying how wonderful the coaching has been and how so much has changed for him.

I notice myself wanting to back away from Pete (mode 6). I feed this back to him.

Pete: That is exactly how I felt. I said he had made the changes, not me, and I wanted the good work to be located in him not me. And I guess I am bringing it here because there was something rejecting about the way I did it. So yes, I wanted to back away.

As he is talking, I notice something very strange: I feel sexual. Not what I expected or wanted! How am I going to feed this back? I have to. It is a good job I have been with the group for two days. I don't know where this is leading. It is not how I feel towards Pete. That would have made it even more difficult.

Robin: I notice, Pete, as you talked, I felt sexual. Can you make any sense of that?

There is a long pause – I feel exposed and vulnerable. Finally, Pete says that his client is gay and that he didn't know whether to share that.

Robin: I notice I feel relieved when you say that. What are you making of all this?

Pete: Actually, I am relieved too. I think I am beginning to make sense of what happened. I think I somehow picked up that his positivity was, well, how shall I say it, a form of flirting. And then, right at the end, I threw it back at him. There was something quite aggressive about the way I wouldn't take any credit and wanted to hand it all to him. Thank you, that feels so much clearer.

We do the usual appreciations and difficulties. As often happens, what I appreciated was also what I found most difficult – the sharing of feeling sexual.

Pete says what he found most difficult was whether to share that his client was gay and what he most appreciated was the sense of relief that he could make sense of his behaviour, which felt out of character. (*This was about him, not my work as a supervisor, but I let it go.*)

The group comments on how quickly we got to the heart of the problem. I notice I don't want to receive the compliments – an obvious parallel process.

I think it might be a good idea to do another example, hoping it might be a bit trickier – I would like (and not like) the group to see me flounder. I ask for another volunteer. Max begins to describe one of his clients and I interrupt quite quickly (role-modeling something that is not usually done in normal conversation).

Robin: I notice as you talk, I do not feel engaged.

Max continues to talk as if he has not heard what I said.

Robin: I notice that I feel frustrated – as if what I am saying is not going to make any difference.

Max agrees that is what happens with his client but continues to talk about his client. At this point I could happily strangle him and wonder if he is getting me to feel the feelings he has for his client. I interrupt again.

Robin: Nothing I say has any impact on you (*I decide to water down my feelings of aggression*).

Max is about to continue in the same way, so in the end I just say: 'You are wiping me out. I've had enough.' This catches Max's attention.

Max: Yes, that is how I feel. I am glad you know how I feel now. (*He pauses.*) You know, now I have been on the receiving end of your comments, you have given me permission to listen to myself more, although I would not be able to feed it back in the way you did. But at least I understand a bit more of what was happening.

The group is both fascinated and wary. How can they interrupt like this? What if it is just their stuff? They say it's alright for me, I have practised this, but it is a big leap for them. I agree and suggest they try it, which they do in their groups of three. The feedback is very positive – the supervisors find it much easier than they thought, and the supervisees also say the sessions are useful.

We are now almost at the end of day 2 and it's time for home groups and finishing together. I think both are important – home groups so they can process the day and finishing together so we can get a sense of community. Sometimes I structure the end – I ask what they have appreciated about the day, and if they found any of it difficult.

∽   ∽   ∽

Day 3

I welcome them and outline the day, which will be more practice as a group on the seven modes, and then in triads, and then we will return to their identified learning needs and see what has been left unfinished.

I explain that we will do tag supervision, which they will have done with Joan in the Core Course (see p65). The focus is to show the use of all seven modes, and I ask for a volunteer supervisee.

Maryam volunteers. She comes to the front where I have placed two chairs facing each other. She sits in one and the other will be taken by different group members, each taking a different mode. I thank Maryam and explain to the rest of the group that I will allocate each of them a mode. I will invite them to come to the front in any order, occupy the empty chair and make their intervention, after which they can clap themselves out, or we will clap them out and another person will take their place and try their mode.

I go around the group, assigning a mode to each person. As it's a large group, there are two people for each mode. I briefly go through each mode again, so they only have to remember their own. Then I ask Maryam for her opening sentence.

Maryam: I've been seeing Trevor for two years now.

Robin (to group): Where shall we start? Mode 1 – find out a bit more about Trevor? Mode 3 – find out a bit more about the relationship? Mode 4 – find out why Maryam is bringing him? Mode 6 – explore our own feelings (*I notice myself suddenly feeling sad*)? These are all possible. Which shall we start with?

Mode 4 person: I'd like to go with mode 4. (*She goes and sits in the empty supervisor's chair.*) Why are you bringing him?

Maryam: Well, he originally came because of a bereavement – his wife of 40 years died, he was lonely and isolated and the sessions seemed to be helping. But now I feel stuck. I feel he is dependent on me.

Robin (to group): This tells us a little about the client and the relationship, which is mode 3. The modes overlap.

Mode 4 person: You say he is dependent on you. How do you feel about that?

Maryam: Actually irritated. He says things like, 'I have been looking forward to the session all week.' I hadn't realised I was so irritated.

I clap mode 4 out and ask which mode should come next. The group agrees it should be mode 3. One of the mode 3 people takes the supervisor's seat.

Mode 3 person: Can you give me an image for your relationship? Say you were planning a holiday together (*Maryam shudders*). I think we have an answer already – I notice you shuddered.

Maryam: Yes. I realise now that I am finding something creepy about him. He asked for a hug a few sessions ago and I said no. My goodness, I think he is getting me to feel uncomfortable – getting me back for not hugging him. Is that possible?

Robin: Yes, it is possible. So which mode next?

A mode 2 person takes the supervisor's chair.

Mode 2 person: Can we look at what other options there might have been when he asked for a hug? What happened when he asked for a hug?

Maryam: I said no. I think I was quite sharp because I was taken by surprise. And now I can see he looked hurt. And the next session he was ill and cancelled at the last minute.

Mode 2 person: So, what other options could you have taken?

Maryam: I could have said something like, 'Gosh, you took me by surprise then.' That actually feels good. It doesn't reject him and is honest about what is going on with me.

Mode 2 person: Can I try another mode 2 for the future? Now that you have tracked some of the dynamics between you – your saying no, your irritation – I wonder how you could use these in your next session?

Maryam: I could do the same – I could say to Trevor, 'I notice that, since you asked for a hug, I have felt shut out and stuck. Can we go back to that moment?'

We clap mode 2 out and I ask what could come next. One group member suggests mode 3 or 4, and to focus on what this means to Maryam. I acknowledge this but ask that we try modes we haven't used yet. A mode 6 person volunteers to take the supervisor's seat.

Mode 6 person: I felt judgemental of you just now – I'm not sure why.

Maryam: I'm not surprised. I feel like that towards Trevor. (*She has spontaneously worked out the parallel process, mode 5.*)

A mode 4 person claps herself in.

Mode 4 person: I am wondering if this client or the situation reminds you of a previous situation?

Maryam: Yes, I remember my first thought when I saw the client was that he reminded me of my stepfather.

It is tempting to follow this up, but I decide this is not a good idea as we would be going into supervision, rather than demonstrating the modes.

A mode 7 person claps himself in.

Mode 7 person: I know nothing about his support system or who else is in his life outside this counselling relationship. Can you tell me about that?

Maryam: One of his children lives in Scotland and the other has moved to Switzerland with his Swiss wife. He thinks they are quite selfish – when his wife, their mother, was dying, they never bothered to come and see her.

At this point I clap out the mode 7 person and suggest we have a mode 1.

It is interesting how often mode 1 comes last. You'd think it would come first, but in my experience you can start with many of the others. As I touched on earlier, we could say that there is no client – only the supervisee's version of the client. Many people might not agree with this, but I ask the group to consider it as a possibility. Sometimes, paradoxically – and why we go to supervision – the supervisor can see the client better than the supervisee because the supervisee is too close.

Mode 1 person: Tell me three things you would like me to know about Trevor.

Maryam: The first thing that comes to mind is that he has very long fingers. I don't know why I thought of that. Second, that he is bitter.

I comment to the group that, if I were to go into this more, I would ask how she knew that, but I suggest we leave it at face value now.

Maryam: And he limps because he had polio as a child, and he was bullied at school.

Robin: Thank you. It is interesting to see what comes to mind.

The second mode 1 person claps themselves in.

Second mode 1 person (to Maryam): If you imagine yourself as the client, how do you feel in your body? Perhaps you could go out and come in as them, as that may help you.

Maryam (as client): I feel hunched and angry – no, that is not quite the right word. I feel entitled. Like the world owes me something.

Second mode 1 person (talking to Maryam as if she were her client, Trevor): What is the hardest thing to share with Maryam? (*He turns to me and asks if that is a mode 3, not a 1. I reply that the modes overlap, as talking about the relationship between supervisee and client also tells you about the client.*)

Maryam (as client): I don't tell her that I fancy her. (*She shudders and comes out of role and says she knew that but didn't want to let herself really take it in.*)

At this point I intervene and thank everyone. It's tempting to go into the case more, but I want to ensure that we stick to learning the modes. I invite all the supervisors to each say an appreciation and a difficulty, in the usual way.

They do this and then Maryam says to each one what she appreciated and anything she found difficult about their intervention. She reports that, with each intervention, she seemed to get more insight. She adds that she felt very exposed when she articulated her disgust at the idea of planning a holiday with her client, and especially appreciates that intervention.

I ask them to go into their threes and have a supervision session where they put all the modes together in a seven-way stretch, or to pick a mode where they feel least comfortable and just use that (Joan gave an example of this on p63).

They practise for the rest of the morning.

At the end of the morning, someone asks if we can do more on mode 7. I give a bit more theory.

In the 1960s there was a move from individual psychoanalysis to family therapy, which placed a bigger emphasis on the context of the patient rather than just their internal world. So, a child might be carrying something for their family; in a workplace team, a conflict between two people could be carrying something for the whole team, or different departments could be carrying something for the organisation. So, a useful question might be, 'Who else is in the room that we have not taken account of? How might the situation be seen from their perspective?' In family constellation work, when something has not been recognised or acknowledged, it comes out later as a symptom. We look at this more in group supervision and the advanced course but, even in one-to-one supervision, the supervisor can set up empty chairs and ask the supervisee to sit in different seats.

We break for lunch.

After lunch I ask them to go back to their home groups and look at their learning goals and to have a supervision session on anything that has not been covered.

When they come back together, I suggest they have some time on their own and write about what stood out for them in the course, and one thing they might do differently as a result of being here. Then I suggest they pair up with the person with whom they did their sparkling moment and share what they have written. At this point, I ask if any of them want to form peer groups to meet after the course. A few people put up their hands and I suggest they meet at 4pm to discuss this. In the past, a number of groups have continued to meet for many years after a course.

We then have a round of appreciations of self, each other and the course, and anything they might have found difficult. I also acknowledge Peter Hawkins, who first wrote up the model in 1985 before we wrote about it together in 1989, in the first edition of *Supervision in the Helping Professions*. Since then, Peter, Joan and I have developed it, and I think we all really appreciate what this map has brought to the supervision world. There is much appreciation for Joan's cakes. I think there is something there about feeling taken care of.

The final part of the course is to hand out the certificates and take a group photo.

Over the years, my teaching on the seven modes has changed. Initially I went through the modes one by one and then put them together at the end. I have now found that the seven-way stretch demonstration at the beginning, where they watch and score, followed by a practice of each mode separately, and then a tag supervision at the end, best embeds learning how the modes fit together.

Summary of exercises/techniques

Sparkling Moment (p76)

Name and something you would like us to know (p79)

Needs and sabotage (p79)

Seven-way stretch for all modes (p82)

Mode 7: Map of stakeholders and ghosts (p89)

Mode 1: Use beginning of session (p90)
    Become client (p91)
    I see, I imagine, I feel (p91)
    Three things you would like me to know about client (p93)

Mode 2: Stuck moment (p94)
    Brainstorm options, especially wild ones (p95)
    Role play and switch roles (p95)

Mode 3: Desert island (p97)
    Both animals (p98)
    Going on a journey (p98)
    Ask supervisee to play client and see relationship from their perspective (p98)

Anyone who has not... Normalising (p98)

Count to 20 (p99)

Mode 4: Brainstorm how supervisee is affected by their client (p100)
    Exercise client A and then client B (p100)
    Different kinds of countertransference (p101)

What do you not like about your client, how do you want them to change, what can't you say to them? (p102)

Modes 5 and 6: Using the here and now, particularly body sensations (p103)

Tag supervision (p108)

Foodnotes

Banana cake

This is an ideal way to use up bananas that you've kept too long. I have even used ones that I've frozen, and it has still worked. It is a bit like supervision – revisiting old stuff and habits and working them into something nourishing.

> 4oz/112g butter or margarine
> 6oz/170g sugar
> 8oz/227g self-raising flour
> 2 eggs
> 2 large or 3 medium very ripe bananas

1. Heat the oven to 180°C/350 °F/Gas mark 4.
2. Grease a 2lb loaf tin.
3. Mash the bananas with a sturdy fork.
4. Cream the butter and sugar together and mix in the eggs.
5. Mix together the two yellow sludges you have created.
6. Mix in the flour.
7. Pour the mixture into the loaf tin and bake for 40 minutes, then reduce the temperature to gas 150 °C/300 °F/ Gas mark 2 and cook for a further 30 minutes.
8. Remove from oven and turn the loaf out onto a rack to cool before you devour it.

References

Allen J, Allen S (2012). *How Love Works*. Croydon: CPI Group.

Bettelheim B (1993). *The Art of the Obvious*. London: Thames & Hudson.

Bion WR (1970). *Attention and Interpretation*: a *scientific approach to insight in psycho-analysis and groups*. London: Tavistock.

Buber M (1923/2000). *I and Thou* (Smith RG, trans). New York: Scribner Classics.

Cooperrider DL, Whitney D (2005). *Appreciative Inquiry: a positive revolution in change*. San Francisco, CA: Berrett Koehler Publishers Inc.

Dass R, Gorman P (1985). *How Can I Help? Stories and reflections on service*. New York: Alfred A Knopf.

Hawkins P (1985). Humanistic Psychotherapy Supervision: a conceptual framework. *Self and Society* *13*(2): 69–79.

Hawkins P, Shohet R (2012). *Supervision in the Helping Professions* (4th ed). Maidenhead: Open University Press.

Hawkins P, Shohet R (1989). *Supervision in the Helping Professions*. Milton Keynes: Open University Press.

Jones J, Wilmot J (2002). *The Boxing Clever Cook Book: twelve recipe books in one*. Findhorn: J&J Publishing.

Martin E (2002). Giving, taking, stealing: the ethics of supervision. In: Driver C, Martin E (eds) (2002). *Supervising Psychotherapy*. London: Sage (pp121–131).

Rowan J (1983). *The Reality Game*. London: Routledge.

Stewart J (2002). The container and the contained: supervision and its organisational context. In: Driver C, Martin E (eds) (2002). *Supervising Psychotherapy*. London: Sage (pp106–120).

Winnicott D (1947/1964). *The Child, the Family, and the Outside World*. Harmondsworth: Penguin Books.

The group supervision course

This is our third three-day course and we limit the numbers to a maximum of 18 as this divides into three groups of six for the group supervision practice.

Facilitating and teaching group supervision is perhaps where I feel most at home, as the group begins to work together for the benefit of the supervisees and their client(s). It means the group will come up with insights and understandings of the client and the supervisee that the supervisor on their own would never have seen so easily, if at all. How to use the group as a resource and the safety of the participants are very important here. Many, if not most of us have had difficult experiences of our first group – namely, our family of origin – and our experiences of school can also make us reluctant to be vulnerable in a group.

I welcome the participants and say that several of them will know each other from the previous two courses, because people can take the modules at any time, so each group has a different but overlapping membership. I start with an exercise that, like the Sparkling Moment, comes from Appreciative Inquiry (see p44) (Cooperrider & Whitney, 2005). I ask them to pair up and one to be A and another B and to ask and answer the following question, taking two to three minutes each.

- How has supervision enriched your life?

I wonder if you, the reader, might like to jot down a few ways in which supervision has enriched your life. Of course, it doesn't have to be just supervision; you could apply it to anyone or any aspect of your life.

As is obvious, I am a huge fan of Appreciative Inquiry. It is not that it avoids difficulties; it is that, once appreciation has been shared, the difficulties do not loom so large.

When A and B have swapped roles, in the usual way I ask them to share what they appreciated about themselves, each other or the exercise. They share what a pleasure it is to listen to each other and to remind themselves of how important supervision is to them. I ask them to turn to the back of their course manuals and fill in the sections on 'What I want personally, professionally,' and 'What a supervisee might want you to learn' and 'What your team/organisation might want you to learn.' I give them about seven or eight minutes and then ask them to form groups of three – these will be their home groups. I ask them to share their learning needs and, as in the previous courses, pay particular attention to their sabotages.

They do this and come back together in the whole group. I ask them to share their sabotages. They include:

- I will switch off/withdraw.
- I will feel that everyone knows more than me.
- I will either get self-critical or critical of others.
- I won't mix with everyone – just with those I already know.
- I will find myself wanting more theory and will criticise you for not giving it.
- I might want more structure than you give, even though I love how you use what is happening now.

Throughout there are nods. Again, addressing you as reader, what might be, or has been, difficult for you in group learning situations? It is really interesting how much we all have in common around these.

I thank them and say I am glad they have felt safe enough to include comments about me. I remind them of the basic idea of groupwork, that everything belongs to everyone. So, for example, I ask: 'Is there anyone who has *not* withdrawn or felt everyone knows more than them, or has not been self-critical?'

I think it is important to repeat this question in this module, even though I mentioned it on the Seven-Eyed Model course (Chapter 4), as this idea really contributes to safety in a group. And the phrasing is so important: 'Is there anyone who has not….?' If I were to ask, 'Who else has felt critical of others?', for example, people might be unwilling to own up at the beginning of a group. By normalising such statements, we can then use everything as data and belonging to us all.

I ask them if they are OK with the good will contract (see Chapter 3, p54). I then ask them to go to the page in their manuals where they will find the figure reproduced overleaf. I explain that this is the structure of the course – that we start with creating groups of six in this instance (*a group can be bigger or smaller*) and then go on to facilitate group responses. By this I mean we will demonstrate techniques for doing group supervision. On the second day we look at group dynamics, and on the final day we look at supervision in organisations.

Figure 5.1: Group supervision module structure

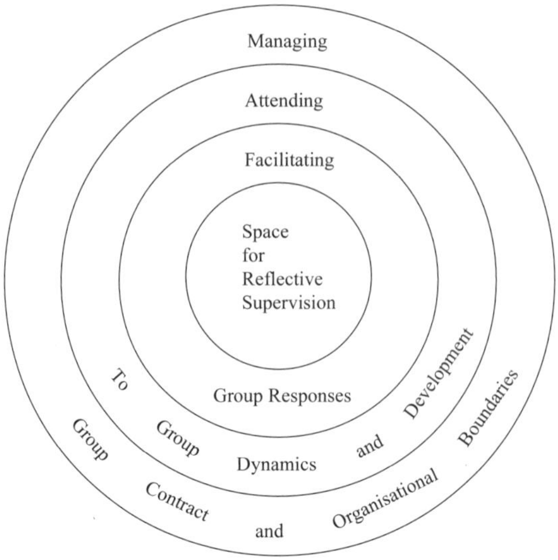

Managing

Attending

Facilitating

Space
for
Reflective
Supervision

To

Group

Group

Group Responses

Development

Boundaries

Contract

Dynamics

and

Organisational

and

I explain that we are going to start with a tag supervision on the seven modes (see Chapter 4, p108). I will give each participant a mode and they will come up to the empty supervisor's chair and try it out with a supervisee. This is a refresher from the previous course but will also give some theoretical basis for the way I do group supervision. Next, I will do two demonstrations in front of the whole group and then ask them to practise it. This will take up all of the day and some of the next day. Then we will move on to looking at difficult situations and, finally, on the last day, explore supervision in organisational contexts, as this is far more complex.

I ask how many of the participants work in an organisation. Five people out of the 18 put up their hands and I remind the group of the stakeholders and ghosts exercise that we did in the last course (p89), and that there are always dozens of people in the room.

When I've explained the rough shape of the course, we do the tag supervision and then have a break.

ᔥ   ᔥ   ᔥ

Group demonstration

After the break we go straight into a group supervision demonstration. I move into the middle of the group and ask for five people to join me.

Robin (to the rest of the group): I want you to make sure you can see and hear me, because once we have started, I will forget about you. (*People shift their chairs to get a more comfortable view.*)

Robin (to the small group in the middle): The way I do group supervision is basically using mode 6 – paying attention to what is going on inside you. So, when someone presents, I want you to pay attention to what is happening inside you. It could be a feeling – for example, feeling sad or angry. It could be a physical sensation – a knot in your stomach or tension in your neck, say, or you notice a restlessness in your leg, or a pain in your heart. It could be an image of some kind. The important thing is that you pay attention to what is happening inside you. You don't have to worry whether it is relevant or useful or not; just report on it. And don't censor. For example, if you notice yourself switching off or feeling bored, from my perspective that could be very important data. It could indicate, for example, that the client or the supervisee might not be engaged and you are picking that up. So, I want to give you permission to listen to yourself.

The second principle is that, when I ask for feedback, you give your feedback to me, as supervisor, and not to the supervisee. This is very important and I will insist on it. If I am asking you to share whatever is going on with you and not censor, then the supervisee could feel overwhelmed or even criticised and take it personally if you direct your comments to them. If you feed back to me, then the supervisee can just listen and take what is useful or what resonates. This sometimes takes practice. The aim is to give you permission to share whatever is going on with you and for the supervisee to feel free just to listen and take what they need. And giving the feedback directly to the supervisor helps this.

The final point is that I will interrupt. As soon as someone begins to share, we will have responses, but we don't usually pay them much heed as we are either paying attention to what the other person is saying or rehearsing what we are about to say. Now that you will be paying attention to your responses, you will notice yourself having reactions immediately, which is why I will interrupt to help you catch and vocalise them. Doing this also moves us away from content (the story) to process (what is happening in the here and now).

I then ask who would like to present a client.

Sometimes there is a pause; sometimes people jump straight in. Usually there are two or three who want to share. To get a rough idea of who to choose, I ask them to rate themselves between 0 and 10 for how much energy they have for presenting. This is by no means a perfect guide: some people will naturally give themselves a high mark for whatever reason – they might want attention, for example; some might give themselves a low mark, having been conditioned not to put themselves first. But I use my own feelings and pay attention to their tone of voice when they ask for the space. Words like, 'I suppose I could bring someone' might indicate low commitment. Ultimately it does not matter because, whoever we choose, there is plenty to learn. This happened recently at a conference where I chose the first person who volunteered and did not do my usual checking out. We got really stuck and the participants said how much they learnt from watching someone with my experience get stuck.

In this group, one volunteer who is not sure drops out. Another, Julia, gives herself a six and another person rates himself a seven. I ask Julia how she would feel if the other person went first, and she suddenly says in a strong voice, 'I would mind.' We all notice this, and the person who has rated himself a seven says it is OK with him if Julia goes first.

> *I make a mental note that there could already be a parallel process – for example, the client Julia will bring may have difficulty asserting themselves until they realise they will lose out.*

Before we start, to help us with our awareness, I ask everyone to close their eyes and repeat the sentence, 'Now I'm aware of...' out loud.

Robin: 'Now I'm aware of the traffic outside. Now I'm aware of tension in my neck.'

> *I choose an outside awareness and an internal one.*

The group follows:

- Now I'm aware of my feet on the floor.
- Now I'm aware of feeling anxious.
- Now I'm aware of waiting to see what people say.

> *And so on – mixtures of body awareness, feelings and cognitive labelling. I do this awareness exercise to show how accessible our internal states are, because sometimes people say they could never use mode 6 with their group – they are just beginners or they are chief executives and would not be able to or are not used to doing this.*

Then I ask Julia to tell us about her client.

Julia: The person I want to bring is a 35-year-old housewife with two children, who is very depressed.

> *I could stop her here because we will already have picked up a lot. I hesitate for a second and decide to go for it. I know it is early, but I want to show how quickly we pick up things.*

Robin: Let me stop the group here and ask what you are aware of.

Participant 1 (P1): I notice I am feeling angry (*said slightly awkwardly as if this is unexpected and could be irrelevant*).

P2: I started to slump in my chair. I felt defeated.

P3: I notice I was thinking, is there a husband?

P4: I was thinking of one of my clients of about the same age.

At this point I have a choice. Sometimes I share what is going on with me and sometimes not. The reasons vary. Sometimes I am paying a lot of attention to what is happening or has just happened in the group and am not specifically focusing on myself. That could be relevant, too, in that the supervisee might not be present with themselves, for example. I also don't want to influence the group too much – I see my job as holding the space and letting the responses of the group be the primary material. And sometimes I do share. But I prefer to see if the group can find their own way. In this instance, I choose not to share, although I notice I am thinking about the children and feeling paralysed.

Julia: Gosh, so quickly. Yes, she does feel defeated and I think very angry. And I am certainly angry with her husband.

I notice Julia's countertransference and am tempted to ask why she is angry, but the structure of supervisee talking and the group feeding back needs to be honoured. Otherwise I am falling into the trap of being the supervisor and this is not what I want to do. I want the responses of the group to be the supervision.

I ask Julia to continue.

Julia: Well, the husband is a workaholic and often comes home late, sometimes after the children have gone to bed. My client has confronted him, but he says that's how they can afford to send their children to private school. Recently he has been staying away overnight, saying that a merger at work means he has to visit other branches of his firm. The elder daughter is 10 and has recently started to fall behind at school. She has been unwell a few times and stayed off school.

My mind is whirling. Husband having an affair, child staying at home to protect mother, child a carer in the making, a potential therapist, need for marital therapy... It is amazing where our thoughts can go. Anyway, it's time to go round the group. I start them in reverse order.

P4: Sorry. I'm still with my client.

I am curious about this but don't ask. However, she volunteers.

P4: When I was that age with two children, I suspected my husband of having an affair and have felt guilty ever since. My stuff is coming in big time, not just with this client but with my own client.

Robin: That's fine. This way of working and giving the feedback to me means the supervisee can take what he or she wants and ignore if it is not relevant.

Julia: But it is very relevant. She is checking his phone and his pockets and feels terrible. He has been a very good provider.

Robin: Good. Let's hear other responses.

P3: Well, I am feeling worried about the child.

> *P3 says this directly to Julia and I insist she says it to me. P3 apologises. I say I know it is an unusual way of communicating, but it gives the supervisee time to take what is relevant. It also means that the supervisee does not have five supervisors and it gives us a chance to free-associate without having to take too much care of the supervisee. I go back to the group to get more responses.*

P2: I notice I feel helpless.

P1: I feel sick. And a bit dizzy.

I turn to Julia and ask where she is with these responses.

Julia: Yes, I feel helpless and I think my client does too. And I worry about the child. Amazing what you have picked up already. Shall I go on?

> *Now that we have established that the method of going round and sharing what is going on for us is quite effective, I think it might be time to ask what Julia has wanted from bringing this, which I do.*

Julia: Well, the word 'helpless' really rang true. She goes on and on about wanting to check up and feeling guilty and resentful and I find myself stuck. I guess I am also worried about the 10-year-old. I don't know what I want really. Help with feeling unstuck.

Robin: Let's stay stuck for a while. And keep noticing what is happening for us.

P2: I want to cry.

P4: I feel like I am ashamed and want to hide.

P3: I am so resentful of my husband's freedom.

Julia (excitedly): Yes, of course. My client was a promising dancer and gave up a possible career to support her husband and look after the children. We have been focusing on the possible affair and not looking at how she can go back to her passion now the kids are a bit older. I feel much better now.

> *I notice that this may or may not be a 'solution' in that it could be a way of not sticking with the helplessness, but it has given Julia a burst of energy and*

I think we have done enough to show how the method works, which was my aim.

I suggest we leave it there and do the feedback in the way we have done in other courses: what we appreciated about the supervision and what we found difficult. This is a way of structuring the feedback to ensure we do not get into the case material. We feedback:

- supervisor to themselves, as we are here for supervisor learning
- supervisee to supervisor, for the same reason, and last…
- group members to supervisor.

Robin: I appreciated suggesting we stay stuck a while. I found it difficult to hold in all that was going on with me and not to offer 'helpful' suggestions, especially around the child.

Julia: I appreciated feeling very safe and that my client got held and, without trying, we got a new direction. What I found difficult – well, nothing really. That I had not seen this before.

This is not actually about the supervision itself, but I am not too bothered by this.

The rest of the members of the small group supervision then feed back.

P2: Initially I was irritated that you interrupted so quickly but that is the thing I now appreciate.

P3: I really like the method of going round and sharing what is going on with us. What I found difficult was that I wanted to ask lots of questions about the daughter.

Again, the feedback is not about my work as a supervisor. I point out this is about supervisor learning and ask if they have any comments about what I did or did not do.

P4: I can't think of anything, except I was glad to see how useful it was to Julia.

I get feedback from the larger group, where there is a lot of appreciation for the power of the method and some difficulty around just observing and holding the powerlessness of being on the outside.

I open the discussion out and participants ask questions such as, 'How do you know when to interrupt?' This is a good question and I say there are no easy answers. Sometimes it is when I have a strong feeling myself; sometimes it is when I notice something happening in the group. The principle is to interrupt the story (content), which is familiar to the supervisee, and move on to the process, which is new, because it uses the here and now and can open up fresh lines of inquiry. I suggest that, when they supervise, they give themselves permission and don't wait too long. There is always something happening. Another question asks, 'What if people are not comfortable feeding back what is happening inside them, or think that it is not relevant?' I suggest that a lot of it is confidence – I have always found people are able to do that and, because I expect it, people have done it. But we will look at other techniques later, as this is not the only way to do group supervision. It is the way I started 40 years ago, and I still find it very useful.

It is time for lunch and, to get a feel of the group, I ask them to shout out a word, any word. They offer words like 'stimulated', 'excited', 'hungry', 'buzzing', 'I could never do that' (*not a word but it generates laughter in the group*). We break for lunch.

∿   ∿   ∿

Following lunch, we go straight into the second demonstration of group supervision, with five new participants. Liz asks to present her client.

This one is very different and involves a client who has lost a daughter in a car accident. She had been knocked down by a speeding driver. The driver was prosecuted but the father of the daughter was obsessed and blamed the judge for not putting the driver in prison. He wanted to appeal and was constantly having outbursts of rage and grief. He was very stuck, or at least that is how it appeared to Liz, the supervisee. (*In this instance, unusually, I let the supervisee give a lot of story before I interrupt.*) We do a round of sharing what is going on for us, and people share feelings of wanting revenge, feeling kicked in the stomach, shock, an unbearable pain in the neck. We have another round and one person in the group rather timidly says:

P1: I have had this phrase going round in my head and I can't make any sense of it.

Robin: What is it?

P1: It's my fault.

Liz (almost shouting): Of course, of course!

It turns out that, when he first told his story, the client had shared that he had been supposed to give his daughter a lift home, but had asked her to come to his workplace because he was working late. He had not told his wife because they were estranged and his workaholism was one of the reasons for the marital breakdown.

Liz: Now it makes sense. He feels responsible because she was walking to his workplace when she was knocked down.

The group lets out a collective sigh of relief. It was as if we had all felt incredibly tense and now something has relaxed in us.

> *We recognise that this will not bring his daughter back, obviously, but this sense of it possibly being his fault has not been explored. He feels guilty that he might have been indirectly responsible for her death. And he could not share this with anyone. The supervisee had missed that he had mentioned it in passing and had not made the connection, as she was too caught up in his obsessing about revenge. So, a sentence that did not make sense is a clue for opening up a whole new line of inquiry. He did not dare share with his ex-wife that he was working late and didn't go to collect his daughter as planned. There are still loose ends – losing a child is one of the most traumatic of experiences anyone can encounter – but the supervisee is feeling more compassionate and has a possible direction for the work.*

We gather in the feedback of appreciations and what we might have found difficult, in the usual way.

It is now time for the group to practise supervising in groups of six, and I say there will be time for everyone to have a chance to be supervisor. The practice is based on the demonstration and I go over the steps. Someone presents and other group members pay attention to what is going on inside them (mode 6). The supervisor stops the supervisee and asks the group members to feed back their responses, ensuring that the feedback is to the supervisor. And, to finish, the supervisee shares if anything resonated. There can be three or more rounds of this. I like all three groups to stay in the main room, as that keeps the energy in. I ask if there are any questions before we do go off into our small groups. I suggest 20 minutes is enough and say I will give them a five-minute warning so they can get the feedback in.

When the groups come back, I ask them how it went.

Group 1: It went really well (*nods from the rest of the group*).

Robin: What did you appreciate most?

Member of group 1: Sam [*the group supervisor*] took charge and we felt really held.

Robin: This is important. I think we are sometimes reluctant to take authority but, when we go on to look at group dynamics, we will see that there are always natural anxieties about being in any group, and especially a new one, so it is important that the facilitator is in charge at the beginning.

Supervisor of group 2: I struggled at first. I did not want to interrupt and probably let the supervisee go on too long. Then I did not insist that the feedback was given to me and there was a dialogue between the supervisee and one of the group, which sort of broke up the group. And then I had a flash, because I am not usually so unassertive, that perhaps there was a parallel process and the client was reluctant to assert herself – a bit like the first demonstration. And the supervisee agreed and from then we were fine.

Robin: You spotted and used the parallel process.

Member of group 2: This parallel process seems like magic. In fact, the whole thing does. Does it ever not work?

Robin: If you remember from the material we covered on projective identification in the last module, we have suggested that what is brought to supervision is something that has not been digested. So, it seems that this way of working enables us to pick this up. But I can't say it always happens. Anything from the third group?

Nothing much emerges from them. They say it all went fine. I noticed when they were working, they seemed to be quite a tight-knit group. I make a note to ask them first next time as they may feel as if their feedback is not as interesting as that of the other two groups.

It is time for tea, and I ask them to go straight into the same groups after tea and do another session. This time I ask the third group to feed back first.

Member of third group: Well, we ran into difficulties. Last time, when Jeni was facilitating, the energy was quite low. And the same happened this time. And I guess we did not spot the parallel process because it took ages to decide who was going to be supervisee, and that seemed to demoralise us. Now I can see that, in your words, it was all data, but at the time we did not see it.

Robin: Thank you. I really appreciate your sharing that. It's hard to feel that everything might not be going as well as you hoped. Once you get the idea it is all data, and can share that at the time without blame, just as information, the stuckness is useful. It could be parallel process. But whatever it is, I appreciate your sharing that as we learn more from stuckness than when everything is going well. As you have reminded us, it is all data.

Supervisor of third group: You know, I think it all went wrong because (*hesitates*) I think I wanted to work with Zelina – the energy was higher, but somehow we worked with Alan – no offence (*looking at Alan*) – and I did not share that because I felt it was my fault.

Alan (supervisee, excitedly): The client was bringing in sibling rivalry, so we just replayed it (*parallel process again*).

The group is relieved and there is learning for everyone about how everything can be used. I mention that tomorrow we will be looking at difficult situations such as being stuck, which happens to all of us. I get feedback from the other two groups and then it is time for home groups. We finish in the large group as I think this is important. People report that they are tired, full, full of questions; that this seems like magic and is this usual?; that they feel stretched, curious, and looking forward to more. I remind them that we start half an hour earlier tomorrow and hope they have a good evening.

∾   ∾   ∾

Day 2: attending to group dynamics and developments

I start by asking if there is anything from yesterday anyone wants to share or ask about. Somebody asks why we are focusing on just mode 6 and not using other modes like mode 2, where the session finishes with an action plan.

I reply that sometimes just doing a mode 6, as we have done, can leave the work apparently unfinished. My belief and, I add, my experience is that the supervisee will continue working on it afterwards. I suggest that the need to have a mode 2 action plan at the end could reflect the supervisor's need to have a result.

I tell them about one occasion when the supervisee felt unfinished after the demonstration group supervision like the one we just did. As it was a demonstration of mode 6, I let it be. The next day, the supervisee reported he had woken up in the middle of the night full of shame at how he had presented his work and realised that was how his client felt about his own work. In other words, leaving the supervision apparently unfinished left the space for something to emerge afterwards. As I mentioned, there is a danger that the supervisor might like to have everything tidied up.

I am asked if I ever finish with an action plan and I say there is obviously a place for that but, for the moment, we are using mode 6 and how to use ourselves. I say a bit more about the thinking behind this method.

I think it is important that we come to the sessions as empty as possible so we can allow ourselves to be filled with what needs to emerge in the moment. And what I say now, only semi-jokingly, is that I am not the slightest bit interested in you. That may sound shocking, but if you empty yourselves, when you feed back what is going on with you, you can be a transmitter of what is in the field. It's not personal. The emptier we are, the less static there is. Of course, because the supervisee can take or leave what you say, it does not matter if your feedback is full of your stuff, but the more empty we are the more we allow ourselves to be a channel for what needs to emerge.

I suggest one more practice just on mode 6 for 20 minutes. After this third session, they come back and I ask them how it was.

Member of group 3: Our group is really getting the hang of this. It seems to be working well and each time the supervisor seems to be more confident. I was quite cynical at first about it being enough to just report what was going on inside us using mode 6, but now I see how powerful it is.

Robin: I discovered this way of working 40 years ago, before the formulation of the seven modes. It seemed to me the obvious way of working and comes naturally, but I also realise that might not be true for others, so I appreciate your being willing to give it a go.

I suggest it might be time to move on to other modes. I ask for the first group with whom we did the demonstration to move into the middle again and recap the story of the 35-year-old woman who is depressed. Her husband is away a lot and she suspects he is having an affair and hates herself for being so suspicious. She is also resentful as she has given up a potential career in dancing to support her husband and look after the children.

Robin (turning to Julia): Is that right?

Julia: Yes.

Robin: OK, I want everyone in the group to become part of the client and supervisee's system – a mode 7. So, someone could be the wife, someone could be Julia, someone could be the husband and so on. It does not matter if two people become the same person. Just choose someone and feed back as them.

There is a hesitancy in the group, so I start – not as a person but as the client's dancing, to show that we can become any part of the system.

Robin: I am the client's dancing. I am really sad that she does not bother with me anymore. I think it would really help her depression. But more than that, she will value herself again. I can't wait for her to find me again.

P1: I am Julia, the supervisee. I am relieved that I have a way of working now whereas before I was stuck.

P2: I am the daughter. I want Mummy to be happy.

P3: I am the husband. I feel very unrecognised as it was clear at the beginning that I was going to be the breadwinner and that we wanted the best for our children.

P4: I am the husband's place of work. We have noticed that he has been a bit preoccupied recently. We need him to be at his best in this merger, and if he doesn't produce, we may have to let him go.

Julia: Gosh. That all makes so much sense. I am much more able to both support and challenge my client – support her around her dancing and challenge her paranoia. He may or may not be having an affair, but the point is that she is not fulfilling herself. Thank you.

I find group supervision very rich as you have the whole group as a resource. A clear structure is important. So, in the above intervention, each group member says something to the supervisor so no one is either dominating or not speaking. In this way the group begins to build cohesiveness.

I ask the second group to enter the circle. This is the one with the daughter who was knocked down and killed and the father who was vengeful.

Robin: This technique is not mode specific. I want us each to ask Liz a question, which she will write down but not answer now. The questions are not factual – eg. 'How old is the client?' – but something that will take the supervisee deeper into their work. The reason I don't want Liz to answer now is that I want her to reflect on them and come back with her answers tomorrow. If it were an ongoing group, the person would bring the answers to the following group the next week or next month, or however often the group meets.

I ask Liz if she is ready for the questions, making sure she has a pen and paper to write them down.

P1: Why do you think you blocked out that your client had asked his daughter to meet him at his workplace, even though you had the information?

P2: If you were really critical of your client, what would you say?

I like this question, indeed any questions that encourage supervisees to get past their professional censors.

P3: Do you like this client? And I have another – are you frightened of your client?

I suggest that it might be useful, as well as asking Liz if she is frightened, to ask what might be making her frightened. (*I always check with the person who has asked the question if it is OK when I suggest a change. P3 nods.*)

Liz: I can already answer that – he reminds me of my father, and I was scared of him. And now I can answer the first question – I didn't want to remember the change of arrangements as I felt I might not be able to deal with his reaction.

Robin: Great. But still, write down the question as I would like you to reflect on them all and come back to us tomorrow. Any more?

P4: What would be the best outcome from your work with this client?

I thank the group for their input.

In this exercise, I prefer the questions to go via me, but I am not insistent on this. The reason is that sometimes I can clarify the question or build on it a bit if it is not clear, as in the case of P3. Sometimes there is space for more than one question per person, which is fine.

I suggest we leave the question technique here and go on to another technique.

Robin: There is another technique I would like to give you. That is, we give the supervisee a piece of advice. It is a kind of mode 2 group brainstorming, where we allow the group to come up with suggestions, however wacky they might be, safe in the knowledge that the supervisee just listens and takes what is useful. Let's try it.

P4: Tell him to confess everything to his wife.

P2: Put his daughter on the empty chair and get him to talk to her and then swap places.

P3: Yes, I like that. I was going to say, ask him to write a letter to his daughter.

P1: Get him to go through what happened to see if there really is any justification for his guilt. I suspect there isn't but, either way, it would be good to go through everything he did.

Robin (to Liz): How are those?

Liz: All good. I especially like the empty chair, as I can facilitate a dialogue between him and his daughter. Gosh, I have been shut down on this. Thank you all.

Robin: This technique is good for all of us who like to give advice. What it does is make this advice-giving explicit rather than giving feedback like, 'Couldn't you try...?', which is telling without owning it. And actually, there is another technique I would like to show you. I have used it when I have been really stuck, but you can use it at any time.

I ask the supervisee to move her chair slightly outside the group and invite the group to close the circle.

Robin: Now, what I want us to do is to gossip about the supervisee and their client. I am here to make sure that the gossip stays respectful but, after the rigour of going round and each person reporting what is going on with them, we can free associate.

There is some discomfort about this – it is countercultural to talk about someone when they are in earshot.

P1: I was wondering about the whole topic of forgiving oneself. Really hard to do. I know that I have struggled with some of the things I have done.

This is a really generous way to start. P1 has taken a topic that is universal and applied it to herself.

P2: I kept wondering about the family dynamic – the estranged wife, his workaholism.

P3: I think that is quite external, in one way. The point is that he has not been really able to trust anyone with this information. He got (*pointing to the supervisee, Liz*) to know and not know this. Thank goodness it has come out.

P4: I found myself not liking the sound of him. All this revenge stuff. I found it distasteful, even though I can understand it and might well be the same if it were my child.

Robin: I notice we have begun to focus on the client, which is fine. I find myself wondering about the supervisee's relationship with her client (*mode 3*) and want to ask her for an image for their relationship (*client and supervisee*).

P1: Funny you should say that. I thought, he has killed the supervisee off – or is that getting too analytical?

Robin: We are free associating, so it is all fine. The supervisee will take what she needs. Let's ask her back in.

Robin (to Liz): How was that?

Liz: Very interesting. At first I thought I would mind being excluded but it felt very safe. And you are right (*turning to P1*) – I have felt killed off in some kind of a way. Paralysed with all this anger stuff.

I say it is time for a break and then we will have a fourth practice session, using any of the techniques we have demonstrated – mode 6, mode 7, being part of the system, questions, advice and, finally, gossiping.

After the fourth session they come back full of energy. Someone asks about how much control the supervisor has, in that the feedback from the group goes to them and they also decide when to stop the supervisee's narrative. Is this not quite controlling?

Robin: On one level it is, but that structure can take care of some of the many anxieties there are in such a group. Once the group has settled, then if someone is bursting to say something, they put their hand up and, as facilitator, I am usually happy to stop the group then. If I think it will break the flow, I wait. I would rather the facilitator is too much in charge at the beginning than too little, like a teacher with a new class. Moreover, after a while and when the group is really settled and used to the way of working where people are reporting what is going on for them, I don't even ask them to put their hands up. People just come in with their comments and it is rarely intrusive – in fact, it is more flowing than my stopping the action.

It is time for lunch. Afterwards, we will look at difficult situations in group supervision.

After the lunch break, I suggest we do a warm-up in which only three people are standing at one time. When one sits down, another stands. I let them do it for a while. Sometimes there are four people standing and one has to hastily sit down. The secret is to do it in slow motion so there are clear signals when someone is about to sit down, so another can take their place, and if two people go to stand, there is space for one to back down. We draw parallels about the value of slowing down in supervision.

Then we get back to group supervision. I ask five volunteers to come into the middle of the larger group. We are going to improvise a group. I don't suggest a topic or situation, although we have done it that way in the past. By improvise, I mean that the group has to use whatever data each other brings – to remember if, say, one person says this is the second session, or that someone wasn't at the group last week. So it means listening quite carefully to what each other says and the roles they have taken on, and to the possible history of the group. I say that they can use their own names or choose another name or gender.

The purpose of this improvised group is to roleplay a difficult situation where the supervisor (in this case, me) is taken by surprise and to see how they cope and what strategies they use. I intend to start with a first session, but someone jumps in ahead of me.

Diane (turning to the only man in the group): I was really pissed off with you answering your mobile last week. (*Turning to me*) And for you for allowing it.

This has really thrown me as, in reality, I would never have allowed it. I have to think quickly on my feet.

Robin: Thank you, Diane, for bringing this. I had forgotten to mention about mobile phones at the beginning and, as it was almost the end of the session, when Peter went out, I thought it would be too disruptive to go into detail about this. If you remember, I apologised for not mentioning this and said we would look at it next time. Thank you for bringing this up straight away, as I was intending to, but I get that this is important for you.

Diane: Yes. I felt Joanna's work was interrupted and your saying that it was parallel process felt a whitewash. (*Turning to Peter*) You always do this in groups.

Oh my goodness. Now they have 'previous'. This group is really testing me out, much to the amusement of the outside group.

Peter: There goes my phone again. There is an emergency at work so I said they could phone me any time. I'll be as quick as I can.

This is getting worse by the moment. The outside group can hardly contain their amusement.

Robin: Wait (*I say this in a very strong voice that contains in equal measure, I think, panic, irritation and a determination to not let this happen*). Let it ring.

Peter: I can't.

Kamala (to me): Who do you think you are? Can't you see there is an emergency?

Peter: Thank you. I'll be as quick as I can.

This is getting farcical now. I know it is only a roleplay but I am being really tested. I turn to Peter.

Robin: I wonder if you were the one in your family everyone could depend on?

This is really left field and a long shot. Not surprisingly, Fiona comes in hard.

Fiona: How dare you give him this psychobabble stuff? This is not a therapy group.

Peter (looks thoughtful): No, wait a moment. He's onto something here. In whatever team I work in (*looks at Diane*), I seem to play this role of being a compulsive rescuer, and, would you believe, I had never connected it with my mother being suicidal.

Having really tested me, Peter in role is now being generous. So far, the group has brought up faulty contracting (I didn't mention about phones), so-called emergencies, previous relationships coming into the group, and now the fact that I have brought in a mode 4 intervention, which is seen as therapy. This group is really making me work.

Robin: Peter, can I start with you? I really appreciate your honesty in making the connection with your past. So where shall we start? You may remember last time (*my turn to invent something now*), when I said that supervision is here to help with our work with clients.

Fiona: But that's what Peter is doing – being available to his clients.

She is not going to let go easily.

Robin: I agree. But the purpose of supervision is to look at the best options for helping. Being on-call may create a dependency.

Fiona: I suppose so.

Robin (turning to Peter): What makes it an emergency?

Peter: We have a suicidal young person and I am their key worker. I only got to come here because I promised to leave my phone on.

Robin: And what can you do on the end of the phone that someone else can't? Don't you trust your other workers?

Peter: That was below the belt. You are double-binding me now. Either I have to say I don't trust my workers or that they can cope with it. Yes, but it was on that condition that I was able to come to this group.

Robin: Sometimes it is a question of 'pass the hot potato of anxiety' and you are very used to carrying that hot potato. Any sign of distress and they know they can count on you to sort it out. They leave you with all the stress.

Fiona: People like Peter are the salt of the earth. Why have you got it in for him?

Kamala: Robin hasn't got it in for him. This is the first time I have seen Pete not in heroic mode.

Peter: I don't know what to do. I really want to phone back but what you are saying about creating dependency rings true.

Joanne (who has been quiet up to now): Just text back to say you are getting some good supervision on whoever it is, and if they wait a couple of hours, you will ring as soon as the group is over. You are just asking and let's see where that goes. (*Out of role*) This has been really useful for me.

Robin: OK, let's call an end to the role play and do the usual appreciations and difficulties. I appreciated rolling with what a mess I had apparently made in the previous session. What I found difficult was adapting to what a mess I must have made last time.

Peter: I know this is a role play, but there is always some of us in the roles we choose and I do have a heroic rescuer in me, but far more subtle than the role I played, I think. What I found difficult was putting you on the spot like that, although I have to say I enjoyed it too.

Fiona: You were never judgemental and you thanked everyone for their contribution. What I found difficult was playing that role. I felt quite obnoxious.

Robin: I don't know if this make sense but it is as if the group elects people to play roles in groups – if there is unease in a group, someone often lands up the challenger of the facilitator. I have found myself in that role – being used by the group so they can sit back and pretend there is nothing wrong with them. Suddenly I am the 'baddy' in the eyes of authority. That could have been happening to you in your role.

Fiona: Yes, that makes a lot of sense. I find myself behaving in a way I don't really want to sometimes in a group. Just as you say, being elected to challenge.

The other three give their feedback. Joanne says she has already said what she appreciated and found nothing difficult. Diane says that she felt very well handled – that her anger with Peter was acknowledged and appreciated, and she in her role wanted to be appreciated for her courage. Kamala says it was useful to be challenged on the use of the word 'emergency'.

We go back to the larger group, who are generally appreciative. I am asked why I stopped it there. I say that it was the end of the allotted time, and I confess it was getting too much. 'Too much of what?' asks someone, and I say it was too much to hold at that moment as I saw so many teaching points. The group asks what would have happened if I had continued. I said that I was frightened of forgetting the teaching points that I needed to share with them. They persevere and ask what would have happened if I had forgotten? Didn't I trust them to pick up what we needed? Was I in parallel process – feeling I have to do it all? We laugh together.

I share the dynamics I have picked up:

1. *Clear contracting.* In the role play, it became the third session so, with no first session, I had to improvise with what I had been given. In a first session, I would ensure that they understood the purpose of supervision – to enable them to be as present as possible for their clients. However, it is worth saying that we often miss something, and paradoxically that can be more useful than if we hadn't missed it, if it is then acknowledged and worked through together.

2. *People having what I call 'previous'* – that is, they know each other and carry baggage. This takes us back to the contract, where I ask people to be in the service of the work and to keep personalities out of it. This is sometimes easier said than done.

3. *The question of emergency* – I dealt with it in the moment with an interpretation on rescuing, which Peter accepted, but it is a much bigger question. I have a copy of my book *Passionate Supervision* with me (Shohet, 2007), and I read out the relevant section (page 198) to promote a discussion. It involves a psychologist who claimed there was an emergency at her workplace and, on further questioning, she turned out to be covering her back.

4. *People carrying something for the group.* In a role play of a difficult group from a previous course, there was one woman who was playing the role of being consistently angry. Different supervisors clapped themselves in and out (we did it as a tag supervision). The person playing the supervisor changed the dynamic when she turned to the person playing the angry role and asked if she was carrying anger for the group. This person also wondered perhaps

whether she (the angry person) was being used not only by this group but by other groups. This intervention brought about a real shift in the person playing the angry role and everyone could see the value in understanding that we have a valency for carrying things for others in a group. If this is not understood there is a great likelihood of scapegoating. (For an excellent description of this, see Ivor Browne's *Music and Madness* (2008: 198–206).)

Difficult situations in group supervision

I ask them now to brainstorm difficult situations in a group. This is their list:

1. Personal antagonism between group members.
2. People having to attend.
3. Not having the option to tell people to leave.
4. Competition for the facilitator role and dealing with the feelings that might generate.
5. A member of a group being unethical or incompetent and being unaware of it.
6. Death of a supervisee's client, particularly suicide.
7. Two people having an exclusive pairing in a group.
8. When members are very cognitive and task-orientated.
9. Supervision being offered as a tick-box commodity.
10. Dealing with 'perfect' people.
11. People having fun undermining the facilitator.
12. Pre-existing hierarchy.
13. Breaking confidentiality and codes of conduct.
14. People not taking the group seriously.
15. A lot of different norms in the group.
16. Someone walking out of the group in a dramatic and/or distressed way.

I suggest they vote on which they would like to focus on. The top three are 5, 15 and 6, although 1, 2 and 3 get a lot of votes too.

Robin: Let's go for number 5. Can five people join me in the middle?

I am going to go straight into role-playing this – I know this group can do it. I think it is more powerful than talking about it.

Robin (to the group, improvising): This is team supervision with an outside consultant. You are all staff at a day centre. Louise, you have been counselling this male patient and have been seen having a coffee with him after work. This is creating tension in the centre as your client is telling everyone and boasting that he gets hugs from you. The other clients are jealous and confronting their counsellors about being too rigid with their boundaries.

I decide to do it as a tag group supervision (briefly, group members clap each other out of the supervisor role – see p65 for a detailed explanation). I had thought of facilitating another group supervision myself but decide it would be far better to see what the group comes up with as I think they will manage it. I vacate my chair and say, 'This is the supervisor's chair, who would like to sit in it?' Pretish volunteers.

Pretish: I am an outsider here, but what are the centre's guidelines about seeing people outside work time?

Caroline: They are very clear. We do not see people outside work time.

Louise (to Pretish): I know why you brought this up. Once and only once, I was having a coffee and this client came in and asked if he could join me. I didn't feel able to say no. What's going on here (*said in a suspicious tone*)?

Pretish: Yes, you are right. I heard about this and instead of asking the person who told me, I thought I needed to do something.

Cynthia: I was the one who told Pretish. (*Turning to Louise*) Your client is telling everyone you give him hugs and that he has had coffee with you.

Louise (to Cynthia): Why did you tell Pretish and not me directly?

Cynthia: I was frightened you would get upset.

Louise: Not half as upset as I feel now. (*To Pretish*) I don't feel safe here.

Pretish is clapped out of his role by Dorothy, who now sits in the supervisor chair.

Dorothy (turning to Louise): I can well understand that, Louise. I have a big ask of this group. That we notice how we feel right now and feed it back.

Louise: Unsafe.

Cynthia: Caught out.

Caroline: Annoyed.

Pretish: Curious.

Dorothy: Thank you. Now here is the ask. We see everything as part of the system. I want you to imagine you are different parts of the system.

Both these interventions are very skilful. In the first one, Dorothy changes the frame from conflict to feelings, taking her cue from Louise saying she did not feel safe. In the second, she depersonalises the whole situation, and asks people to see the bigger picture and how they might be carrying something for the organisation. She also says twice that it is a big ask, thereby inviting the group to rise to the challenge.

Continuing with Dorothy's intervention, people become the other clients at the day centre, the receptionist, the hug (we are not given enough recognition), Louise, other counsellors, policy, the manager (people can take more than one role). Even though this is a role play, the participants are actively engaged.

I end the role play here as I think there is plenty of learning already. I thank the group for volunteering, Pretish for being brave enough to volunteer to go first and Dorothy for stepping in. The appreciations and difficulties are a way of de-roling.

The learning centres round not carrying something for someone else – ie. the supervisor could have asked Cynthia, 'Why are you telling me this?' Denise, who is sitting outside the group, says she has a policy of insisting that if there is any correspondence between groups, then it must be brought to the group. So she would have started the group with, 'Cynthia, you emailed me between groups. Please tell the group what you said.' This has quite an impact, and we look at the question of contact between groups.

We have not looked at the question of dual roles either. Does the supervisor feed back to a training body, so if the Louise role is incompetent, what is the supervisor's responsibility? A lot seems to be about clear contracting, which we will revisit later.

Robin: We have been sitting a while so I suggest that if anyone has a strong desire to choose one of the difficulties we've listed (*above*), they get up and others join them. In this way we will have three or four groups around a difficulty and you choose a supervisor, with the proviso that it is someone who has not supervised before, as I want everyone to have a turn.

There are a few logistics to work out, and we end up in three groups and roleplay the difficult situation and/or discuss how we might cope with it. This is adding roleplay to the other techniques we have already used.

The feedback afterwards centres around really using authority, being willing to admit mistakes and not be defensive and finding a positive way of reframing all contributions.

It has been a full day and there is no time for home groups. We can start with them tomorrow, as it gives us a chance to review how the course has been and what they want from the final day. The feedback has been around challenge and learning and many say how important the safety has been. We agree to start with home groups first thing next morning.

Day 3: managing group contracts and organisational boundaries

I welcome them and we start with home groups. They then go into their final practice session to integrate what they have learnt. When we reconvene, I ask how they are doing with their learning needs and they report feeling much more confident about taking their authority in groups. I say it is time to look at the outer circle from the diagram (p118) – supervision in an organisational context. I ask if anyone has something that relates to supervision and the wider system. I ask for five people to form a supervision group with me, in the middle of the whole group.

Five people join and John volunteers to be the supervisee.

John: I would like to bring my supervision group. I have been running it for over a year. The old manager was charismatic and the staff in the supervision group were devoted to her. There is one newcomer who has not met the old manager and was appointed by the new one, and they don't contribute much to the group.

Robin: There are plenty of stakeholders and ghosts in the room. It sounds as if the new person might feel excluded as they were appointed by the new manager and don't know the old one and the older group members might be feeling resentful at losing their old manager. This will affect how they bring their cases, as well as the group dynamic.

Robin (to John): Why have you brought this?

John: My supervisor says that my job is to supervise the group and not to get involved in politics.

Robin: Who pays for the group?

John: The organisation.

Robin: You are in a three-way contract: you, the group and the organisation. You can't take the organisation out of the equation. It can be very easy not to pay enough attention to the system (mode 7).

Like his supervision group, John is irritated by the new CEO. I guess his group will have picked this up and there may be a collusion between him and the group around this new CEO. I suggest the exercise where people become part of the system and different people play the roles of the new person, the new CEO, the old timers, the client group and the supervisee himself. The supervisee, John, watches with interest, especially the person playing the new CEO, who does it quite sympathetically, showing how she is in a set-up, coming into the organisation after the old CEO, who may have relied on her charisma to bypass formal structures.

Of course, this is guesswork but my experience is that people very often tune in and, if they do get something wrong, their input does not need to be taken up. However, sometimes the so-called wrongness can highlight something that has been hitherto hidden.

John says he has had a light-bulb moment and that he has allowed himself to be part of the split in the organisation. He says that he does not know what he will do next, but that his attitude has changed. I leave it there and we complete the feedback in the usual way, starting with appreciations and then difficulties.

We have a break and continue looking at the wider system. I refer back to the team supervision roleplay that we did earlier. A group that works together in the same organisation obviously has a different dynamic to one that only comes together for supervision. What can happen is that there is more baggage, because they know each other better from other contexts. I remind them of my starting point when I told the groups that they are there to be in service, and they serve best by emptying themselves and letting what needs to emerge about the case come through them.

I have an exercise that is useful when working with teams because it quickly highlights what can't be talked about. I invite the team members to complete the following sentences, but I stress that they will not be asked to share the answers; I say that just allowing the answers into consciousness can change the dynamic:

- What I can't say in this group is… and
- I can't say it because… and then
- What I think we can't talk about is… and
- I think we can't talk about it because…

I suggest that we do this exercise now, but we will just do the last two: 'What we can't talk about as a group' and, 'We can't talk about it because…' I ask them to write down their answers and stress that they do not have to share them.

In fact, this group is very willing to share their answers, and what emerges is competition, fear of not looking good, and sex. The woman who mentioned sex says that she fancies one of the men in the group, but that she is bringing up the topic because of something that is happening at work. She is pretty sure that two people in her team are an 'item', but they have not declared it and this is having an effect on the rest of the team.

We explore her fears around mentioning it at work – her fear of being wrong or their going into denial and being angry with her. Many people identify with her, which seems to give her permission to dare to risk it when she goes back to work.

We talk about the work of Wilfred Bion, who writes about pairing (1961) – when two people form an exclusive relationship – as having a detrimental effect on a group as a whole; it is a form of splitting.

I turn to the issue of competition, and ask the group to do another exercise involving finishing a sentence on paper.

- I am not as good as everyone else because…

I give them a few moments to write 20 such sentences. Only two or three manage 20, but they get the point. Comparison is a trick of the mind where you cannot win. If you are worse, you lose. If you are better, you lose but indirectly as you fear envy or being found out or being dethroned.

Then I ask them to write 20 sentences using the following root:

- I am better than everyone else because…

Doing this has reduced some of the charge around the topic as we can see how all our minds are doing it, but we can become the witness of the mind rather than at its mercy.

We have touched on several aspects of group dynamics – people carrying things for the group, conflict, pairing, how to begin working with what can't be named, the contract with the group and perhaps with the organisation, and dual roles. We have covered a lot of ground since we started with mode 6, and the latter stages have reminded us how complex group supervision can be. However, I think the format of going round and having everyone feed back can avoid potentially difficult situations, such as people not contributing or someone dominating. I really encourage the group to take their authority, especially at the beginning. And I reiterate that there is so often fear that can't be named and there is always the potential for shame from some of the past 'ghost' experiences in groups.

We break for lunch. After lunch we look at applications, which can include how to get a group going, fears about taking authority and more on difficult situations and the difference between groups and teams. We then break again for tea.

When we return, it is apparent that the group has been 'gossiping' over tea and several of the women are saying they miss Joan (she has done the first and second course with some of them). I ask why and they say that she is willing to be more vulnerable than I am and stay lost for longer. At first it irritated them, but they grew to like it, they say. I thank them and say yes, I can resonate with that.

They go into home groups and then we finish together in the large group with appreciations of self, other, group and the course.

I really appreciated the feedback at the end – that they felt able to say it. I actually do feel vulnerable – that somehow I haven't given enough or in the right way – and I reflect on the parallel process of the world outside, where there are several invitations to not feel good enough. I notice that the level of needing to get it right has changed over the years. The world felt kinder about experimentation when I began this work. I suddenly feel sad and wonder if the gap between me and the participants is too big. It's no use being falsely modest: I do have a lot of experience. That has pluses, of course, but I can see there are disadvantages, too. I am not as raw as when I started; I am more polished. I don't like that thought. I take this to my own supervision, and my supervisor confronts me with how I keep people at a distance and that my not going down to tea with everyone else, like Joan does, reflects that. This group obviously minded. And, once again, I see the strengths that come from my family position – being on the outside, and able to witness – and the weakness – I am less involved and not willing to be vulnerable.

And finally remembering you, the reader. What shall I say to you? Or what have you to say to me? Have I conveyed the richness of the group and its huge potential? In truth, with some group supervisions, I have been able to sit back and watch the group unfold. I hope some of that came across. I have just been re-watching a video of the orchestra conductor Ben Zander[1] talking about his relationship with his orchestra, and I think this is a wonderful metaphor for group supervision. The conductor does not make a sound but brings out the sounds of everyone else.

Summary of the techniques

Supervisee presents. People share what is going on inside them (p119)

Supervisor makes sure that all comments are addressed to them (mode 6) (p119)

Supervisee presents and we all become part of the system (mode 7) (p128)

Supervisee presents. Everyone asks one or more questions (p129)

Supervisor makes sure these questions are framed in a useful way (not mode specific) (p129)

Supervisee presents and we all give a piece of advice (not mode specific) (p130)

Supervisee presents. Supervisor asks them to sit back and the group gossips (p130)

Supervisee is asked back in and comments (not mode specific) (p131)

Postscript

The night after finishing this write up, I had a dream about Princess Diana and breaking confidentiality. I dreamed it did not matter in the end because she was in a large group supervision demonstration I was giving. This reminded me of the power of mode 6, and how this emerged very vividly at a real event I gave.

I was giving a demonstration of mode 6 to about 60 people, and the set-up did not allow me to follow my usual technique of creating a small group in the middle of the whole group as there was a lecture theatre and a stage. So, I did a one-to-one supervision on the stage with microphones for me as supervisor and a volunteer supervisee. I periodically stopped the session and asked the audience for their mode 6 responses and someone wrote them on a flipchart. This proved as useful to the supervisee as the small, more intimate group structure, and demonstrated how sensitive we are to each other even in such a setting.

---

1. See www.youtube.com/watch?v=qTKEBygQic0 (accessed 29 October 2019).

Foodnote

Gluten-free lemon drizzle cake

The gluten-free cakes emerged when Robin became intolerant to gluten a few years ago. I wanted to find a recipe that was even better than the regular lemon drizzle cake, rather than a poor imitation, and I think I've succeeded with the one below. Just for comparison, we cook the regular one too. Can you ever have too much lemon drizzle cake? I think not.

Robin has recently started to make this cake himself for the group. He says, if he can do it, it must be virtually foolproof.

> *For the cake*
> 200g butter
> 200g golden caster sugar
> 4 eggs
> 175g ground almonds
> 250g mashed potatoes
> Zest of 3 lemons
> 2tsps gluten-free baking powder
>
> *For the drizzle*
> 4tbs granulated sugar
> Juice of 1 lemon

1. Heat oven to 180°C/350°F/Gas mark 4.
2. Butter and line a deep 20cm round tin.
3. Beat the sugar and butter together until light and fluffy.
4. Gradually add the eggs, beating after each addition.
5. Fold in the almonds, cold mashed potato, lemon zest and baking powder.
6. Tip the mixture into the tin and bake for about 45 minutes until golden and a skewer in the middle comes out clean.
7. Allow the cake to cool for 10 minutes and then turn it onto a wire rack.
8. Mix the granulated sugar and lemon juice together and spoon over the top of the cake, letting it drip down the sides.
9. Leave the cake to cool completely before cutting.

Ordinary lemon drizzle cake

> 225g unsalted butter, softened
> 225g caster sugar
> 4 eggs

225g self-raising flour
Finely grated zest of 1 lemon
Juice of 1½ lemons
85g caster sugar

1. Heat oven to 180°C/350°F/Gas mark 4 and line a loaf tin with greaseproof paper.
2. Cream together 225g butter and caster sugar until pale and creamy.
3. Add eggs one at a time
4. Sift in flour and add lemon zest.
5. Spoon the mixture into the tin.
6. Bake for 45–50 minutes until a skewer inserted into the cake comes out clean.
7. While the cake is cooling, mix together the lemon juice and caster sugar.
8. Prick the warm cake all over and pour over the drizzle – the juice will sink in and form a lovely crispy topping.
9. Leave the cake in the tin until it has cooled.

Duke of Cambridge Tart and Lemon Meringue Pie

I had to put both these recipes together – the first from my Auntie Jean and the other from my Mum, Alma – because the shortcrust pastry works for both, the egg yolks go in the Duke of Cambridge tart and the egg whites in the lemon meringue pie … perfect fit!

225g (8oz) short crust pastry, half for each pie (half fat to flour plus water to make a dough)
125g (4oz) raisins
50g (2oz)glacé cherries
75g (3oz) butter or margarine
75g (3oz) caster sugar
2 egg yolks (egg whites can be used for the lemon meringue pie)
2 tbs rum or brandy

1. Preheat oven to 190°C (375°F/Gas mark 5).
2. Line two 18cm (7in) pie dishes with pastry.
3. Prick with a fork and blind bake for10 minutes.
4. Cover raisins with cold water and bring to the boil.
5. Allow to stand for 5 minutes and then strain.
6. Put raisins and cherries into the pastry case.

7.   Melt butter or margarine and sugar in a pan and bring to the boil.

8.   Remove from the heat and add egg yolks and rum.

9.   Pour over the raisins and cherries.

10. Bake for about 30 minutes.

11. Serve with cream.

Lemon meringue pie

For the filling (using the other pastry case)
2 lemons
35g (¼ oz) cornflour
25g (1 oz) butter or margarine
4oz caster sugar
2 egg whites

1.   Grate lemon zest.

2.   Squeeze juice of the lemons and add water to make up to 12 fluid oz and add to pan.

3.   Mix cornflour in a bowl with a little of the lemon liquid.

4.   Put rest of liquid on to boil. When boiling, pour over paste, stirring continuously.

5.   If it hasn't thickened, put back on a low heat until it thickens.

6.   Add butter or margarine and stir until melted.

7.   Add half sugar and add egg yolks.

8.   Allow to cool for two or three minutes and pour into pie case.

9.   Whisk the egg whites until stiff and fold in the rest of the sugar.

10. Spread the mixture over the lemon base.

11. Bake in a slow oven for about 20 minutes or until golden brown.

References

Bion W (1961). *Experiences in Groups and Other Papers*. London: Tavistock Publications.

Browne I (2008). *Music and Madness*. Cork: Atrium Press.

Cooperrider DL, Whitney D (2005). *Appreciative Inquiry: a positive revolution in change*. San Francisco, CA: Berrett Koehler Publishers Inc.

Shohet R (2007). *Passionate Supervision*. London: Jessica Kingsley.

6

The advanced course

We must trust our feelings and risk the challenges of new experiences.
Let's rededicate ourselves to provide learning communities that kids love
and that are so rewarding for adults. To accomplish that goal, we must
step back and trust our students and ourselves and give us all the freedom
to learn. (Rogers, 1983: 375)

The advanced course is our final three-day course. Much of it centres around the
use of video, and the rest is co-created with the participants. We have between
12 and 16 participants, who will have taken from just over a year to around five
years to do the complete training. By this course, most will be working in some
capacity as supervisors.

The module is run in the form of a learning community. We have started
the chapter with the quote from Rogers as, for us, it clearly states how a learning
community and creating conditions where people feel able to trust themselves
enhance or complement each other. On this course, we invite teaching input
from the students if there is a topic in which they have expertise.

Apart from the making and watching of videos of people supervising, each
Advanced Course is totally different as it is co-created afresh each time. We have
included details of the most recent course at the time of writing, as it produced
some interesting dynamics and issues. We have altered the style of writing slightly
and have not used direct quotes from group members.

First morning

We are running the course at our usual place, but for the first day we have been
allocated a room on the seventh floor of the building, and there is no lift. The room
we usually use for our courses has been changed because of the organisation's
graduation day. We were warned, but we forgot. Worse still, as we are working with
video, we need two breakout rooms and we have not been given them. We think we

may have to re-arrange our whole programme. The person responsible for room allocation is not coming in until lunchtime, so we will have to wait until then to sort out the breakout rooms, and there is nothing we can do about the seventh floor.

It is not yet 10am, it is already hot, and the air conditioning is not working. People arrive already sweating and out of breath. The last person is red-faced and, we guess, furious, which adds to the heat of the room.

We were going to start with the postcards exercise from the Core Course (p43), but instead choose an exercise that involves sharing in pairs what we need to leave behind to be fully present, which we very much need to do.

When we come back together, some of the group share what they are leaving behind. We share our distress about the room we are in and the lack of breakout rooms and reflect with the group. What are we upset about? If we are building a learning community, then this is a good opportunity to see how we can collectively manage this. Is this a cop-out? We own that not telling the group about the room was our oversight, but the group are more interested in learning than apportioning blame. We look at the role of apology in our work. If we apologise too soon, are we robbing the clients of their feelings? Are we saying, 'Don't be too angry with me, it wasn't my fault'? Someone shares a situation where she did not apologise immediately and the client was furious and how beneficial this was to their relationship. We look at how the normal rules of polite society might not apply to therapy. This is not easy, because it could be construed as an avoidance of responsibility, but we are collectively grappling with apology/responsibility/blame in relationships.

Joan writes on the flipchart a quote from James Carse's book, *Finite and Infinite Games* (1986: 23):

> To be prepared against surprise is to be trained. To be prepared for
> surprise is to be educated.

We have a lively discussion about how we are trying to make our lives and work risk-free and the cost of that: how we can be so easily thrown by the unexpected, and whether training gives us a false sense of security? We mention our interest in improvisational drama, where we accept the unexpected and surrender to being out of control. With the group, we look at a culture of unrealistic expectations that can lead to a culture of blame when something goes wrong. It also adds to a culture of entitlement: 'I am entitled to a risk-free life.' We look at how this is relevant to supervision – supervisees can want us to sort things out, to pass responsibility on to us.

There is much learning from all this and we both notice we feel more relaxed now. In fact, someone has suggested that the doors at either end of the room be left open so air can go through, and it is less hot.

I (Robin) decide to share something about myself here. There are no 'rules' about self-disclosure – only to check oneself out really carefully and ask in whose interest it is to share this. The group has been talking about blame and I decide to share an insight I have had. I had been looking for ages for a writing retreat in Malvern and I found almost the perfect place, with magnificent views, right next to the hills. I moved in and sat on the steps inside the flat, which led to the sitting room. Suddenly I was consumed with self-hatred. A voice said, 'You are so selfish, you are taking the family's money, you just do what you want without taking others into consideration, you are wasting money renting when you should have bought, but really neither renting nor buying is right', and so on. This was violent, and I sat there paralysed.

Gradually it dawned on me how this self-attack was stopping my appreciating the flat and I could focus on that. I started to allow myself to feel gratitude for what the flat was offering. I felt much better and started to write. I reflected on what might have contributed to this self-attack, and realised that it came about because I had got more or less exactly what I wanted, so there was no one to blame. Once that source of projection had been cut off, I was left with what was under the surface, behind blame, revealed in all its starkness: how much it can suit us (me) to stay blaming another so we (I) don't look inside at this self-hatred. I thought that perhaps this experience was not just personal but universal. It would explain why blame has such a strong hold on so many of us. It can save us from seeing the self-hatred underneath.

I would not have wished this self-attack on anyone. It would have been far easier, in one way, if Joan had tried to stop me renting the flat, so my energy could have focused on her, on blaming her for not supporting me. I could see the payoff for blame cycles. We avoid the self-hatred and get to feel self-righteous, and I believe that the need to justify oneself, to be seen to be in the right and morally superior, is at the root of most conflicts. But in attacking others, we pave the way for them to attack us, because we project that they might be doing to us what we are doing to them ('Judge not lest ye be judged'). So we feel vulnerable to the outside attack that really started inside us. Allowing myself to experience the self-hatred, staying with it and letting it move to gratitude was a profound experience.

For a second I wonder, was this OK? The group seems to be present with it. Was it my way of saying, 'Don't attack us for being in this room but find your self-hatred'? I hope not. I think I was grappling with my wish to blame someone for the breakout room cock-up and saying to the group, 'I don't want to go there.' It is not the deeper truth (in fact, it was all sorted at lunchtime).

There is a pause. We are adjusting to being with each other and our environment. We decide to move on for the moment and see what comes up later.

We explain about being a learning community that has already started, and about the videoing. Someone asks what it involves, and we give an outline. The person says they want more detail. Other people nod.

We wonder if any amount of explaining and reassuring will work, and so ask them to complete the sentence:

- What worries me most about the videoing is…

The answers come up:

- I will be seen as boring.
- I will be seen as a fraud.
- People will think I am repulsive.
- People will realise I don't know what I am doing.
- People will see something in me that I won't know about.

This is quite deep sharing, perhaps facilitated by my (Robin's) self-disclosure, and it feels that a spirit of trust has come into the room quite quickly.

Once again, we remind them that what belongs to one belongs to all. Who, for example, has not felt a fraud? Normalising is such an important intervention in groupwork; otherwise, those who have shared deeply can feel exposed.

We move on to an Appreciative Inquiry exercise on supervision, working in pairs. Readers may like to fill this in for yourself or, even better, pair with a colleague and do it for 20 minutes each way.

Appreciative Inquiry on supervision

1. Think of a time in the past year when you felt you were supervising or being supervised well, perhaps in a way that left you feeling good about yourself, your skills or the work, or however you would like to frame the positive experience. Picture that scene as if it were happening now, in as much detail as you can, and feel the feelings that are associated with making it good. As you see it in your mind's eye:

- Where are you?
- What are you doing?
- Who else is there? What are they doing?
- How are you relating to yourself, others, the environment?
- What makes it such a good experience for you?

2. What strengths, skills and relevant life experiences do you bring to your work as a supervisor, and, if you are in a team, to the team?

3. What values are important to you in the delivery of supervision? How have these values supported what you do?

A colleague has pointed out that there might not be a correlation between values and behaviour. Many organisations whose behaviour is questionable subscribe to high values. Nevertheless, we keep the question in because it promotes interesting discussions about what is important to people.

4.   How has supervision enriched your life?

5.   If you were to describe supervision to someone who knew nothing about it, how would you describe it in a way that left them wanting to know more, or even have it for themselves?

6.   Imagine it is a year from now and you have changed something about your supervision practice as a result of your dedication to ongoing learning in and around supervision. Take a moment to see yourself in your mind's eye. What have you done? How is your practice different?

After the pairs have completed their conversations, we ask for feedback on what they appreciated about themselves, their partner or the exercise. People report how good it was to be reminded of their strengths, to feel listened to, to recognise how big a part supervision has played in their lives.

We then divide the large group into three groups, which will vary in size between four and six, depending on how many people are on the course. We ask them to share their partner's stories for question one. The rest of the group collects key words, which they write on Post-it notes, and we look for themes. This is a standard format for Appreciative Inquiry and brings positive stories into the room. We ask for a couple of stories to be shared in the larger group.

We suggest that, once the story has been told, it belongs to all of us and the answers to any questions that might come up will be here, in the collective wisdom of the group. We introduce the idea of positive gossip – we are going to talk about each other in a positive way. We mention how useful it is to do this in teams or staffrooms where people have not talked together in depth or have fixed ideas about each other. We have seen these radically change through doing Appreciative Inquiry.

For the second question, we ask one partner to tell us all about a strength, skill or life experience that stood out for them as they listened to their partner.

For the question on values, we ask each person to choose their core value, write it on an A4 sheet and carry it in front of them. They then go to someone who has a similar value, or a different one that has aroused their curiosity, and have a dialogue about their own and each other's values. Sometimes there is a cluster of people around a particular value. It is a way of enabling people to share what is important to them and to be curious about others.

For the fourth question, 'How has supervision enriched your life?', we share the answers in the larger group and write them up on a flipchart.

- I feel really held by my supervisor and always come out feeling better.
- I get clarity with my cases.
- I feel most myself when I supervise.
- I enjoy it.

- I see things differently after supervision – it really is super vision.
- I admire my supervisor. She is a role model for me in the way she listens.
- I learn about myself as well as my clients.

This leads into the fifth question, which is about describing supervision in a way that makes them want to know more. In our work with different teams and organisations, we ask people to make an advert for whatever topic we are exploring. So, if it is a team awayday, they 'sell' their team. Here it is supervision, and we enjoy people exaggeratedly 'selling' supervision and, in the process, discovering a hidden talent of singing, drawing, or dancing even, to sell their 'product'. For example, one group did the popular reality TV show *Love Island*, which threatened to descend into a scene from William Golding's book *Lord of the Flies* until someone had the idea of introducing supervision. Harmony was instantly restored.

We then take a break.

After the break, we ask them to divide into home groups. This time we suggest that they do it geographically, in case they want to continue meeting afterwards. In the home groups, they share their learning needs. The last question from the Appreciative Inquiry, sometimes called 'The Miracle Question', will have helped them to formulate what they might want from this course. We ask them also to think about what they might want to offer the group, which may have been helped by talking about their strengths.

We come together as a whole group and (as in the previous courses) invite people to introduce themselves by their names and share one thing they want to work on/learn about/challenge themselves with, anything they would be willing to offer, and how they might sabotage their learning. As we have already seen, the sabotages often cluster around switching off, comparing oneself unfavourably or generally not feeling good enough and holding back or withholding, and are remarkably similar to those on the other courses – the human condition. We have already touched on this with the responses to the video. It is good that we can share these without shame because we have recognised they belong to us all. We write up the learning needs and what people are prepared to offer on the flip chart.

> *Over the years we have had suggestions for a rich variety of topics, which we list in the appendix at the end of the chapter. It is at this stage of the training that the students give workshops themselves in something in which they have expertise or they want to try out before doing for real.*

The next part of the morning is a tag supervision (see the detailed explanation in Chapter 3, p65). We include this as a refresher for the seven modes, as people will be practising supervision in threes or fours for some part of the course. Briefly, each trainee is allocated a mode. We invite one person to volunteer to be the supervisee, and they take one chair. The rest of the group are supervisors, each of whom has chosen a mode, and they take turns to clap themselves in and out of the other chair and try out their mode.

In the final part of the morning, we explain the logistics of the videoing.

We always have four groups, which here we will call A, B, C and D. After lunch, for the first session, each person in group A makes a video lasting about seven minutes. Joan manages the process. Sometimes people say it is not enough time, but we have seen how much can be done in seven minutes through the tag supervision. The making of the videos lasts about half an hour for three people and 40 minutes for four people, to allow for setting up. Meanwhile, group B practises supervision in a triad or foursome on their own for half an hour, or 40 minutes. They then switch so group B makes the video and group A practises supervision.

Groups C and D stay together for the whole hour (or hour and 10 minutes) and do group supervision with Robin. After the afternoon tea break, group C makes a video, group D practises supervision, and they then switch. Groups A and B stay together and do a group supervision with Robin. So by the end of the day, everyone will have made a video, practised supervision in triads or fours and had a group supervision.

Kagan and interpersonal process recall

Below is a very brief summary of Norman Kagan's work on interpersonal process recall (IPR) (Kagan, 1980), on which we based our video work. His theory and findings build on our work on intent and impact, non-verbal communication, transference and countertransference and using modes 5 and 6. We think that the theory relates to other relationships besides supervision. There is a universal quality about the dynamics that are described.

Kagan discovered that, when people watch a video recording of an interaction, they are able to recall thoughts, feelings and underlying motives in amazing depth. This was even more effective when it was facilitated by an outsider (a role we play). He and his associates found that people perceive and understand much more from their communications with each other than would be suspected from observing their interactions but are often afraid to act on their perceptions. They also tuned out – not seeing or hearing the other person. This usually occurred when the student was especially concerned about making an impression. (We have found that our students are mindful of our watching and try to show they know about the Seven Modes. They laugh when we all realise how performance anxiety comes in, even though they know intellectually we are not assessing them.)

In Kagan's research, the inquirer would ask such questions as:

- 'How did you want that other person to perceive you?'
- 'Were there any other thoughts going through your mind?'

- 'What feelings did you have and are those feelings located physically in some part of your body?'

Kagan found that the inquirers usually learnt, often to their amazement, that they could be both confrontative and supportive; that questions or comments raised by the interviewer, which might be embarrassing or bold in most social settings, were appropriate and productive in a counselling/supervisory session when accompanied by concern or interest. (Perhaps so-called everyday life could benefit from a bit more robustness?) In fact, it was not just the inquirer who became more direct; Kagan found that the counsellor/supervisor was more willing to share the here and now in the sessions (this supports our encouragement of supervisees to make more use of modes 5 and 6). After watching themselves on video and using IPR, Kagan's students were more involved, more concerned, more assertive and more honest with their clients, who in turn were better able to understand their relationships with others in their lives.

Another interesting discovery was that people feared their own and others' aggressive impulses and being (or the other being) too seductive or intimate.

Karen Rowe (1973) developed a theory that she found helped students not just with IPR but with their lives. Here is a summary of her work, which has application far beyond supervision.

1. **People need each other**. People are the best, the most complete potential source of sensory stimulation for other people.

2. **But people learn to fear each other**. Just as people can be the most potent source of satisfaction for each other, they can also be the most potent source of horror for each other.

As one's earliest, most impressionable imprinted experiences are when we are very small beings in a large person's world, many of the 'gut-level' feelings eventually admitted to in the IPR sessions appear very infantile. Fear of people usually clusters around four basic themes: 1) 'The other person will hurt me,' or 2) 'The other person will incorporate or seduce me.' Similarly, we learn to fear our own potential to 3) strike out or to 4) incorporate others. These fears are usually vague and seem irrational to us because we cannot adequately ascribe them to a reasonable source. These basically opposed states – the need for people and the fear of people – manifest themselves in a variety of behaviours. This approach-avoidance behaviour seems to characterise most human interaction.

The movement towards and away from people appears to establish a psychologically 'safe' distance that is unique to each individual. The individual's movement toward and away from others may be summarised as an attempt to find a balance between the pain of boredom and deprivation when contact is too distant and the experience of anxiety when the interpersonal contact is too close. The greater the fear, the further is the distance we establish.

Those who gain most easily from psychological 'growth' experiences are those who already are able to be close with others. ('To those that have, more shall be given.' Matthew 13:12.) Those who are most resistant are those who are most frightened. The fears people have of each other foster a self-fulfilling prophecy in which people make their nightmares happen. It's as if you paint a picture and then put yourself in it.

One of the manifestations of the approach-avoidance dynamic is in the way in which people send and receive messages. People have an almost uncanny ability to hear each other's most subtle messages, although they acknowledge and label only a small part of what they perceive and react to. Kagan sees this 'feigning of clinical naïveté' as an almost universal characteristic.

Another manifestation of the approach-avoidance dynamic is in lifestyle – the basic interpersonal patterns that people characteristically rely on to survive in a world they need but perceive as dangerous. These range around different styles of 'attack' and 'withdraw'. The conclusion Kagan draws is that less effective people tend to rely on a particular interpersonal pattern and posture, which limits their repertoire of behaviour. They experiment in very limited ways and with much fear, whereas one of the characteristics of more effectively functioning people is not only their ability to establish and maintain interpersonal intimacy but also their flexibility in being able to use a variety of response modes, depending on the situations and their goals within the situations.

So, to conclude, Kagan believes IPR is an effective learning programme in several ways. First, most people simply have never had opportunities to develop adequate skills that enable and facilitate interpersonal communication. The IPR programme confronts this problem with exercises in skill definition and skill practice. Second, people are helped to face their fears by coming face to face with their most feared nightmares. If these can be experienced from a place of maximum safety, it is possible for people to overcome them. Third, by coming together with other people, we learn that others may share some of our nightmares, thus reducing feelings of aloneness and shame. (We did this on the first day when we shared fears about being seen on the video.) Fourth, the examination of an actual behavioural sample gives us an opportunity to recognise the daily expressions of our own ways of interpersonal distancing. Also of benefit, the recall process is in itself a practice of new behaviour. Given support in the recall session, it is intriguing to hear how astute the students are. Truly people are the best authority on their own dynamics and the best interpreters of their own experience. To sum up, it would seem that the programme has several direct and supportive ways of addressing fear, which is the biggest block to intimacy and communication. (For a complementary approach to the topic of fear see Chapter 8 of this book.)

Joan's account of using IPR

The advanced course when full is 16 people, which means four groups of four. On our last course there were 13, so we had three groups of three and one of four. Also, we have made the video group and the home group one and the same on this course. Sometimes we separate them so that the members have a chance to work with the maximum number of people, as in the other courses.

Over the years, video cameras have become smaller and we now record onto memory cards, using a small camera on a tripod, and play the videos back through a computer afterwards.

I set up the camera and tripod during the lunch break and arrange the two chairs facing the camera more than usual, so we can see more of the supervisor. The focus is on the supervisor's learning, so the camera is mostly focused on them. As previously described, the four groups are numbered A, B, C and D. A group comes with me, B group goes off to practise supervision in a triad on their own and groups C and D work with Robin.

I take group A into the room with the camera. Each participant will have a turn in each role – supervisor, supervisee, observer and camera person. If there are three in a group, the observer doubles up as the camera person. I give a brief demonstration of how to use the camera –basically, how to record and stop and how to zoom to get close-ups of the supervisor as well as shots of the supervisee and supervisor together. Robin and I were trained in regression work early on in our careers and it was helpful in reading non-verbal language, particularly around the face, as well as from the tone of voice and the actual dialogue. The sessions are seven minutes, with one minute for feedback, which is not recorded.

My role for the afternoon is managing the logistics of the filming and people's fears about exposure, which are massively relieved by actually doing it. Also, as many of us have fears around the technology and being a camera person, some of the fear can get projected onto that instead of the session. It is interesting what we fear and, even though we know it isn't real, how difficult it is to let go of it. I never liked hearing myself on audio recordings, so was pleasantly surprised to find I preferred video to audio. I still have to be pulled away from criticising my appearance but it has faded and most of my anxiety now focuses around the equipment – whether it works or, more to the point, doesn't work. Even though it has pretty well almost always worked, I still have this fear, so it must stem from something around my core beliefs or forgotten trauma.

Overnight, we download the recorded videos and check the sound quality, but we don't watch them, as we want to see them fresh with the participants. The following morning is given over to watching them. I watch with one group and Robin watches with another group. Meantime, those who aren't watching form a peer-led group to either do supervision or focus on one of the topics that has been named the day before. We have a tea break and then the other two groups watch their videos and the first two groups do supervision in the main room. The watching time is approximately 20 minutes per person.

When watching the video, we invite each supervisor to look at the beginning of their session and then pick a moment in the seven minutes. When we have made time for people to watch the whole seven minutes, they tend to zone out, and also the macrocosm is really in the microcosm, so there is no need. Watching the video is like taking the supervision to supervision.

Robin and I have different styles with the watching, so I will leave him to describe his way and I will describe mine here. I use the questions taken from IPR, which I have produced below.

Key questions in IPR

These questions are adapted from Kagan's work and his IPR method, which we described above. They can be used by the inquirer to help a supervisor or therapist review a video of their work. We have both in the room on our courses – supervisor and supervisee – but other courses bring in pre-made videos. Either way, the focus on the here-and-now relationship helps clients and supervisees 'understand their relationships with others in their life'. The inquirer asks the supervisor:

1.   What did you feel at this point (mode 6)?

2.   What were you thinking (mode 6)?

3.   What bodily sensations did you have (mode 6)?

4.   What did/would you do (mode 2)?

5.   What other options might you have had or might there have been (mode 2)?

6.   What problems or risks would there be if you did take one of these other options (mode 4)?

7.   What sort of person does this supervisee see you as (mode 3)?

8.   Does this episode remind you of any past situations (mode 4)?

9.   Do you have any images or associations in relation to this episode (mode 4)?

10. Does the situation provoke any other feelings or thoughts in you (mode 4)?

We have added an 11th question that is specific to supervision, as we have found that what is going on in the supervision session is a mirror of what might be happening between the supervisee and their client. In accessing what is going on for them and feeding it back, the supervisee can gain insight about their client, even though the client is not being directly referred to. So the final question is:

11. How might what is happening be relevant to the supervisee's work with their client (ie. parallel process, mode 5)?

As the supervisor looks at herself or himself on video, they start answering the questions spontaneously: how they were feeling, what they were thinking. I ask them what body sensations they remember. As we move through the questions, they see that the thoughts, feelings and sensations that they have taken solely as their own belong to the client and the supervisee. The client's feelings and life experience are conveyed not so much by the words of the supervisee as they give a history of the client but in the experience of the supervisor as they supervise the supervisee. And this starts happening before what they think is the beginning of the session – the parallel process is already at work.

For example, in one video on this course, we saw the supervisor trying to get comfortable in their chair, which was uncharacteristic of them, but the supervisee said that was just like their client, who could never get comfortable in the session and didn't feel at home in their body generally. The supervisee hadn't noticed this at the time but did when we started watching the video. It as if the client is transmitting through the supervisee to the supervisor and particularly through the body. To use technical terms, the countertransference, parallel process and projective identification are the processes that are in play for the supervisor and supervisee to have a felt sense of the client.

Other interventions arise spontaneously and there is an opportunity for the supervisor to discover what unconscious beliefs led to the interventions they made, or beliefs they held that were both blocking the work and pointing to what was wanting/needing to be attended to. It is like chocolate-mousse supervision, it is so rich. Sometimes people carry on using the tool once they have tried it for themselves. Nowadays, when many people are taking holiday videos on their phones, it is more mainstream to film ourselves. Video can be used in sessions and sometimes clients will ask for it. Participants have asked in the past if they can take their recording home but it hasn't been possible, as several have been recorded onto the same memory card. In future, we will suggest people bring a memory stick so they can download their own session if they want and if the rest of their group agrees. However, the recording is probably most useful when it is fresh and you have a supervision group to watch it with. So it's probably best to go home and make more videos with your supervisees and clients.

Robin's account of using IPR

I would like to acknowledge that I was very resistant to using video. I can only say that I was mistaken about its value. Since reading about Kagan, we have found others who have used video with huge benefit.[1] It is very much in keeping with our philosophy of slowing everything down as much as possible, looking at intent and impact, and commenting on the here-and-now relationship.

Over the years, we have seen many themes come up. The supervisor's fear of how they will be seen gets transferred onto us. Will we judge them? As they watch, they realise how preoccupied they are with trying to remember the modes, and

---

1. See www.videointeractionguidance.net

often laugh at themselves as they see how much this has affected them. No matter how much we say our role is not to assess, our conditioning around assessment is hard to overcome.

As Joan mentioned, together we spot parallel process. The session has barely begun before either the supervisee or the supervisor has taken on aspects of the client, and this can be seen clearly. The benefits of watching with both supervisor and supervisee together are shown when the supervisee exclaims, for example, 'I am talking/sitting just like my client!', or when the supervisor sees themselves behaving atypically and asks if this is how the client behaves. Sometimes people report that they knew they were having atypical thoughts or feelings at the time but did not trust themselves to feed them back. So they might have felt not fully present, switched off, but instead of using that to wonder about the supervisee–client relationship, it leads them to try harder. The supervisee feeds back that they realised that the supervisor was not fully present but did not want to comment. They can now see that they were re-enacting how they were with their client.

Our experience is that using video has led to many transformative experiences. Three examples come to mind. One is where a female supervisor was quite confrontative and critical of her supervisee. At the time we were watching the videos together and felt quite uncomfortable – which is actually a euphemism for critical: we were being critical of the supervisor in the same way as she was with her supervisee. We asked her what she saw as she watched; she focused on how she saw her supervisee as resistant. We paused the replay and asked her to look at the expression on her face, saying, 'That expression on your face almost feels as if it does not belong to you. Like a mask. What do you think?' She paused and then told us a story. Her mother was Irish and conceived out of wedlock. The family pressure meant she had to marry the father and give up her career, as they moved to another town to avoid the shame. As a result, she always resented her daughter. The supervisee realised that she had introjected her mother and was doing to vulnerable others what had been done to her. She saw that the expression on her face was one she saw regularly on her mother's. It was as if she had been carrying a huge weight and was released; her face visibly softened. A few months later, when she came for a tutorial, she reported how much more relaxed she was in her practice.

In the second example, I (Robin) was watching the supervisor. I asked her what she noticed as she watched the video and she said she heard a very bossy tone in her voice. I asked her what else. She said she also remembered wanting the supervisee's approval, and saw how she was checking out his reactions. She commented that she was giving double messages. As the inquirer, I fed back that I was confused by her manner, which seemed to me both dominant and placatory at the same time. I shared my impressions and an unusual question occurred to me. I asked her where she came in her family and, as she told the story, she touched on a grief that had been with her all her life. It turned out that her elder brother had died when he was three and she was a few weeks old, and the family had never really mourned or even talked about this. So she was both the eldest and the second (there were three younger siblings). Besides being in touch with her grief now, this aspect of giving double messages helped her understand better some of the difficulties she was experiencing at work.

The final example centres around using a supervisee's reaction to watching herself. She said she hated watching herself. I (Robin) noticed that she was incredibly self-critical – far more than the so-called normal. I knew from working with her that her parents had died young, and a thought just came to me that perhaps being critical of herself was her way of parenting herself. This had a huge impact on both of us as I realised that, although my parents had not died, I had felt left to parent myself, so could identify with her.

These are examples of watching videos taken from previous courses. Returning to this course, which so far has only made the videos, we are at the end of the first day. The participants meet in their home groups, and then the whole group comes together to share, as we like to finish with the large group. People usually report that making the video was less scary than they thought and they had enjoyed it.

ಌ   ಌ   ಌ

Day 2

On the second morning, we watch the videos with the students from groups A and B for the first session while groups C and D self-manage. Then, after the break, the groups switch. As mentioned above, at the end of each session we come together briefly to share our different experiences in a fishbowl. This is a very useful technique when two groups are joining up or an individual or individuals are joining a group. The group forms a large circle and four or five chairs are set up in the middle. A few members from one group go into the middle (leaving at least one empty chair) and talk about their experiences of being in their group. A member from the other group then goes in and asks questions. The groups switch. The idea is to always have an empty chair, so that people can come and go.

After lunch we start with another fishbowl and find out what the group who have not been watching the videos have been doing and the video groups share their experiences. It seems that making the videos has uncovered core beliefs and we discuss these as a whole group.

In brackets are questions that take us deeper:

- I need to get it right (For whom? What happens if you don't? How do you know what right is?)
- I must appear to know what I am doing. (In case? What could happen if you didn't? Who told you that? What does that phrase mean to you?)
- I can't trust my intuition (Because? Trusting my feelings means?)
- I will look stupid (Who says? What is the purpose of this belief?)

- It will lead to a break-up of the relationship if I say what is going on with me (*this fear often emerges in the Love and Fear workshop described in Chapter 8*).

The last one leads us to think about how people often know anyway what is going on with the other, so why are we trying to hide it? The fear of losing a relationship by being too direct also applies to all relationships, as the work of Kagan and Rowe (above) has indicated. The first half of the afternoon is working in supervision triads. We suggest more practice only using mode 6 and the supervisor simply feeding back what is going on with him or her. It is one of the foundations of our training as it is immediate and leads on to understanding the parallel process. The video has highlighted the value of doing it. After the sessions, supervisors are glad to have more practice in this and report feeling more confident using it. The supervisees report feeling held – that so often what is going on with the supervisor is going on for them, or for them and their client.

After tea, we have one more practice session and then we look at the outstanding topics that we have collected on the first day, and there is a strong wish for a constellation, based on the work of Bert Hellinger, which Joan says she would like to start with the whole group the next day. We finish with home groups for people to integrate what has happened for them during the day.

∾   ∾   ∾

Day 3

I (Joan) start the day by setting up a constellation where someone has volunteered to explore a supervision relationship within a charity for which they work. She is the supervisor in this charity. The process involves choosing members of the group to represent members of the charity. I limit the number of representatives to six and ask the person setting up the constellation (the issue-holder) to begin by choosing someone to represent her, then asking her to choose other members of the group to represent other members of the charity. In this instance, there are people to represent her supervisees who she saw individually, the client group, the manager, the owner and the investors. These representatives are placed by the issue-holder one by one in a position and facing a direction in the room. I ask the issue-holder to sit down where they can see and hear everyone in the constellation and then go round each representative one by one and ask each to report on what is happening for them, particularly focusing first on sensations, then feelings and any thoughts. Time and again, what the representatives report, with absolutely no prior knowledge, corresponds exactly to the person or group they are representing.

I then check out with the representatives whether there could be one change. In this instance, the manager moves alongside the issue-holder. I then ask everyone whether they feel better, worse or the same. Most feel better, more connected, and see the manager as more part of the organisation. Finally, I ask the issue-holder, who has been watching, to step in and replace the person playing her and ask her how that feels. She reports that it has been useful to see how fragmented the charity is, and the separation between her and her manager, and how that might have contributed to her supervisees not being open.

We discuss what to do next. We notice the energy is a bit flat for the constellation and Robin decides to share that he does not feel connected to the group. He asks if there is something that he and Joan have missed or not understood.

> *This is a very useful question. It comments on the here and now. It offers to take responsibility for the disconnection experienced, while also inviting the group to own if there is anything they are not saying.*

There is a pause and one woman feeds back that she had felt misunderstood the previous day in her sharing about her family situation. She was not going to mention it, but she left feeling angry at the end of the day. There are a couple of nods from others, so this is obviously important for others as well. We thank her for sharing it. As we listen, we notice our wish to explain and justify as we check that we have understood. We talk about intent and impact. After a few moments we check to see if the woman feels heard, which she does. Someone else shares that we have underestimated how difficult it is for people to feed back what is going on in the moment. We make it look easy and they feel inadequate when they struggle with it. We wonder if we have been insensitive around other issues as well as this, and someone else shares that we downplay the fear of assessment that is always around. We really appreciate people sharing their difficulties and notice we are feeling more connected.

Certification process

It is a good time to discuss the certification process as there is almost always some confusion around it, possibly triggered by anxiety. We refer to the work of Ben Zander (Stone Zander & Zander, 2000), referred to in the Core Course, and how he gives his students an 'A' when they start (see p29), mindful from our previous discussion how strong the fear of failing can be.

> *In their book,* The Art of Possibility, *the Zanders describe how you can give an A to anyone – the drivers on the road, your mother-in-law, the waitress at the café. For us, his work is not so much about assessment as reinforcing the idea of relationship and co-creation. Below is an example of this where I (Robin) describe how I was able to introduce this into a postgraduate diploma in supervision. The account is taken from an article I co-wrote for* Coaching Today *journal (Shohet et al, 2019).*

I was asked to be an external moderator for the Ashridge/Hult Business School supervision postgraduate diploma. This involved my reading written work by the five students and grading them along with three other tutors before the live practice assessment day. On the day in question, I along with one other staff member from the course were meeting with the five applicants. Each was to make a 20-minute recording of a supervision session in another room which was live streamed to us as the two assessors and the four other students. All seven of us were there for the whole day, watching and giving feedback.

After checking with the other moderator, we agreed that I would introduce the day by telling everyone that they had passed. There was a catharsis of laughter and relief. I noticed that I felt a little uneasy – as if the words had not really gone fully in, so I fed that back and added that there were no tricks but the mind can do funny things like, 'This diploma can't mean anything if everyone passes' or, 'I am better than x, so if they pass that means that I have not been recognised' or worst of all, 'He is just saying that. I don't really believe him.' This was particularly true of one student who had had bad experiences of assessment. It seemed to me that she was not willing to move into a new possibility, so I suggested she might be willing to forgive those previous experiences. This, she later shared, had a big impact and enabled her to let go for the day.

I gave a rationale for this way of working. As part of the day was students giving feedback to each other, there would be a fear of giving robust feedback to each other, in case it contributed to a failure. The way it had been set up was that students gave their feedback on a particular recording, and then the two moderators made the final decision. The new way meant that we could all be part of all of it, as there was no final decision to make. The power balance, an unfortunate concomitant of most assessments, was altered, and we could get on with the task of learning together.

As well as reducing the fear of giving robust feedback and reducing fear generally, the impact of passing everyone from the beginning meant they could enjoy their sessions and therefore were more likely to do good work. They might be free to take risks, rather than play safe. These reasons seemed to us a good justification for this way of working, and is based on the tenets of Appreciative Inquiry, that we are more likely to both find, and create, good practice if we actively look for it and encourage it, which is what this way of assessing aims to do.

I will not go into detail about the day, except to say that one person who had been dreading the assessment shared that it had been the best day of her year.

The purpose of writing this short piece was to begin to challenge conventional ways of assessing which I think are unconsciously designed to keep those assessing in a power position under the guise of maintaining standards. What it teaches students is how to second guess the examiners, to divine their 'currency' and give them what they want to get through; a legacy from our school examination system which there is no need to perpetuate.

There is a bigger discussion to be had here. Our intention is to bring to light how assessment increases fear and thereby reduces opportunities for learning, not to suggest that this should be a universal approach.

We decide to try a different way of explaining the certification process (the certification process itself is described in the next chapter). We do a role play with Robin as the student, asking the sorts of questions we get asked, and the course members answering them. This is amusing, but also will help embody the process.

We talk about the Interdependent Supervisors Network (ISN),[2] and a forthcoming conference to launch it. In the early 1990s, Robin was instrumental in organising two conferences to look at the dynamics of accreditation, out of which grew the Independent Practitioners Network (IPN),[3] with a membership now of more than 200 people. The ISN is based on the same principles as the IPN. The idea behind both is to form peer groups where members are accountable for each other's practice, and in this way use accountability to build community. A complaint against one person in a group would be a complaint against the whole group, so there is a great investment in being clear and open with each other. To increase learning and to lessen the opportunity for collusion, groups would from time to time send a delegate to another group to challenge and support.

> *You will have gathered how important to us it is to encourage as much self-direction and community as possible. Over the years, we have watched as various professions have become increasingly regulated and, while there might have been good intentions, we have felt the process has been run by a zeitgeist that asks us to be out of relationship. We see the ISN as offering a possible alternative.*

Ethics

Ethics comes up as a topic, and we look at how we can best support ourselves when a question of ethics is involved. The list below is taken from a talk given by Robin in 2016 – they were a precursor to some of the principles outlined in Chapter 2.

1. *Know thyself.* We are all capable of anything, so jumping to an ethical conclusion based on judgement and moral self-righteousness is unlikely to be a useful or honest position. But if we do not know ourselves, and even if we do, we are capable of the most intricate of rationalisations and justifications, so that in itself is useful to know. Macbeth, debating whether to kill Duncan, says: 'To know the deed would best know not myself.' We refer to an excellent book called *Wilful Blindness* (Heffernan, 2011), which shows our propensity for fooling ourselves – a prerequisite for unethical behaviour.

2. Connected to this is *create a space for reflection.* This is what this book is about – namely, having conversations with others who can both support and challenge.

---

2. www.independentsupervisorsnetwork.com

3. www.ipnetwork.org.uk

3. *Help to create a moral community.* We can't be ethical alone easily, because the zeitgeist is so transactional. The whistleblower is isolated and very often scapegoated. Get together with people who can tolerate uncertainty and ambiguity. Simplistic thinking is rarely ethical as it avoids complexity.

4. Related to complexity, *see the bigger picture,* which others may need to help you with. What might be ethical in one part of the system might be seen as unethical in another.

5. And because of this, and all of the above, *courage* will be needed. In *Wilful Blindness*, Heffernan shows how the strength of the need to belong can blind us, so it is important to have the courage to stand alone if need be. And, of course, there are the experiments of Milgram (1974), which show how obedience can make us behave unethically. The courage to say no supports ethical behaviour.

6. It is important to *tolerate being seen as a betrayer* by some people in the system, and to be willing to act in spite of that. Otherwise difficult decisions could be avoided or communicated badly or there might be a need to be seen as the 'nice guy', all of which could lead to unethical decisions (Fuchs & Shohet, 2012).

7. *Ask what I am afraid of.* Fear promotes survival patterns, which can very easily lead to unethical behaviour. Our workshop on Love and Fear in Supervision (see Chapter 8) begins to highlight this.

8. *Ask what the system is afraid of.* It could be loss of reputation, financial insolvency, a hostile takeover. Systems have their own dynamic and are as much into their own survival as individuals (Schaef & Fassell, 1988).

9. *Ask what love would do.* Do we believe in the goodness of human nature or that we are basically sinners? This will affect whether our approach to ethics is love-based or more likely to be fear-based and therefore punitive. Our belief is that love connects to keeping the heart open, whatever the circumstances, and this is about a willingness to be vulnerable. And we want to stay in touch with the love that brought us into the work and not let the fears that surround us in the zeitgeist dominate. I believe you cannot reduce the love in a therapeutic encounter to something that can be measured. In the early 1990s, a group of us were very interested in alternative methods of accreditation as we saw dangers in procedures not being face-to-face and in relationship. At one conference, we asked a group of people to talk about the love in their work. It was moving and supported a philosophy of looking for love and building on that to improve standards rather than looking for faults. We propose (perhaps provocatively) that anything that comes from love is ethical and anything that comes from fear will be ultimately unethical, as it

is about survival and not the bigger picture. We know this is a belief and not provable, but it leads to interesting discussions.

10. Finally, *be willing to go beyond simple right and wrong dichotomies.* These lead to blame and the persecutor, victim, rescuer triangle (Karpman, 1968). We quote Rumi again: about meeting in the field beyond right and wrong.

We suggest that, if we feel compromised when someone tells us something, the first thing to do is to ask, 'Why are you telling me this? What do you want to see happen?'

In addition, it is also useful to see if any ghosts and stakeholders in the room (see p89) have not been acknowledged or might be influencing the situation. A technique that we particularly use in groups is to ask different members to play different parts of the system, as described in the chapter on group supervision (p128). Doing this can give a bigger picture and is more likely to lead to a compassionate approach as we then might see that everyone is doing their best. Even if people are acting from selfish motives or watching their back, this approach helps us resist the temptation to oversimplify the issues.

Some of the topics gathered on the first day will not have been covered. We acknowledge this and ask the people who suggested them what prompted them to ask for them and point them to resources that we know of or ask if anyone in the group can help them.

One way of dealing with any outstanding topics that have been collected from the brainstorming on the first day is for everyone to have two votes on what they would like to work on from the list. We do this on the final day and then decide if we want to explore the top topics together as a large group, or to invite someone with a special interest in the topic to stand up and invite others to join them. Sometimes people offer topics in which they have a level of expertise and at other times they are wanting to know more. They make that clear when they stand up and ask people to join them to talk about their topic. Usually, about four people stand up, and others join them. In that way we can cover several topics at a time, and we ourselves are not in the foreground as the participants are facilitating these small groups. After the sessions, each group shares in the larger group a few sentences about what they did.

Ending

We are nearing the end. Endings are an important topic that we could easily bypass, and we have in the past not given them as much attention as they merit. We mention that it is good to have brought endings into the initial contract – how much notice there needs to be from both sides to give space for the ending process. It does not feel good when a client or supervisee announces, out of the blue, 'Today will be my last session.' We look at issues around who initiates the leaving – is it mutual, has the contract come to an end or has one party decided to end it? And what is involved in each of these scenarios? We suggest people take paper and pen and write the word 'ending' around in a circle, like the hub of a wheel, with spokes coming out, and free associate the word, and then share what they want with a partner. Together, we discuss how much baggage we carry around ending – grief, not saying goodbye, regret, guilt, anger, betrayal. This could be a workshop in itself.

An often-used defence against ending is denial. We point out that this could be happening here, as most of them will see us for the follow-up tutorials that are part of the whole course (see next chapter), and some are already in peer groups with each other. We believe that what increases stress in everyday life is not having the time or opportunity to say goodbye properly. Many, if not most of us, are carrying a lot of unresolved grieving, which we take into our next relationships and, as a consequence, don't let them touch us as deeply. This can lead to relationships becoming increasingly transactional as we defend against potential loss of deep connection. To help counteract this, in the group we create a space for people to go around sharing with each other how they might have been important to each other. Our belief is that the more we know about our patterns around ending, the more we can be helpful to our supervisees and their clients. And as trainers, and for us personally, we know how much more work we still have to do.

As we draw to a close, we ask people to go into their home groups and check what they might need for their return to the outside world, and the importance of a good support system. In the Core Course, they will have mapped their support systems. We remind people they can keep in contact with us and each other in our monthly Friday afternoon drop-in groups. (We started running these in 2015, originally for graduates to keep in touch, then for all trainees, and now for anyone interested. They run for two hours. The first hour is on a theme and the second hour is group supervision.) Very often, by this time, peer groups will have been formed from previous courses, and we ask anyone who would like to form one to stay behind to do so.

As we end together, we appreciate the journey we have taken by suggesting we each say an appreciation of self, other or the group, and (if one comes to mind) a metaphor for our journey together. To amalgamate a few from our courses: 'a bumpy ride but wouldn't have missed it, especially with the others on the bus. Stunning scenery. And the tour guides were OK too.'

The Advanced Course is the last of our course teaching. As mentioned above, trainees are asked to attend two tutorials after this to help with integrating their learning into their practice. Most of all we are wanting the students to have confidence in themselves – not a false confidence that hides an insecurity, but one that both recognises their strengths and enables them to be vulnerable. We hope we have been able to model that.

Appendix

Topics suggested by participants on the Advanced Course:

(For us this list shows however much ground we cover, there is always more for us all to experience and learn.)

- A non-dualist approach to supervision
- Working with trauma: the inner world of trauma
- Supervision for those working with children
- Pre- and perinatal influences in supervision
- Supervision using creative modalities (art, drama, music, dance)
- What constitutes an emergency, and working with other agencies
- Ethical dilemmas
- The work of Byron Katie
- Family constellation work and how it can be applied to supervision
- Bert Hellinger's principles of belonging, balance and order and conscience
- Dual roles
- Supervision in organisations – three-way contracts
- Not-knowing and the need for answers
- Erotic transference
- Practice sessions of some description
- How fear comes into the supervision work
- Managing complaints
- Assessment and accreditation
- Working with difference
- Co-leadership
- Power dynamics in supervision
- Endings
- Online supervision
- Appreciative Inquiry

Foodnote

Victoria sponge cake

This was the first cake my mother taught me to bake. I was about seven, in the dream world still, beginner's mind – a space to be in for the Advanced Course.

The proportions are very easy to remember: half the number of eggs to the dry ingredients of butter, caster sugar and self-raising flour plus 1tsp of baking powder.

> 4 eggs
> 8oz butter
> 8oz caster sugar
> 8oz self-raising flour
> 1tsp of baking powder

1. Cream the butter and sugar.
2. Stir in the eggs, flour and baking powder.
3. Ladle the mixture into two (or three) greased and floured sandwich tins (depending on their size).
4. Bake in the oven at 180°C/375°F/Gas mark 5 for approximately 20 minutes until golden brown and firm to the touch.
5. Allow to cool and fill with whatever you like – jam, cream, fruit.

Cupcakes

Cupcakes offer a chance to play with the ingredients inside the cakes and the decorations on top; an opportunity, now we have the basics, to improvise or ask the question, 'If we were all cupcakes, what kind of cupcake would I/you be?'

I use the same ingredients as for the Victoria sponge, and put the mixture into cupcake cases. You can play around with colouring and flavouring of the sponge mix and the toppings. You can also make gluten-free cupcakes using gluten-free flour.

Ginger cake with caramel frosting

This was a new recipe that I introduced in 2019. I always do a new recipe for the Advanced Course, to advance myself! Go to the edge and stretch beyond.

> *For the cake*
> 200g (7oz) butter
> 200g (7oz) muscovado sugar

100g (4oz) black treacle
100g (4oz) golden syrup
2 large eggs, beaten
300ml milk
350g (12oz) plain flour
2tsp ground ginger
2tsp bicarbonate of soda
A few chunks of crystallised ginger, chopped

For the frosting
85g butter
175ml double or whipping cream
175g caster sugar

1. Heat oven to 160°C/325°F /Gas mark 3.

2. Butter and line a 23cm, round cake tin.

3. Put the butter, sugar, treacle and syrup in a large pan and gently heat, stirring until the butter has melted and the mixture is smooth.

4. Remove from the heat and cool for 10 minutes.

5. Stir in the eggs and milk and sift in the flour, ginger and bicarbonate of soda.

6. Mix well and pour into the prepared tin.

7. Bake for 50–60 minutes until the cake is firm to the touch and springs back when pressed in the centre.

8. Leave to cool in the tin for 15 minutes, then turn out, peel off the paper and allow to fully cool on a wire rack.

9. Put the frosting ingredients in a small pan over a medium heat and stir until the butter has melted and the mixture is smooth.

10. Increase the heat and boil hard for 3-4 minutes, stirring occasionally. At this stage, the frosting should look like runny custard.

11. Pour into a bowl and leave to cool for 30 minutes. Beat with an electric whisk until thick and spreadable. Spread over the cooled cake and decorate with crystallised ginger.

References

Carse JP (1986). *Finite and Infinite Games: a vision of life as play and possibility*. New York, NY: Free Press.

Fuchs B, Shohet R (2012). Betrayal: an inevitable part of leadership? *International Journal of Leadership in Public Services* 8(4): 232–236.

Heffernan M (2011). *Wilful Blindness: why we ignore the obvious at our peril*. New York, NY: Bloomsbury.

Hellinger B (1998). *Love's Hidden Symmetry: what makes love work in relationships.* Phoenix, AZ: Zeig, Tucker & Theisen Inc.

Kagan N (1980). Influencing human interaction – eighteen years with IPR. In: Hess AK (ed). *Psychotherapy Supervision: theory, research, and practice.* New York, NY: John Wiley & Sons (pp262–283).

Karpman S (1968). Fairy tales and script drama analysis. *Transactional Analysis Bulletin 26*(7): 39–43.

Milgram S (1974). *Obedience to Authority: an experimental view.* New York, NY: Harper Collins.

Rogers C (1983). *Freedom to Learn for the 80's.* New York, NY: Merrill.

Rowe KK (1973). A 50-hour intensified IPR training program for counselors. *Dissertation Abstracts International 33*(9-B): 4525–4526.

Schaef AW, Fassell D (1988). *The Addictive Organisation: why we overwork, cover up, pick up the pieces, please the boss, and perpetuate sick organizations.* New York, NY: Harper & Row.

Shohet R, Birch D, de Haan E et al (2019). Love over fear: an experience of assessment. *Coaching Today 31*(July): 14–18.

Stone Zander R, Zander B (2000). *The Art of Possibility: transforming professional and personal life.* Boston, MA: Harvard Business School Press.

7

The 'fifth' module: the inquiry process, focusing on the supervisory relationship

'The meaning of life is not what happens to people.'

'It's not?'

'No, it's not. The meaning of life is what happens between people.'
(Beck, 2000: 186)

We offer all our students two individual tutorials with one of us after they have completed the four modules and delivered 50 hours or more of supervising and received 10 hours of supervision on their supervision from a senior practitioner.

In the first part of the first tutorial, we reflect on their training and how their practice has been since they completed the modules. In the second part, we go through our inquiry form (below, with our commentary) to make sure it is clear to them. We have devised and modified the inquiry form over many years. It is about the supervisory relationship and we ask the students to complete it individually with their supervisor, two supervisees and a peer – in other words, in four separate conversations. The purpose of this is to promote a robust conversation between the people in question. It is very much in keeping with our philosophy of making the supervisory relationship the foundation on which everything else is built (see Chapter 1) We also look at the practicalities of how they will do this.

In the second tutorial, they report back on these conversations with the four different people. Invariably the conversations have deepened the relationships, which has been our aim. In Chapter 8, on love and fear, we look at other ways of deepening the supervisory relationship – or, for that matter, any relationship.

In line with our basic belief that so much of what happens in supervision is applicable to life, the form can, and has been, adapted for other relationships.

It is really interesting to us that we never set out to have a certificate process. It came about in response to requests from the students and from the field, as employers would sometimes ask for proof of training. The inquiry form is a result of wanting to support learning after the formal teaching has finished. It is not a tick-box exercise, but an opportunity to explore the supervisory relationship.

We have kept to our philosophy of self-direction as much as possible, so students are in charge of when they do the tutorials. We do not ask for written work in the 12 days we spend with them over the course of the four modules, but we do ask for a high degree of introspection and self-disclosure. This form is part of that.

Self/peer/supervisor/supervisee inquiry form[1]

The students are asked to complete this with a peer, their supervisor and two supervisees. People do it in a variety of ways – some do it with their supervisor in the session; some prepare beforehand. We stress that going through the inquiry form is part of the supervision and extra time should not be allocated for this. The doing of it will benefit both parties.

We believe at the heart of supervision is the relationship. The aim of this inquiry is to invite you both to engage in exploring the relationship, how it is co-created and how it serves all the stakeholders and your work. What we are most interested in is the quality of conversation that you have together and we offer the questions below as a way in. Our reflections on the questions are in italics.

Relationship

How would you describe your relationship, both literally and metaphorically? You could use an image or use the questions from mode 3 (see p98) such as 'If you were two animals...?' or 'If your relationship were part of a myth or fairy story...?'

On the course on the Seven-Eyed Model where we discussed mode 3, we asked you to come up with an image, and we suggest doing that here. Perhaps two animals. It is helpful to write down the images first and then share. If you write them down and then find it difficult to share them with each other, share instead why you might find it difficult, and decide whether to share them or not. In fact, all the questions relate to your relationship in different ways.

---

1. Copies of the inquiry form can be found at www.cstdlondon.co.uk

Strengths

What do you think are your strengths? How do you bring them into the relationship? What do you see as the other's strengths? Give some concrete examples.

> *Over the years, and influenced by Appreciative Inquiry, we really encourage a strength-based approach. It is surprising how much these strengths are not given a place as there is such a temptation to focus on what is not working. This is a chance for both parties to remind yourselves of your strengths, which include, but go beyond, supervision.*

Values

What values are important to each of you and how do they show up in your work?

> *We make the assumption that people who are supervising have the best interests of their supervisees and their clients at heart. However, supervisor and supervisee might come up with very different values and a discussion on why these are important to each of you can be very useful. We would suggest that values are very strongly connected to core beliefs, which we invite you to look at later.*
>
> *If we take honesty, it is a value we imagine we all ascribe to. Yet we can all point out examples where we might not have been honest. So, we would like you to be interested not just in your values but in where you might not live them, or where you might not see the other live them. Are your values a source of strength or do they separate you from someone who might not share them?*

Scope/focus/purpose

What is the main scope/focus/purpose in your supervision? How was/is that negotiated?

> *Do you share the same purpose? Was it negotiated and if so how? In the Core Course, we looked at the different archetypes, like teacher, mother, priest, guru. For example, a supervisee may come to supervision looking for answers, and the supervisor may believe that the purpose of supervision is to help people find their own answers. What expectations might not be being met? Can you talk about this?*
>
> *This is also an opportunity to look at the normative, formative and restorative functions of supervision (Proctor, 2010) and see if they match for both parties.*

Core beliefs

We all have core beliefs. Examples might be, 'I should always know the answer' or, 'I must be helpful.' Share some of your core beliefs with each other.

> These can be hard to spot as they seem to us to be self-evident truths. One way of finding out about them is to see where we have a difficulty with anything or anyone. On the Core Course, we described an exercise (see p61): 'What I wouldn't want to say to my supervisor because…' Here we often see core beliefs. For example, someone might finish the sentence with '… they would think I was not good enough'. 'I am not good enough' is a much more common core belief than is acknowledged. If we access these through areas of difficulty, it could mean that any difficulty is to be welcomed, as difficulties can tell us about our core beliefs and blind spots.
>
> For example, we have a core belief that inquiry is a worthwhile activity. There are people who will see it as a waste of time, impractical and so on. And, of course, there is a core belief that supervision works, which is why we like the story of the axe at the beginning of the book (p3). It is the 'proof' that comes from story. (You will find many of our beliefs listed in Chapter 2.)
>
> You might like to share at least five each.

Boundaries

How do you manage the boundaries and the contracting in your relationship? Is there any part of the process you might find difficult or avoid (eg. your cancellation policy)?

Has it changed over time and in what ways? We believe much learning happens on the boundaries and through ruptures – what has been your experience?

> In the section on boundaries we are asking you to revisit your contract together. Are there any parts that are unclear? Can you think of any examples where the boundaries have been unclear or broken and, if so, what do you think contributed to that?

Safety and challenge

We believe that good supervision embodies safety and challenge and that each supports the other. How do you think that safety is created in your relationship? Can you think of an example of a challenge that might have deepened the relationship?

> We are interested in how robust you can be together. We believe a relationship that does not challenge is not a safe one – we think that, by having a way of challenging each other, you are respecting the other's

strengths, whereas backing off in order not to hurt the other is, in some ways, undermining them (assuming they can't take a challenge), or, if you don't feel strong enough, undermining yourself.

Power and deference

How is this operating in your relationship? What leads you to move towards each other and what leads you to defer or retreat? How easy is it to talk about what is going on between you and use this as a resource for the work with clients (parallel process)? As we have mentioned above, a way into this is for each person to write down 'What I can't say in this relationship is…' and 'I can't say it because…' and choose how much of that to share.

> *We think that supervisors can underestimate their power in the belief that they are in a collegiate relationship, which is true but denies the possibility of the supervisee feeling vulnerable as they explore their difficulties. It is well known that people with higher status always underestimate their own status. Is this happening in your relationship? Has the power relationship changed over time? Where was it at the beginning and where is it now? Can it change within a session? What can make it shift? Can you both talk about this?*

Difference

How is difference handled in your relationship and how much is it available for comment?

> *Are topics such as gender, race and class brought into the room? If so, how? And if not, why not? In our training, we emphasise our similarities – how underneath we have the same fears that basically boil down to a fear of death and loss, and that love is our true nature (a core belief) and, as such, we might not have given this topic enough weight.*

The wider system

What stakeholders and ghosts from the system are brought into the room and who by? Can you name a few that relate to you individually, and some that relate to you together?

> *The wider system, as we have seen in mode 7, is always in the room. Are there dual roles in supervision involving assessment and managerial functions and how might they impact on the supervision? A useful question from constellation work is, 'Who in the system has not been given attention and is coming in as a symptom?'*

Use of self

How confident do you both feel in using what is going on with you in the here and now as data? Is the concept of parallel process used in your work together?

This is one of our core ways of working. Is there anything that you might not be able to use? For example, if you noticed yourself switching off, could you feed that back and see how/if it might relate to your relationship or your work with clients?

Vision

It is a year hence. Imagine you have both made changes to deepen and develop your relationship. What have you each done? Can you each give a specific example?

This question is the so-called miracle question from Appreciative Inquiry. We are asking you to imagine that your relationship has expanded and what has enabled that to happen. And then, using that picture of the expanded relationship, we are asking you both to see what steps you might need to take to move towards it.

Transferring the learning

Consider how this conversation you have just had might contribute to your work and your work with your clients. Name three ways.

Our belief is that, once you have had one robust conversation, it will transfer.

Final reflection

How has doing this together been for you? What have you learnt? Is there anything you skipped over/avoided, and if so, why? Can you give each other a final appreciation?

This is an opportunity to reflect together on the process. Our experience is that using this form has benefitted both parties.

Reference

Beck M (2000). *Expecting Adam*. London: Piatkus.

Proctor B (2010). Training for the supervision alliance: attitude, skills and intention. In: Cutcliffe JR, Hyrkäs K, Fowler J (eds). *Routledge Handbook of Clinical Supervision*. London: Routledge (pp23–34).

8

Love and fear in supervision: a one-day workshop

Fear knocked at the door. Love answered and there was no-one there.
(Sufi maxim)

In this one-day workshop, I am inviting participants to look at how fear and love might enter the supervisory relationship. The core belief I have is that fear covers love – a love that is not conditional or ephemeral, but the naturally compassionate essence of who we are. I use the analogy of the sun always being there but sometimes it is covered by clouds of fear. In offering a space where fear can be brought into consciousness and shared together, we can help dissolve it and enter into a loving presence that can bring healing for supervisor, supervisee and client.

As mentioned in the introduction to the book, this workshop was inspired by a combination of my own (Robin's) very early experiences of going past fear to a place of peace, a book called *A Course in Miracles* (Foundation for Inner Peace, 1996), and the inquiry work of Byron Katie.[1] Examining some of the belief systems that keep fear locked in place is very releasing. If we make this fear more conscious and do some work to see some of the beliefs behind it, we make more space for love to emerge. My experience is that fear can take many different forms that are not obviously seen as fear, such as anger, shame, preoccupation with safety, rigid adherence to beliefs, judgement, and rules and procedures. Many of these emerge during the workshop.

In this workshop, I am asking people to question some of their core beliefs that might contribute to keeping them in a state of unnecessary separation. I do this through the medium of the supervisory relationship. I use a technique described in Chapter 3 (p61) of asking people to finish the sentence: 'What I would least like my supervisor to know about my work is…' and then, 'I would not want them to know because…' This can be done for any relationship – you could substitute boss or colleague for supervisor. It can even be extended to

---

1. www.thework.com (accessed 13 September 2019).

'What I would least like x [friend, partner] to know about me [as opposed to my work], and 'I do not want them to know because...' I do not ask the group for answers to the first question but I ask participants to share their answers to the second. This helps them to access some of the fears like 'I will be judged', 'I will be seen as inadequate', and so on. Naming fears such as these, and normalising them, forms the basis for this workshop.

> *To explain my thinking a bit more, I don't want to hear people's responses to the first sentence because they might be reluctant to share specifics about their work, like 'I overrun my sessions' or 'I don't take notes'. However, the second sentence is about process – the **reasons** I don't want to talk about the content. The reasons reveal a lot about the supervisory relationship and the process that is happening to stop open sharing. Whereas the content is more particular to the supervisee, the reasons for not sharing tend to be more universal and, ultimately, I believe, can be traced to fear.*
>
> *Here is an example where the supervisee (P1) shared that he would not want to share what he had written with his supervisor because he thought the supervisor might think less of him.*

Robin: Can you really know that's true, they would think less of you?

> *The question 'Is it true?' is taken from* The Work[1] *of Byron Katie and I have found it really useful in helping to uncover beliefs that do not serve.*

P1: No, I can't.

Robin: And I am guessing that honesty is very important to you. (*P1 nods*). So, by withholding, you are not living one of your values. So somewhere you will be thinking less of yourself.

P1: And holding them responsible.

Robin: Exactly. We all do it. Perhaps also you feel you cannot stand behind what you did?

P1: Oh, I can. But I fear they might not see it my way.

Robin: And then?

P1: Well, I want their approval.

Robin: And perhaps withholding what you have written for the first question means that you can't quite trust you will get it. In a way, in one relationship where we are withholding, we might have an aspect of many of our relationships where we want approval. There is another aspect to this. Perhaps you think less of them?

---

1. www.thework.com (accessed 13 September 2019).

P1: What do you mean?

Robin: Well, you don't think highly enough of them to trust them with what you have written.

P1: That's very clever, but I guess there is some truth in it. And why would they think highly of me if I weren't honest with them? I wouldn't trust it meant anything, because they would only be valuing a kind of mask.

Robin (turns to group): Go there with him. We have all withheld because we think we need approval. But there is a cost to our integrity. And, to repeat, I am not saying share; I am saying, look at the reasons for withholding and then decide. *(To P1)* Is it OK to leave it there?

P1: Yes. You know, I think I could share what I have written for number one with my supervisor. It will feel scary, but I see an opportunity to break a pattern.

It often happens that, with a little inquiry, people realise that their reasons for withholding that are fear based are not valid. And through the inquiry, they are willing to share more openly with their supervisors.

   I mentioned that the responses to sentence 2, like fearing judgement, tend to be universal. When someone shares one of their answers, I ask the group to go there with them. For example, I ask: 'Is there anyone who has not feared judgement?' The fear of judgement belongs to most, if not all of us.

   I share how I came to the very powerful method of normalising so-called negative responses. I have mentioned the actual method a few times already in this book but not how I came to it.

I was at a training with Byron Katie. She asked participants to fill in a worksheet with what or who upsets them, makes them angry. At this training, I was in a terrible state. I could not manage myself, so in time-honoured fashion I projected and blamed. So I wrote: 'I want Katie to drop down dead'. Very hesitantly, in a room of 93 people, I shared this, expecting to be banished by the guru. Instead she thanked me and turned to the group and said, 'Is there anyone here who has not wished someone dead?' Not a hand went up. And she turned back to me and said, 'See, you are not alone.' I learnt there the power of normalising. She didn't judge me, shame me, but recognised that, at some time, we all have murderous thoughts. From that moment on, I felt totally safe. So, I have seen that the answers to question two have probably been felt by dozens of people at different times.

   The next exercise I do is to ask people to write down what they would least like supervisees to say to them – things like: 'You are useless, you haven't helped me, I did what you said and it didn't work'. I then help them access what might be the fear behind hearing these statements, which often amounts to not feeling good enough. And again, I aim to normalise their responses, showing they belong to most, if not all of us. Behind the fear of hearing statements such as 'You are useless' can be a core belief that 'I must be useful', or 'I must have the answers'. There is also often a fear of getting it wrong, or making a mistake or being found out. The issue of complaints can come up here – the supervisee or client threatening a complaint. This seems to be a common fear and prompted me to write an article for the journal *Self & Society* (Shohet, 2017), which I have included in the Resources section (p216).

> The idea behind this exercise is that whatever we would least like to hear can lead us to subtly steer the supervisee in a particular direction. For example, if a supervisor does not want to be told they are useless, they could spend extra time unnecessarily proving how useful they are. I believe it is good to make some of these strategies more conscious. This provides an opportunity to change them if they do not serve.

To explore core beliefs further, I do a sentence completion exercise where people write down the first answer that comes into their heads and share if they want to:

- Men are…
- Women are…
- People should never…
- People should always…
- I must never…
- I must always…
- I can help people by…
- I can damage people by…

It is very curious that most, if not all of us have a core belief that, for example, we should never lie, and yet we all do. We enquire into the origin and purpose of the beliefs that have been uncovered. Often they have been formed as the best way of dealing with a situation when we were young, and they may no longer serve. Bringing them into consciousness can help them be released.

The last sentence is particularly interesting. People report completions like '… by shaming them'; '… by being very critical'; '… by abusing my power'; '… by not listening to them.' I suggest that perhaps they feel they can damage people in the way they have shared because that is how *they* felt damaged. Many people resonate with this idea and see how their fears of damaging another are based on their beliefs about their own damage. By bringing these beliefs, often unconscious, to consciousness, we have the opportunity to change them if they no longer serve. Of course, it is not good to shame or abuse power, but people appreciate how this sentence completion can give them an insight into what might be proving difficult in other relationships, not just supervisory ones.

Finally, we put some of what we have explored into a supervision exercise. People go into groups of three or four and take the roles of supervisor, supervisee and observer/observers. The supervisor supervises for five minutes and the observer(s) observe. I then ask supervisor and supervisee to write down:

- What I have not been able to say is…
- I have not been able to say this because…

The observer(s) have a slightly different sentence:

- What I imagine they have not been able to talk about is…
- I imagine they have not been able to talk about it because…

Supervisor and supervisee choose whether to share what they have written. Observers do not share at this stage.

I then instruct them to continue supervising for another five minutes. After five minutes, I call time and the observers share their responses with the supervisor and supervisee. Last, the group as a whole reflects on their experiences. The feedback is that there is so much more energy in the second five minutes than the first. Once we allow ourselves to know how we are holding back, just knowing this, whether we share it or not, makes us more present.

> *Besides demonstrating how fear might cover love or connection, I am also wanting to show how our minds can trick us into avoiding difficult situations with all sorts of beliefs. This can, on one level, avoid fear but on another perpetuate it. We humans seem to have an infinite capacity for self-deception and I am no exception. However, this workshop can help us develop a witnessing presence to ourselves and, in doing so, deepen connection not only with ourselves but with each other. We share our vulnerability and fallibility.*
>
> *In many ways this approach complements Appreciative Inquiry. In Appreciative Inquiry, we are looking at building on the best. In this approach, we are uncovering some of the fears that stop us connecting and being at our best. Both approaches have a deep belief in the essential goodness of human nature.*

References

Foundation for Inner Peace (1996). *A Course in Miracles*. New York, NY: Viking Penguin.

Shohet R (2017). Exploring the dynamics of complaints. *Self and Society* 45(1): 67–91.

The Beast from the East:
an account of a challenging
supervision training

'To be prepared against surprise is to be *trained*. To be prepared for surprise is to be *educated*.' (Carse, 1986: 23 – emphasis added)

I was asked to run a supervision training at a counselling centre in the west of England. The training consisted of four three-day modules, three of which I ran on my own and the fourth with Joan. The course was completed, and I was asked to run a second one on the same lines. At the time, we also had three tutorials, and now have just two. This will be very significant.

In the following pages are five accounts by participants in that second training, followed by some of my own reflections. I will end the chapter with the sixth account, a poem. My reflections are in italics.

As you will see from Kirsti's piece in particular, right from the word go, the group was testing me around boundaries. I do believe you can get a sense of a group very early and Peter Brooke (1993: 36) describes how actors need to be able to read audiences very quickly. Although I believe it is possible to read a group (or a person or an audience) very early, sometimes I fear I am making it up. Anyway, I 'knew' that this group was going to be challenging. I overcompensated by going into overdrive, introducing a lot of ideas and exercises and not taking time to talk about the tutorials. I hope these comments will give readers the confidence to trust their ability to read a group and not go into unconsciously compensating, as I did. I think that more and more is being asked of people at work, with fewer resources to support them, and I think the supervisor needs not to mirror that by overworking.

I also hope you can use some of the material mentioned earlier in this book on topics like parallel process. For example, I could have said to this group near the beginning, 'I notice I am working really hard here. Almost feeling as if I have to earn your approval. I wonder if this might resonate for

*you and your work?' However, I think they might well have dismissed that. It
is no use trying to avoid stickiness by resorting to naming parallel process.
Sometimes the only way past the fire is through it.*

The four modules for this second course were scheduled to take place in
December, March, June and September. The March one had to be cancelled
because of very bad weather, which the tabloid media dubbed the 'Beast from
the East'. I was very reluctant to cancel it; I sensed that strong feelings might be
aroused, even though it was a sensible decision as not everyone would have been
able to get there.

*Any change in a boundary at some level can easily contribute to a lack of
safety. I sensed that, with this group especially, this would not go down well.*

The decision to cancel was taken jointly by the counselling centre and me, and
I then wrote to all the participants offering a Skype session, to check in with
them. I also intended to explain to them the individual tutorials that had been
scheduled for April, which I would have informed them about at the cancelled
March course. No one replied to my email, so the course participants turned up
for their first tutorial without really understanding what it was for. They were
also unaware that some tutorials were going to be with me, some with Joan and
some with my stepson, Joe, also a tutor from our Centre for Supervision and
Team Development (CSTD).

*When no one replied, I should have sent out another email with the details.
I was baffled that no one had responded to my offer of a free Skype session,
and hurt, as I thought I had been reaching out. I was acting out a narcissistic
wound in not sending out another email. The group and I were acting as
mirrors for each other to the less-known parts of ourselves. I was certainly
finding out about the consequences of not living our first principle (see
Chapter 2) – know yourself.*

The weather intervened again for the April tutorials. Joan had gone down to the
venue the night before, but I was unable to do so. The next morning, I was still
unable to reach the destination, due to overnight snow, and had to turn back
half-way. This meant that Joan saw my tutees as well as hers. Joe had arranged
to see his a couple of weeks later. Even though it was clearly stated in the course
outline, some people were not expecting to pay for these tutorials. This was a
further complication.

*At a push, I could have gone down with Joan the night before, but chose not
to as I was already going out of my way and no one had bothered to write
to answer my email offering a free Skype session. The accounts from the
participants that you will read have been very honest, and I hope I can be so*

as well. I can see how much I contributed to what happened subsequently and I strongly advise people to pay careful attention to the contract (Chapter 2, point 21). I also was carrying an experience of a previous successful course, so was not coming without memory (Chapter 2, point 4), and, as I stated above, I knew myself less well than I thought.

This is background information for the second module, which took place in June instead of March. Liz's account gives some idea of the onslaught I had to withstand, and some of the projections that came towards me. I listened for close-on two hours. I agreed with some of the complaints, but others were either partial truths or plainly untrue. I had not explained the tutorials when we met for the first module, and I could see the students had been taken by surprise by not seeing me for their tutorials, as they expected. (*As mentioned above, I should have written again.*) But, after nearly two hours, I said I had had enough. I owned where I thought I was at fault, but I had a course to teach. And so I taught the Seven Modes, even though we all knew there was unfinished business. This was partly addressed on the third module but really all came together on the fourth.

This is a rare occasion where I was glad there was a syllabus that I was determined to finish. I would describe myself as someone who works with process, but after those first two hours, I just continued through the seven modes and did not leave any more time for processing. The first two hours had felt to me more like dumping than processing, and I don't think we could have resolved the issues if we had continued to process. I certainly was not capable of processing everything at the time, and I think we all needed time to reflect. Also, not to have taught the seven modes would have felt like a hijacking of our contract to teach supervision.

I have been running groups for 42 years, many of them very challenging, but I had never experienced anything like this. What got under my skin were the attacks on our family – on me, Joan and Joe. I felt hurt, misunderstood and furious, and I think probably frightened – not of them but of what I might say or do. Several of the participants confessed later that they did not expect me to come back. Although the degree of rage directed towards me felt almost unbearable, what was worse was to have my intentions deeply mistrusted. I wanted to protest, justify, explain and, of course, attack. I was reminded of how important it is to me to feel trusted and, seeing it from their point of view as best I could, they had reasons not to trust me.

I hope that is enough background and I will let the accounts of the students fill in the picture. All the students have agreed for these accounts to be published.

Caring for cruelty

Liz

I decided to embark on supervision training, anticipating becoming a more experienced and wiser supervisor and learning more theory to improve my practice. I wanted to make the most of it by participating as much as I could and being willing to take a few risks out of my comfort zone – to be braver than I usually am. I often find groups difficult as I become very self-conscious, which tends to silence me and make me struggle to participate. In my own family, I am the middle child and often felt overlooked and shut down. I learnt to please, to avoid my own true feelings and to 'be good and kind' to get noticed. I grew up being told I'd 'make a lovely nurse as I was so kind and thoughtful'. My younger sister took the role of the 'naughty child, being angry and difficult' and my older brother took the role of the aloof intellectual who was idealised for being all-knowing and left for boarding school at 11 years old. My father had been sent to boarding school aged seven by his alcoholic and depressed parents and my mother had struggled with an emotionally absent mother and a father who adored her, to the cost of his marital relationship.

On the second weekend we experienced a cancellation due to extreme weather. Robin contacted us all by email asking us if we had questions or wanted to get in touch in the interim. I had seen the email but didn't reply, thinking I didn't *need* to get in touch – I could *manage fine* with a cancellation – it didn't affect me – in fact it *was good to have an unexpected free weekend*.

At our next weekend some months later, the cancelled weekend was raised and Robin asked if we had received the email. I was really surprised to discover none of us had replied. That struck me as odd. I had assumed someone *who had needed to make contact* would have done – but no one had. Robin was puzzled. A conversation then began about the tutorials that had taken place with Joan and her son, Joe, in the intervening time. I had expected a tutorial with Robin and became aware of a strong sense of feeling tricked or misled. I had not *been aware* that Robin and Joan were partners and that Joe was also providing the supervision tutorials. I was aware of *feeling suspicious and mistrustful*.

I felt an urge to speak out and name my feelings. I said how I had *felt conned or tricked as if this was a 'family racket'* and had not known that they were all related. Suddenly, others in the group began speaking of their negative experiences with the tutorials. I felt panic as I didn't realise so many of us felt this way. The complaints grew with clear, concrete evidence: we hadn't been told, we didn't expect to have to pay a fee, we expected a free book, the supervision was poor, the person couldn't think, we weren't willing to pay, Robin hadn't bothered to turn up... the list of concerns and complaints grew longer and louder. I was aware that no one else seemed to be as concerned about the family relationship between the supervisors as I was – I wasn't sure why this bothered me so much but I was aware I felt very indignant about it and very unsafe, as if I was on the course *under false pretences*.

The weekend ended very painfully. Robin was challenged and attacked. I left concerned that *this course was not professional and that I wasn't sure about going* back. In the interim we thought in our small groups and again I became aware of my indignation about the relationship and confusion about why it bothered me so much. I found myself *looking for reasons to question the integrity of the training and the trainers – I could find nothing that relieved me of my irritation.* I became increasingly aware that it was mine.

Our third weekend was very difficult. Emotions ran high. There was anger, upset, pain, rage and vulnerability. I was challenged for the comments I had made. I felt overwhelming shame. I was horrified when I realised the extent of my attack and was really challenged about why I had said what I said in the group. I felt I had twisted and distorted good intention. The generosity of Robin's family in being willing to travel out of London for some distance to allow us to receive supervision locally had got lost and twisted in my mind to exploitative, manipulative trickery, whereby I felt duped or conned. I had been part of opening the door to let the cruelty play out in the group. I felt very exposed and panicky – looking to locate it somewhere else. I apologised but was aware that the attack was cruel and my initial response had been dismissive and minimising. I had not been able to feel the impact of what I had done at the time I had done it. I had safely protected myself with the 'kind and thoughtful' false self, intellectualising about the dynamics while dismissing Robin and his family's experience of the attack on them.

> *Robin – I remember Liz apologising and felt gratitude for that, but also remember my saying that I did not want her to take all the responsibility. I think she was a spokesperson for something in the group. I think, as a general principle, it is good not to locate anything in any one individual but to keep referring to a group dynamic being expressed by an individual (see Chapter 2, point 13). One of the best accounts of an individual carrying something for a group is in Ivor Browne's* Music and Madness *(Browne, 2008: 200–204), in which he describes how a nun appeared to be basically quite stupid until the group was challenged on what they were letting her carry and then she was transformed. Ivor Browne's account is the clearest exposition of group dynamics I have read – I recommend it. This does not mean the individual does not take their share of responsibility and Liz relates how I challenged her. But I did not want her to be too hard on herself and take on something for the whole group.*

I went home from the third weekend shattered. I felt exposed, raw and saddened about what I had been part of in the group. I also was aware that there was great forgiveness in Robin and others in the group and I was humbled by this. I knew that this cruelty had entered a part of me that I had kept deeply hidden and not wanted to know before. I became aware in our small group of a childhood experience of being publicly shamed as a 10-year-old. I had been on stage, in front of the whole school, standing in at the last minute for another child who was off sick. I had tried to read a passage from the Bible but was nervous and unprepared and it came out wrong. I had been shouted at and shamed and told to return the following week having prepared it properly. I became aware of a parallel – the school had been run by a married couple who had duped the parents and had been very cruel to the children, caning and humiliating them in front of each other. I became aware of a part of me that was terrified of being exposed and that my cruelty had to be deeply hidden and wrapped in shame from witnessing cruelty to others and doing nothing about it.

I feel I had managed my cruelty by dealing with it in others, by working with parents who have abused their children and with children who have harmed and hurt others. In doing this, I could maintain my 'good and kind' role by being compassionate to others who had struggled. I was aware it was much easier to forgive others and have compassion for them than it was to forgive myself. I became aware of a cruelty towards myself and a sense of shame that I struggled to get beyond. I was aware that *I had been duped by myself. The unprofessional false pretences were my own. The family racket was happening in my own family in splitting dishonestly into individuals in a way that true selves could not be integrated and accepted.*

I felt very anxious about our last weekend together. It was one of the most moving experiences for me. I felt held by the group. There was a sincerity and genuineness in others' capacity for compassion and sharing. I felt a true love to and from others and a shared sense of vulnerability. There was a strong theme of abandonment of fathers and brothers who had been absent through boarding school experiences and death. There was a sense of having to hide true feelings of sadness and abandonment and a sense of putting on a brave face and not being needy.

I wondered how much the shared sense of abandonment from a boarding school experience had been stirred up by the unexpected cancellation of the weekend and then reinforced by the unconscious expectation that it would be our father who would be making a special visit, not 'some other family member'. I wonder about the importance of fathers for me and of having an absent father who struggled to raise a family after a boarding school experience. I don't know where the cruelty he experienced at boarding school went. It seemed like it wasn't held in our family and managed in a safe way but became projected into my sister or played out through distancing and intellectualising and dismissing felt experience, which kept the rest of us from having to feel or own it.

The experience during the supervision course was profound. I learned to challenge myself and to own aspects of myself I really didn't want to see or to be aware of. It gave me a very different experience of compassion and of being in a group and feeling understood alongside others who could feel the emotional pain of having to take back aspects of yourself you had disowned and projected into others. I now really appreciate the firmness and love with which Robin handed back cruelty to me and challenged me to own it in myself. I felt the intense urge to resist it, to refuse it, to force the door closed on it, to make it belong to someone else, anybody else but me. But the paternal strength to reveal it, to hold it, make sense of it and to firmly hand it back was one of the most moving and challenging personal experiences I have had.

My experience of supervision has changed. For me it is a personal sense of ownership, of responsibility and of awareness of what gets pushed and pulled across the boundaries between self and other; the importance of capturing the trickery of the mind and our shared urge to disown and disallow thinking about aspects of ourselves and others that we find most unsettling. It is a holding firm and a handing back with love and compassion and clarity of intent. It is about the universal sharing of human experience and a willingness to make a leap of faith. It is about managing anxiety and holding out for truth. It is about a capacity to see beyond the usual horizons and to seek out a different landscape within which you are a part. It is about a shared learning and a quest for true integrity. It is really about yourself and your relationship to your own authority.

> *Robin – Just this account would have made it all worthwhile but others also generously contributed. Next is Kirsti's account. I had worked with her before, but we became strangers as the group dynamic took hold and it was only towards the end that we reconnected.*

Rumblings of the collective shadows in supervision

Kirsti

I have started this piece of writing several times, both as a document and in my head. Where do I start? What to include? What parts do I remember and what have I forgotten/missed out? So, I have decided to start at the beginning and see where I end. This in itself is part and all of what has been brought, stirred and experienced within the supervision training.

I begin by acknowledging that I had already been working as a supervisor for a couple of years before attending this supervision training. I had trained in Bristol and had found the initial training informative but very assignment-based and quite heady. What I felt I had missed was the process work.

A year or so later, I heard that Robin would be running another supervision training in my home town the following autumn. I was delighted by this news and kept my eyes open for when the training would be open for bookings. I was possibly the first person to sign up for the training.

As the weekend approached and finally arrived, I entered the 'classroom' filled with excitement, anticipation and a sense of finally being able to learn from Robin 'how to be a supervisor'.

Looking around the room at my classmates, I was curious as to who these people were. Did I fit in? Would they be better than me? I was also a little nervous, as this training was in my home town, there were a few familiar faces in the room and I wondered how this would be too: would I hide from them, or they from me? This now feels very close to home, is that OK? Many thoughts but the overall feeling/thought for me was, 'I have arrived.'

Within the first couple of hours, as we were beginning the forming of the group, boundaries were already being challenged and pushed. Someone wanted us all to stand up and move every 20 minutes, another wanted lunch to be longer than planned, another for the ending to be extended. Robin very calmly and clearly stated that the beginning and ending of the days were the boundary and structure and would not be altered; that what happened within this structure could have an element of flexibility, but not the beginning and end. At this point, we didn't know or appreciate the significance of these first boundary challenges. The power of the collective in fact did result in us over-running and broke Robin's strong boundary setting of the day, on day one.

By the end of the first weekend, I recall feeling inspired and full of the new learnings and people.

As the second weekend approached, all was set and looked straightforward. However, mother nature and her creation of the storm, which was dubbed by the media 'The Beast from the East', meant that other plans and forces were stirring. Snow fell in abundance and, with great reluctance, Robin and the training establishment made the decision to cancel the weekend the night before it was due to begin. We were notified by the training establishment and we also received an email from Robin. The impact and eruptions of this set of circumstances were lying in wait for us just below the surface, still unknown to us.

A few weeks later we were due to have tutorials with Robin, Joan and Joe, and again, on the surface, things appeared to be unfolding as planned. However, again, mother nature decided to intervene; Robin was stranded in a town some 30 to 40 miles away, resulting in cancellations and/or merging of tutorials and confusion. The stirrings of the shadows, our individual shadow selves and the collective shadows of the group, were beginning to move closer to the surface and finding ways to leak out in the first rumblings of confusion, disgruntlement and Chinese whispers.

As the rescheduled weekend approached, I noticed that I had uncomfortable, awkward feelings – feelings of disappointment, of trying to process some of the fall-out of the ruptures; feelings about the cancelled weekend and tutorials and acknowledgement that I had felt glad and supported by the 'peer group' in the interim.

As we began the first morning, Robin apologised and expressed his deep reluctance to cancel the previous weekend, and that in all his 42 years of delivering trainings, he had never before needed to cancel a course. He was aware that ruptures might well have been caused by the cancellation. He inquired how we were and also whether anyone had received his email in relation to the cancelled weekend and his offer to meet with us for a Skype session. Out of the 17 people on the training, possibly only one person had responded to him! Quite bizarre.

> *Robin – as already mentioned, this had an impact on me that I did not fully acknowledge to myself at the time.*

What followed could only really be described as two hours of dumping and disgruntlement; the shadows of ourselves and the group had finally been able to come to the surface and were finding energy and freedom in expression. Robin sat there, on the receiving end of these shadows and accusations. Not one of us stopped to say, 'Hey, wait a minute. What are we doing? What is going on here? How was this from Robin, Joan and Joe's perspectives?' The shadows were so great and so present that they didn't feel like they were going to cease. After two hours, Robin said that it was time to stop for a break. It felt to me that something was entering the room, the group, us as individuals, that was visceral; there but not there, real but not real, and shocking.

The weekend's topic was the Seven-Eyed Supervision Model; a content and structure needed to be followed. On several occasions, the group tried to voice some things in relation to the first morning, but Robin held steady in fulfilling the commitment on delivering the content and structure. By the end of the last afternoon, the tensions in the room were too great. The shadows had been abated but were fighting to be freed. Robin could not tolerate it any longer and let us all know how he felt and how he had experienced us, the group, this weekend, the projections that we had dumped on him. The accusations and the distortions had been something he had not experienced before and he needed to go, earlier than expected, breaking his own boundaries, so that he could somehow survive. I was in shock and shame. Had I been a part of something that would do something so cruel to someone I so admired? How could I tolerate being named and classed as the cruellest group that Robin had ever worked with? Would this be how we/I would be remembered? I too couldn't leave the room quickly enough.

> *Robin – Yes, I do remember saying this. Not a good intervention. I was close to feeling that I had lost my sanity and was reminding myself (and the group) that I was an experienced group worker. In telling them they were cruel, of course I was being cruel. Normally I don't mind groups being angry with me. I take the view that either they are right, in which case I am grateful for the feedback – or they might be mistaken in some way (for example, around the contract), in which case we can process this together. The fact that the attack got so thoroughly under my skin told me that something very deep was going on.*

My feelings of apprehension as the third weekend approached were present and strong. I felt supported by my peer group, but I was uncomfortable about coming. Parts of me had been seen, parts of me that I didn't like, let alone know that they were there and had been stirred and seen. What was this weekend going to bring, and how? Within the first few hours, it became clear that the group, I and we, could not go forward until some of the shadows, projections and hidden elements were processed. Robin held fast, with much skill, determination, courage and balls. He held us in our unfurling of secrets, shadows, polarities, cruelty, compassion, love, death, and of each other. It was a tough, tough weekend, and by the end of it I was exhausted. I had cried many tears, I had expressed things that had made me feel toxic, violent and cruel, and I had expressed wisdom, truths, love and compassion. Am I too much or not enough?

The final weekend, the 'Advanced Module' weekend, offered reparation and understanding. As we muddled through the aftermath of the massive ruptures of the volcano of the shadows, we were able to acknowledge that we had all, as individuals and as a collective, been through and survived a powerful process of group inter-dynamic projections and altered states. In fact, it wasn't until the last hour or two of the last afternoon that I noticed that finally I was feeling like 'me' again. I was separating from the group, or was the collective power of the group separating from me, and are there really any similarities or differences?

> *Robin* – Once again, I refer people to Ivor Browne's account of group
> dynamics. It is possible in a group to literally not feel oneself, which – on the
> positive side – is why groups are so full of potential for transformation. On
> the other hand, people not being themselves can lead to atrocities, as we
> well know.

I came away a changed person from completing this supervision training. The different layers of learning will be filtering down and landing for some time. In relation to being a supervisor, I feel and believe that this experience and all its learning will enable me to be with my supervisees, their clients and the fields around us all with greater awareness and recognition of some of the stirrings of human nature and society. I wanted to learn from Robin and wanted to be him. I realise now that I cannot be him, as he is himself and has had all his learning and life to get to be him. How could I possibly be all of those things? I can only be me, in my learning and life and my own configurations, and as such I step forward in my own shoes and persona.

I thank Robin for all he has offered, held and enabled, his wisdom, stubbornness and humour.

I thank each and every one of the members of the group for the 'trip' and for being there for and with me, and I feel that, with all our new learning, we will do good work. Yay!

Much love (and a few tears).

> *Robin* – Re-reading Kirsti's account, I am again touched. I think most of us
> in that group were changed in some profound way, facing our demons and
> having the courage to share them. Next is Gary's account. He had been silent
> throughout the second group. I was puzzled and wanted him to contribute.
> What was he feeling as he witnessed the attacks? When he finally did share

his lack of trust, I understood why he had been so reluctant to contribute. And because almost everyone has had a difficult experience of being in groups, we could empathise. His sharing of his mistrust opened the way to a deeper trust in the group.

My musings

Gary

A tornado just went through here… What just happened? I didn't see it coming.

I thought I had enrolled on a supervision course. I see clearly there are some issues people have brought that they need to work through. I say to myself, 'Stay with it and see where you can contribute to help the process move forward, so we can get to the proper teaching and learning'. It is taking a long time. I'm sure we will get on to the 'real' work soon.

Yet another weekend. Oh, the stuff gets thicker and thicker. This is heavy. I'm trying to do self-reflection. I can't see how I played a part in the onslaught on the tutor and his colleagues that I am witnessing, but… maybe I did. No, I didn't… the group dynamics did… I am a part of the group and so I collude with the group… must accept my role in the group and what I bring… well – I suppose so, but I don't like it.

Robin said something to me like 'stay with it'. Something about not being aloof from the dynamics of the group process. I can do that. Oh my goodness. Really! Really! What has that got to do with this supervision course? It does. I can see it.

This is my first time being in a group of other therapists and being vulnerable among them, after being savaged by a group of therapists and the organisation for which I worked years before. I don't like this, but there may be further healing in this most unlikely process – which is supposed to be about supervision!

> *Robin – Gary actually wrote about his early experience and I have chosen to omit it. Suffice to say, if it had happened to me, I would never have gone near a group of therapists again. But, as the rest of the piece shows, some really deep healing occurred.*

So, I learn to present 'a part of me only'. Not safe to present all of me – at all. The realisation dawns on me that I have to share my past with the supervision group. This is my first time being back in a group of therapists and I don't trust therapists.

I chose to take a risk and invest all of me into the group and share my realisation. It was handled well by the group. A first foray into carving out a different way; towards completing my healing, maybe.

I needed to capitalise on that gain. Having a joint lunch with the group (despite preferring my own space after group sessions) was a necessary next endeavour. Done. That was nice!

So, the supervision training – certainly group dynamics were happening all along and I had nearly missed them! Supervision training was happening, and I nearly missed it!

> **Robin** – *The thing about being process orientated is that teaching can be more implicit than explicit, and for people expecting a how-to, tools approach, it might be easy to think nothing was happening. At first, my experience was that Gary did not seem open. Although we did work with techniques, an exclusive teaching at that level would have enabled Gary to keep hiding. It is harder to hide when the group works with process and using the here and now, but doing so I hope enables students to be more confident as supervisors. They can work with the unexpected and welcome it, instead of fearing it. As in the quote from Carse at the beginning of this chapter, we can be educated as well as trained.*

Has the course impact caused me to now prefer group supervision to individual? Maybe that is going too far… or not…Weeks later, following the end of the course, I read some posts by therapists on CAPPPCHAT. Let me test out my new-found appetite to interact with therapists and post a reaction. I did it… The closed-off part of me wanting to get out, having been given permission to be free from the shackles?

> *Karin's account is next. I remember at one point early on, her saying, 'I am not sure this course is for me. I want a more spiritual course.' I looked at her in complete bewilderment as we had looked at love and fear based on* A Course in Miracles *(Foundation for Inner Peace, 1996) and touched on* The Work of Byron Katie.[1] *What constituted spiritual? I remember thinking, 'This woman will never understand the way I work.' I am delighted to have been so wrong. I felt her move from an individual perspective to grasping group dynamics. Her account, which speaks for itself, gives me an insight into why she might have thought the course was not going to be spiritual. I love that she sees it in such a wider historical, artistic and spiritual (!) context. She sat close to me, as she is deaf in one ear, and I felt her almost co-leading as she tuned in to herself, me and the group and the spirit that seemed to move through us.*

Karin's account

When I see the clear starry sky, I connect myself to the vastness of the cosmos and to the inherent lawfulness of the zodiac and planetary rhythms. I feel at one with it all, my soul expands, unfolds its wings and I take my place within it.

In contrast, when I contemplate the inner space of my soul, I perceive a chaos of changing weather systems, wind, hail, storms, thunder and lightning,

---

1. www.thework.com (accessed 13 September 2019).

and sometimes also an eerie calm and immovability. I can be engulfed in this ever-changing weather system and feel myself at the mercy of unknown powers.

Yet behind these forces that cloud the sky there is also a space of clarity that allows access to another perspective. The process that I experienced during the course of the four modules felt like an invitation to place my conscious awareness into this space of clarity beyond the clouds, to perceive these weather patterns from the other side as it were, freed from the point of consciousness of my personal ego. It means to bring compassion, recognition, discernment and understanding towards both myself and others in a way that goes beyond the daily standpoint of judgement or even condemnation.

Robin calls this perspective 'looking at data' – collecting information from the phenomena presented rather being caught in the 'story' of daily experience. This recognition led to a quite explosive and powerful insight into the nature of the huge barricades that I had erected to protect my 'precious' world view. In that moment it felt as though scales fell from my eyes – and I could literally laugh about it, about my tiny everyday self that considered itself to be so at peace when it was not.

This experience conjured up in my mind an image depicted in a work of art painted towards the end of the Middle Ages (see figure 9.1). It is of Saint Anthony being assailed by terrible demons.[2] He has fallen to the ground and is being kicked, punched and made fun of. He recognises the demons as a reflection of his own vanity, delusions of grandeur, mockery, pride and so on. Yet his garment remains intact and he is – yes – laughing about it! The image I refer to is part of a huge winged altarpiece painted by a relatively unknown artist by the name of Matthias Grünewald. It employs the imagery understood by the people of that time, who were mainly illiterate. St Anthony being assaulted by demons is therefore presented in the form of religious images. Yet, what is so remarkable about this altarpiece, in fact, is that it was not painted for the church but for its healing power. It was placed in a hospice for people suffering from incurable skin diseases; people who in those days were also social outcasts because of the fear of contagion.

The fierce assault of 'our demons' happened in the process of our training during the first three modules, before being able to look them in the face individually and collectively as a group. This was painful and sobering and was no doubt experienced differently by each one of us. There were some tender moments too, as we recognised how we are embedded in our own family and cultural histories.

The companion image to the assault by the demons in the altarpiece is the depiction of a 'supervision session', to use our modern term, in which the one who had experienced his demons converses with his mentor, St Paul. We see a beautiful language of gesture and, between the two of them, the touching image

---

2. These two images are part of the Isenheim Altarpiece, painted 1512–1516 by Matthias Grünewald. The altarpiece is on display at the Unterlinden Museum in Colmar, France. The images are from *Der Isenheimer Altar: Geschichte-Deutung-Hintergruende*, by Michael Schubert (ISBN 978-3-8251-7534-4) © Verlag Freies Geistesleben & Urachhaus GMBH Stuttgart, Germany, and are reproduced here by kind permission of the author and pubisher.

Figure 9.1: The temptation of St Anthony

Figure 9.2: Visit of St Anthony to St Paul

of a deer listening. The 'therapist' (St Anthony) is invited to look at his own process in this protected space and, in speaking and listening, finds his inner truth revealed. The 'supervisor' (St Paul) looks beyond the specific situation presented and makes the bigger picture available to the other.

We think of therapy and supervision as being young professions, as indeed they are. They belong to our time, where we are tasked to develop a heightened level of conscious awareness. But great works of art have always had a prophetic quality and this one speaks in a particularly strong language about the process of supervision as I experienced it on this course – the radical honesty needed and the ability to look beyond the personal. And so it was that I recognised in these images my profound inner journey with Robin and my fellow travellers.

My deepest gratitude goes to all of you.

Next is Cassie's account. I felt particularly pleased that she relates that she learnt much more than about supervision, because that is always my aim.

Supervision training with Robin Shohet

Cassie

Supervision training seemed such a simple concept, but I did not know what awaited me. Was this supervision training? On paper yes; in reality it was a rollercoaster ride of group process with personal development, all turbo-charged by Robin's tenacious hold on us.

The first, seemingly innocuous weekend session was a tumult of boundaries wanting to be broken. The storm clouds were swirling. The Beast from the East unleashed its venom before our next weekend and postponement was the only option. This opened up a whole can of worms, with the group engaging in attacks on Robin and his family. Those not in direct attack mode were definitely not in defend or 'call-it-out' mode but stood by while this played out.

There was bafflement at the hostile dynamic, but a respect and admiration for Robin's ability to stay with it. Robin poked the puppy paw of pain to remove the thorns as the group snapped and snarled at him. Difficult relationships, resentments and frustrations between us and within us emerged, merged and disgorged into the group. As time passed, however, truths were revealed and understandings of what may be happening to all of us became clearer.

Yes, I did learn about supervision, but I discovered far more about myself and the power of the group; my own pain forced from me into others; my repressed anger; my desire to contain shame until it could be contained no more. I witnessed this in others too. This experience has been moving and developmental; I am changed and the universe is on fire with potential. It sounds grandiose but there is truth in it.

There was play in this process too. The generous improvisation session allowed me to let go of myself and just be. Learning about supervision has tapped into a spiritual dimension so long resisted, but in this experience I was able to sense something beyond the personal, something profound that I may have previously dismissed.

Thank you, Robin.

And thank you, Cassie, and all the other students on the course. As trainers, all too often we are asked to give learning outcomes for our courses. Could we have written, 'To go through a period of disorientation, fragmentation and not knowing in order that we might get a possibility of transformation?'

I believe the need for certainty hides a deep fear of chaos and we certainly entered into a space where we faced some of our deepest fears. How else can transformation happen? I think some of our current thinking might be depriving of us of such opportunities.

Some of what got me and us through was:

1. I liked them. I think the topic of liking/not liking can almost be a taboo as we are expected to like our clients, which is why I mention this here (Winnicott, 1949). For sure, there were times when I hated them collectively – a very edgy thing to acknowledge, never mind own publicly. I felt this when I was not with them and I could not hold them in a loving space in my mind. I came to realise it was not them but the sense of powerlessness I experienced that was my problem. And certainly I liked them individually. This definitely helped me to hang in there. The whole experience really illustrated Chapter 8, how fear can block love, because by the end love was certainly in the room.

2. I knew my stuff. So my competency was not in question.

3. I knew I had been careless around contracting and not explaining the tutorial system. As I have mentioned, I had successfully run a previous course at the same venue, so thought just turning up would be good enough, as it had been on that course. Fate was kind enough to not let that be. It is a paradox that, if we can own something without blaming ourselves, we are free to hear criticism without being reactive.

4. I knew that, however unfair some of the accusations were on the surface, I had something to learn. I was not so wise as to be able to laugh (see Karin's testimony), but could see, even at the time, that it was about my own attacking energy as well as theirs. I knew how I might be similar to many of the people in the group who had been quite outspoken in their criticisms, as I myself had played that role in groups. In other words, I saw the group as a mirror of an attacking part of myself.

5. I had a supervision group that both supported and challenged me and helped me own how I had acted out hurt feelings around my good intentions not being understood. It meant I could really own an unconscious wish to punish them for not appreciating and not replying to my offer of a free Skype

session. In fact, I was able to take this training regularly to supervision and feel heard but not colluded with by my peer group. I needed the group's help to get a sense of perspective.

6. I knew that surviving was really important – if I had gone under, as I was close to doing, this would be really letting them down. Not turning up again would be abandoning them, in fact.

7. I had enough theory about projective identification to know they were letting me know how scared and hurt they were behind the attacks – ie. they were getting me to feel how they felt. It later turned out that abandonment was an issue, as 11 out of the 15 had either been to boarding school or had a parent who had been at boarding school.

8. I knew that, even in supervision, transference gets elicited. So I both took it personally but also knew it was not just personal. My supervision group pointed out that a family business would elicit family transferences, which was very helpful.

9. I knew that, if we got through it, the group and I would learn so much about groups and group dynamics. There were times when the group felt to me demonic and I had a felt sense of how a group could behave psychotically, taking leave of their senses. Images of Rwanda and Nazi Germany were used, and many of us owned the potential to split off our cruelty (see Liz's account). I had worked in a therapeutic community and been part of a group dynamics training. This meant that, although at times I was emotionally floundering, I was able to make sense of what was happening. My thinking capacity had not gone. Eventually, we as a group were able to understand how concepts such as splitting, scapegoating, projective identification and people carrying things for others and for the group had been acted out.

Finally, a poem by Mike. Like so many of the others, he was able to share with the group some things he had kept hidden, and his sense of shame. I think the topic of shame in supervision (see, for example, Zoe Cohen's 2016 article, 'Shining a Light on Shame') has not been written about enough. For more on shame, I recommend the work of Brene Brown – particularly her book, *The Gifts of Imperfection* (2010).

Gold of future kingdoms

Mike

Wondering in a dark wood,
Nothing sounds but blood
In your head
And gravel
In your throat.

Layers of fog, pierced through
By shafts of sun, a temple
Rising in the mist. 'Come in'
Says a voice.

'Take up your tongue of fire,
Ignite the darkness with your breath'
You hear
A rumbling
Of forgotten dreams.

Frightened, you turn away,
Running from dying, flying,
Fighting!
But your shadow
Keeps reappearing.

Frightful dragons, demon hosts;
Fighting in the chambers and hills...
Forest in tatters...
All seems death, until
That clear voice
Calls, 'Take the sword out of your heart.'

Bending your head, reaching down, you take the hilt and pull.

Slowly, fear begins to thaw,
Warmed by flames of trust.
Looking deep,
You drink in the image
Of your other-self.

The mask has fallen to the forest floor;
Instead a figure.
You kneel
Before the lost child,
And tenderly
Remember the art
Of parenting.

The gold of future kingdoms
Firms its foundations
In your heart.
'Thanks for returning me
To myself,' you say,
As the dawn reaches in.

As I finish writing this up in the early morning, my preferred time of writing, watching the sun rise over the Severn Valley, the dawn reaching in, I can think of no more beautiful ending for Mike, Joan, me, the course members, for supervisors, supervisees, and their clients, perhaps for you the reader, and for life than this.

Thanks for returning me to myself.

References

Brooke P (1993). *There Are No Secrets*. London: Bloomsbury.

Brown B (2010). *The Gifts of Imperfection*. Centre City, MN: Hazelden Publishers.

Browne I (2008). *Ivor Browne: Music and Madness*. Cork: Cork University Press.

Carse JP (1986). *Finite and Infinite Games: a vision of life as play and possibility*. New York, NY: Free Press.

Cohen Z (2016). *Shining a light on shame*. e-O&P 23(3. https://www.med.org.uk (accessed 29 October 2019).

Foundation for Inner Peace (1996). *A Course in Miracles*. New York, NY: Viking Penguin.

Winnicott DW (1949). Hate in the countertransference. *International Journal of Psychoanalysis* 30: 69–74.

Beyond otherness:
supervision as spiritual practice

I have come to realise that on those rare occasions when we are fully met by another; when we are both truly seen and understood, the illusion of separation disappears and love is all that remains.
(Student on one of our courses)

We are each other and we are the world.
(Eisenstein, 2013:18)

Mike's ending to his poem in the previous chapter could have been a good place to finish, but we wanted to build on it. And herein lies a paradox. If we accept the idea of our all being interconnected, then, in returning us to ourselves, we are returning ourselves to everyone else.

Beyond the personal 'I'

Many of us have had an experience of realising there is more than just this personal 'I' and inevitably it comes with an experience of some kind of peace, awe and gratitude. Almost invariably, the personal 'I' reclaims its kingdom, but somewhere inside us this experience lives on. It is this transcending separateness that supervision can offer us (see Shohet, 2019).

To expand, we have chosen to identify ourselves as separate individuals. I am Robin, you are Joan, John, Mary, Francoise, whoever. This is so apparently obvious that to even question it seems absurd. There is an exercise where you sit opposite someone and say, 'Tell me who you are,' over and over again. You go past the layers – I am a man, father, therapist, husband – and eventually you get to a point where the mind has nowhere to go. When this happened to me (Robin), I did not know whether I was in the world or the world was in me. There seemed no separation; there was still an 'I' but it was so much vaster than anything I (the separate I) could have imagined. In that state of being, fear would have no place. It would be like the fingers of the hand being frightened of each other, or each finger saying, 'I am the only one who counts', or, even worse, wanting to cut the other fingers off as each finger might feel threatened by the others.

The Upanishads, ancient Indian holy texts, have a saying that where there is another, there is fear. If I see you as 'other', then I will feel on guard, fearing potential attack. Recognising our interconnectness would change that, but, as we have seen in ourselves and others, the idea of joining elicits strong fears in itself.

When something is brought to supervision, whether client, colleague or workplace, one way of framing what is brought is that it has become 'other'. The supervisor's job is to help the supervisee become more present to this other, so that he or she can join this otherness and not make it 'other'. In doing so, the apparent difficulty will resolve itself, because the difficulty was not in the situation but *in the creation of otherness*.

> Conflict and suffering arise from introjected misperceptions that engender and then project the feeling of being a separate self... They are messengers which signal that misperception, introjection and projection are taking, or have taken, place. Conflict and suffering are not something to get rid of. Rather, they are signposts that point out the underlying misperception that is holding the belief in separation in place. When this belief is exposed and deconstructed, conflict and suffering disappear, having served their ultimate purpose. (Miller, 2003: 224)

Or more succinctly:

> If you want to know the truth, get an enemy. (Byron Katie, undated)

Both these quotes seem to point to the insight that whatever is disturbing us is an opportunity to see how we have separated from a person or situation. An enemy is an extreme version of the separation that goes on much of the time. In understanding how we might have separated, we open ourselves to interventions that are fresh and belong to the here and now (mode 2).

Supervision as meeting otherness with compassion

When a situation is brought to supervision, we listen carefully to how the supervisee is presenting their issue. Are they seeing the client as a problem to be fixed? Are they looking for a solution? Both of these are focusing on the problem rather than the person. So, as we have seen in mode 1, we wonder if they can imagine themselves in their client's shoes and might ask them to go out and come in as their client. How able they are to do this might completely change the supervisee's perspective. One supervisee was complaining about her tyrannical boss. She was asked to play her boss, and in that role reported: 'I feel scared'. By becoming her boss, she gave herself a totally new perspective. There might still be issues between her and her boss, but they would now be approached by the supervisee with compassion, rather than with fear and anger. She could no longer identify with making her boss so 'other'.

As we have also seen, it can be useful to ask if the supervisee might be similar to their client (mode 4) – or perhaps, more likely, 'How are you similar to your client?' or, 'Who does the client remind you of?' or, 'Was there a situation where you have felt like this before?' In the above example, the supervisee saw her boss as her tyrannical father and was shocked to see how much of that relationship was still present for her in this current situation. How could her boss be anything but 'other' if that was going on? I (Robin) mischievously suggested she ask her boss for forgiveness for not seeing her, while acknowledging my need to do the same with some people in my life. Physician heal thyself.

We believe on one level it is true to say *there is no client,* only a version presented by the supervisee, which is why helping them see differently can of itself resolve a difficulty. We can choose the lens we look through but the context of supervision offers us the space to inquire into the way we are looking.

Seeing the wider system and thinking systemically (mode 7) is also an important practice that loosens the Western tendency to see separate individuals. So, in the above example, the supervisee saw that her boss had been put into a double bind as the boss had been appointed CEO of a family business while the founders still had an enormous influence. This again had the effect of her seeing this boss less as 'other' and more as someone who was also subject to the dynamics of the organisation.

Finally, of course, there is the supervisor/supervisee relationship (modes 5 and 6). As supervisors, we pay close attention to how the presentation of an issue by the supervisee impacts on us. This can be done even more powerfully in a group, where we have several sources of information. We take the view that what a supervisee is bringing is something they have not been able to digest or something or someone they have made 'other'. We use our own feelings as a guide to what might not have been digested, being present to what has been made 'other' to enable the supervisee to do likewise. Our experience is that supervision can offer a place of inquiry to help dissolve this otherness and the fear that goes with it, and thereby take us to a place of compassion and connection (Shohet, 2019).

Building community – the new story

In early July 2019, we had the launch of the Independent Supervisors Network. The name was queried – independent of what? We realised that otherness was embedded in the very name, and we had just taken the name from the Independent Practitioners Network (IPN), and simply changed the word 'Practitioners' to 'Supervisors'. So we changed the name to Interdependent Supervisors Network. This reflected the idea that we are all interconnected. Our wish is to build a community of supervisors that offers support, mutual learning and challenge by sending representatives from one group to another and having get-togethers three times a year. It would seem that the creation of otherness is deeply rooted in our psyches, so we are curious as to how this will pan out. Whatever the outcome, it represents our philosophy that being in a community of peers is a very potent resource. As Charles Eisenstein writes:

> In the face of a whole society that pulls us into the Story of Separation, we need allies… People cannot hold a new story by themselves. A story can only be held in community. (Eisenstein, 2013: 110)

This book is our 'new story' of supervision, inviting us to go past the old story of separation and otherness and the need for control this otherness creates. We are always asking ourselves and our clients, supervisees and students to inquire, pushing ourselves and them to go beyond technique, to take risks, to not know – in the words of a colleague, to 'break the box' (Encke, 2007). In the giving, receiving, training and reflecting on supervision, we have come to see it as a form of spiritual practice, with awareness, inquiry and relationship at the core. And in the creation of ISN, we have added community.

We would want you to join us in seeing the potential for transformation in the supervisory conversations you have and the connections you make. As the late supervisor of one of our colleagues said: 'Supervision should be a conversation you have not had before.'

And, finally, we would like to echo the words of John Rowan:

> There is no spiritual being who can be so useful as a good human supervisor. (Rowan, 1983: 170)

References

Eisenstein C (2013). *The More Beautiful World Our Hearts Know is Possible*. Berkeley, CA: North Atlantic Books.

Encke J (2007). Breaking the box. In: Shohet R (ed). *Passionate Supervision*. London: Jessica Kingsley (pp16–32).

Miller R (2003). Welcoming all that is: nonduality, yoga nidra, and the play of opposites in psychotherapy. In: Prendergast JJ, Fenner P, Krystal S (eds) (2003). *The Sacred Mirror: nondual wisdom and psychotherapy*. St Paul, MN: Paragon House (pp209–228).

Rowan J (1983). *The Reality Game: a guide to humanistic counselling and psychotherapy*. London: Routledge.

Shohet R (2019). Supervision as spiritual practice. *Coaching Perspectives 22* (July): 40–42.

Part 3

Resources

The versatility of the seven-eyed model

Joseph Wilmot

I was delivering the Seven-Eyed Model to staff from Adult Services in a large English county. The training was mandatory (not always a good start) and the group was made up of half social workers and half IT staff. In fact, the IT team I was training had previously sent details of the training around to staff and nicknamed it the 'seven-eyed monster' after looking at the available content. I didn't blame them. As you can imagine, they weren't used to reflective practice, had no clients and didn't tend to use feelings and emotions when talking about computer programmes or fixing IT problems.

So, what did I do? Well, at first I had a brief internal meltdown! Then I remembered that these were people and so was I. They had feelings and emotions, whether they were used to talking about them or not. Most importantly, I remembered that we always find a way of relating to something, whether we are aware of it or not – and that the Seven-Eyed Model was a fantastic tool for teasing out the relationships we have and making sense of them. I just needed to explain this before they attempted to slay the monster.

Where do we start? Well, normally in case work, this would be the client (mode 1). So I asked them what they were currently working on. They were working on software for a new database for staff to use and keep records on. I made sure I gave them all a chance to speak. I listened, asked questions and gave them space to talk about what the software was, how it worked, what the database looked like and how it would, in their opinion, improve things across the service. I listened and tried to understand. I showed interest; they appreciated this and shared their thoughts with me. We basically did mode one. At this point there were some groans from the social workers present. who were currently meant to be enjoying the new database and spent time entering records. It did not appear that everyone shared the belief that the database would, could or was helping. In fact, they were rather less enthusiastic…

This was great. Here was a chance to enter into some actual live, useful and exploratory supervision. The fact that the IT staff weren't used to looking at the relational dynamics of making people use their software meant that there was a rich experiential vein of knowledge and understanding to be had here and now. We started looking at how they had rolled out the database, how they had communicated it to people, the teams and the wider organisation (mode 2, looking at interventions; mode 7 looking at the wider system). What followed was a very rewarding day of training. I'm not sure who got the most out of it. Perhaps this is the best judgement on a good piece of work you can come away with. We looked at why some teams or individuals struggled or resisted. We explored possible solutions and alternatives. We explored relationships – their relationships to their software and why it was important to them (modes 3 and 4), and I shared the impact they had on me, which was very positive and mirrored their relationship to IT (modes 5 and 6). We looked at the fact that a piece of software could generate so many feelings and emotions, like a client. Most importantly, there was an appreciation from within and without of what everyone was attempting to achieve and the experience of trying to do so, me included. Relationships are truly fascinating, strange and not limited to people.

Paralleling in the supervision process[1]

Joan Wilmot and Robin Shohet

Although this was written more than 30 years ago, we think it accurately describes the process of paralleling, which is the basis for our approach to supervision, and so have included it here.

What we will describe occurs, we think, to a greater or lesser extent in all supervision sessions, be they one-to-one supervision, group supervision or team consultancy. Its very simplicity and effectiveness, once grasped, makes it a very powerful tool for supervisor and supervisee alike.

The concept of paralleling is that the supervisee will do to the supervisor what their client has done to them. Or to quote Harold Searles who was among the first to name this process in 1955 when he wrote about his supervision of trainee therapists, 'The processes at work currently in the relationship between patient and therapist are often reflected in the relationship between therapist and supervisor.' For example, if I have a client who is very withholding (who had a mother who was very withholding, who had a mother or father who was very withholding etc), when I present him to my supervisor, I may well do this in a very withholding way. In effect, I become my client and attempt to turn my supervisor into me as therapist. This function, which is rarely done consciously, serves two purposes for the supervisee. One is that it is a form of discharge – I'll do to you what has been done to me and you see how you like it – and the second is that it is an attempt to solve the problem through re-enacting it within the here-and-now relationship. The job of the supervisor is to work with the supervisee with this process rather than becoming submerged by it; by becoming angry with his withholding supervisee just as the supervisee has become angry with his withholding client. The skill is in noticing one's reactions and feeding them back in a non-judgmental way eg. 'I experience the way you are telling me about this client as quite withholding and I am beginning to feel angry. I wonder is this how you felt with your client?' The process is sometimes quite difficult as

---

1. First published in *Self & Society* 1985; *13*(2): 86–92.

we are working with the paradox of the supervisee both wanting to de-skill the supervisor and at the same time work through their difficulties.

In the following account, we will individually relate some of our experiences of using paralleling.

I (Robin) like using this idea of paralleling in groups because the variety of responses of different members can be used to good effect. I start group supervision where I am the facilitator by asking people to entertain the possibility that we do to others what has been done to us. I introduce the terms 'introjection' and 'projection', explaining that if we swallow something without digesting it properly, we may have to vomit it up later. It is usually these cases that are brought to supervision, where some aspect of the client has not been digested. If members of the group can be aware of what they are experiencing, or being asked to swallow, this can be an extremely useful tool for clarifying what is undigested or unintegrated by the supervisee and the client. By using the terms 'introjection' and 'projection' on an easily understood level, I am inviting all the members of the group to trust their here-and-now reactions as part of the supervision work.

Before going on to particular examples, I would like to say how I came to use this concept of paralleling so regularly in groups. I had been aware of it for some time in my one-to-one work and in relation to the supervision I gave and received; but it was through leading dream groups that I came to see how the unconscious feelings in the dream and dreamer became re-enacted and paralleled in the feelings and behaviour of the group members.

By encouraging people to pay attention to whatever responses they had in listening to someone else's dream, we were able to work with all the different levels that operate, not only in the dream but the dreamer's relationship to their dream and to the group. For example, a man tells a dream in which he can't find something and does not know if it is worth finding anyway. The group switches off and, as leader, I am left trying to 'find' his dream. It is not until after trying to work with the dream for some time that I realise that the group is reflecting his attitude in the dream of not being bothered. By making this explicit, the group and the presenter of the dream are able to decide whether to continue working.

Even with many experiences of paralleling, I am still surprised by the force with which it occurs. Recently, on a supervision course for therapeutic community members, a new, young staff member presented a client with whom she had been having difficulty. After an initial enthusiasm and opening up, the client was either missing her sessions or hardly communicating. As soon as the worker began to present her client, I found myself switching off. I just did not want to be bothered. However, I kept going for about 10 minutes, asking seemingly appropriate questions, until I could stand it no longer. I shared my feelings hesitantly – they just did not seem to fit, and group members seemed very involved. In fact it turned out that the group was split roughly half and half. One half was very involved and the other half had totally switched off too, but like me were trying to appear involved. The presenter was astonished to see how accurately her feelings for her client, of both being very involved and identifying with her and not wanting to know about her, were being mirrored. Besides this process happening in the counselling relationship, it was also happening in the client's relationship with other people in the hostel and in the presenter's relationship with her boyfriend, where she was withdrawing after an initial strong commitment. In this case, she was able to see through her fear of being hurt and was able to see the parallels for her client and why she had been having so much difficulty. The client was doing to her what she was doing to her boyfriend (and to us in the group), and she both identified with her and was angry with her at the same time. This realisation was thus a rich source for furthering the counselling relationship, and for both presenter and client exploring their ways of relating to other people.

I once decided not to use the paralleling model with one particular presentation. It concerned a male resident in a therapeutic community. The worker presented this resident in such a way that most of the group, including me, came up with all sorts of strategies as our way of offering help. I commented that we were not focusing on the resident/worker relationship as we usually did, but this was probably one of the times where it was more appropriate to look at different strategies for dealing with a very disruptive resident. (In his presentation, the worker had said that they had a good counselling relationship but it was the resident's behaviour in the community that was the problem.) However, I began to feel that I was avoiding something and one or two members of the group were becoming restless, sensing something was wrong. The possibility of a defence against homosexual feelings sprang to mind. This proved to be an important clue. I was avoiding looking at my relationship with the worker by opting for a strategic approach, in the same way as he was avoiding looking at his relationship with his resident. The work did not stop with the recognition of the paralleling, but it did stop the flight with which I had been colluding because of my own defences.

(Joan): As a consultant to several different staff teams, I find the concept of paralleling (or mirroring or reflection, as it is also called) essential most of the time. Consciously, a team may want the consultant to stay out of their process and for him or her to give them a dispassionate and objective view. Unconsciously however, they often seem to want her to feel what it is like working there and being part of that particular team. In doing this, they hope they can deposit their unwanted bits in her and have her leave, so that she can provide a sort of dustbin function or laxative and they can label her as a useless consultant.

This can give temporary relief but does not deal with the core issues of the staff group and the issues have to come up again or be acted out by the staff group on an unconscious level. In addition to their own unresolved issues, the staff team is reflecting the unresolved issues of their client group, so in not working through their own, they are also not working through their clients' issues with them. The same can be just as true of the consultant – the unconscious of the team triggers off the unconscious of the consultant – the consultant hopefully recognises this. The task of the consultant is not to stay out of the team's process, even if this were possible, but to experience it without judging and to feed it back to the staff group so that they and she can collaboratively work with it. If they can resolve some of these issues in their own staff group, they will have the means to resolve them with the client group. It is often difficult for a team to move from a position of defending against its own inadequacies, sometimes by attempting to make the consultant inadequate, into a model of sharing responsibility with the consultant in exploring and creating solutions.

Recently I was asked in by an organisation that works with homeless people. Their reason for calling me in was that they thought they could make better use of their worker potential and were aware that workers were getting burnt out from overwork. They were aware that they needed to take better care of themselves, but on the whole unaware of their resistance to doing that. In employing me, who still has issues with taking care of myself, even though I have worked on it, there is a danger that I too could work too hard and have to leave. In one of the early sessions I teach the concept of paralleling and, by way of illustration, feed back my feelings at this point. I notice that I am feeling rushed and having too much to fit in the time we have; I ask if it is like that working at their houses and several of them nod vigorously. The sessions proceed. I notice that I overwork despite my conscious attempts not to – again, a mirror of what they do.

Then, in one session, someone falls asleep. I comment that there seems to be a void in the centre of the group and I feel compelled to fill it. The more I fill it, the more my voice dominates and the more people disappear to the fringes of the group and finally go to sleep. I also remember and share that I had felt tired at the thought of running the session. This turns out to be just like their breakfast meetings where they try to energise and motivate the residents and feel exhausted by it. They also have to prove their worth as workers, just as I was having to prove mine as a consultant. We look at how they are pressurising me because of how they pressurise themselves and how their clients pressurise them, and also how I allow myself to be pressurised because of the pressure I put myself under. This sharing gives us room to move. We now have a common experience, are in effect on the same side, as opposed to being in conflict, and are now in a position to move onto the next stage, which is looking at how we live with and/or resolve this issue. Our experience in the worker group will be the model for how it is managed with the client group.

This was certainly true in the following example from my one-to-one supervision work. I was supervising a social work student on placement to our therapeutic community who was counselling a resident with whom she was having difficulty. He was a man in his forties who had been in the rehabilitation programme in the house for about seven months and was now to move on to the next stage, which was finding himself some voluntary work.

He was well able to do this but, despite the student making many helpful and supportive suggestions, he 'yes butted' everything she said. In her supervision with me, despite her being a very able student, her response to all my interventions was 'yes but'. I took this issue to my supervisor, in order, as I thought, to obtain some useful suggestions with which to help the student. However, despite the fact that I was usually very receptive to supervision, I responded to every suggestion my supervisor made with a 'yes but'. He then commented on how resistant I was sounding and how like the resident in question I was being. This insight immediately rang so true that we were both able to enjoy the unconscious paralleling I had been engaged in and I no longer needed to engage in a resistance game with my supervisor. I shared this with my student, who no longer needed to resist me but was able to go back to the client and explore his need to resist. His issues around needing to feel his power by resisting could then be worked on separately from his finding voluntary work, and he was able to arrange some voluntary work within the week.

Whether it is with a team, a group or a one-to-one session, this way of working focuses on how the relationship between supervisor and supervisee reflects and parallels the supervisee and the client group. By working in this way, we are also emphasising our belief that, however disturbed the client, the solution to any stuckness, for supervision purposes, is with the therapist. The supervisor must not collude with making the client the problem, any more than they should be colluded with in their own supervision, should they seek to make their supervisee the problem. By working in this way, we keep the focus on the here and now and remember that we are working with the supervisee's view of the client, not the client himself. In this way of looking at it, it is the relationship that is being presented,

Our interests in paralleling are many. By focusing on the here and now and the effect that the presenter is having on us or the group, we have the task of using this information for understanding the therapist/client interaction. Without some focus on paralleling, we are leaving much of ourselves out.

We could, as mentioned above, be colluding with the supervisee's description of the client, unless we were used to monitoring our own reactions carefully and using the here and now of our joint experience. This is not to say that other strategies are not relevant. However, our way of working – of combining the here and now (Gestalt) with the relationship (transference and countertransference) – obviously suits us. It is sometimes only a starting point, but can provide the necessary relief for work to continue in a more fruitful way. When used in a group, it encourages members to be aware of, trust and use their responses, which helps them as therapists. It helps the supervisor not to collude or walk into any traps set by the supervisee; and if these traps are walked into, it provides a tool for getting out. Its strength is that the supervisee unconsciously reproduces the essence of the session with their client through their relationship with their supervisor, and this offsets any conscious attempts by the supervisee to distort the content of their sessions with their clients.

References

Searles H (1955/1986). The informational value of the supervisor's emotional experience. In: *Collected Papers on Schizophrenia and Related Subjects*. London: Karnac Books (157–176).

Exploring the dynamics of complaints[1]

Robin Shohet

People have shared their fear of having a complaint made against them.
I wanted to help understand some of the dynamics that could be involved.

Many professionals have a fear of a complaint being made against them. In this article, my aim has been to throw some light on some of the dynamics that might be operating around complaints in order to move towards a more compassionate, systemic view that goes beyond blame. Some of what I have written could be applied to relationships of any kind.

Key words: Complaints, dynamics, countertransference, relationships, inquiry, understanding, systemic view, parallel process, needs, right/wrong

In July (2017), I organised a conference to look at the dynamics of complaints in the so-called helping professions. I start with the premise that whatever position we take around complaints is a form of countertransference. In other words, whether we sit on an ethics committee, whether we start an insurance company for therapists, or even whether we organise a conference on the dynamics of complaints, we are trying to heal something in ourselves by the positions we take.

I started with myself and found more authority issues, a tendency to split, which I saw mirrored in how client and practitioner can be split when a complaint is made, and an omnipotent wish to protect 'my' profession from going down the route of other professions, where fear has dominated to the detriment of all concerned.

Discovering this has helped me be clearer, but I recognise my understanding will always be incomplete. What I want to do now is to share some of my understanding about what could be going on around complaints. You may disagree with some or all of it. You may feel supported in it. But it is the conversation that we might have after you have read it that will be important.

---

1. First published in *Self & Society* 2017; 45(1): 69–71.

1. Our society is becoming increasingly litigious. This is bound to increase fear. From a place of fear, we are more likely to be in survival mode, which lessens the opportunity to combine, to see a bigger picture.

2. It also means we become increasingly defensive. If I defend myself against you, I am implying you are dangerous. I therefore am attacking you, which justifies your attacking me. We are caught in a vicious cycle.

3. Whatever the content of the complaint, there is a process question of 'Why now?' This may (or may not) be connected to a stage in therapy, like ending, or where, just before a breakthrough, a major rupture from earlier in the client's life is often re-enacted.

4. A complaints procedure could be used as an avoidance technique. This does not mean we don't look at the behaviour of the therapist, but we recognise that relationships are also co-created.

5. When we teach supervision, we encourage supervisors not to believe what the supervisee says about their client uncritically. 'I have a very difficult client' would be translated into 'I am finding this client difficult.' I would not believe a client's version of their parents or of their partner uncritically – I would see it as *their* truth but not *the* truth. In other words, I am mindful of a bigger picture. I would want a complaints procedure to hold a bigger picture, however obvious wrongdoing might appear.

6. People often mention so-called bad therapists. So-called bad practice exists in all professions and we may have an omnipotent fantasy it can be stopped.

7. We are the bad therapists too. If there is someone who says he has never done bad therapy (whatever that is), then this is someone who is likely to be doing bad therapy (whatever that is).

8. The people professions are different in that there is not an object involved – eg. a tooth or a car to be fixed or some product that can be exchanged or refunded. We are paying for a relationship, not a product or something to be fixed. The criteria for success or failure are hard to judge.

9. The therapy profession has not been going on as long as medicine, social work, teaching. It may have a wish to prove it has its own house in order. The desire to be accepted by the mainstream has a cost, and this cost may be coming out in the approach to complaints where we over-identify with the complainant.

10. If we look at some of the processes involved in OCD, then the patient is unable to cope with their anxiety. They invent rituals to help them feel safe. The rituals do not deal with the underlying anxiety so become more pronounced.

11. Are we caught in the same dynamic? A complaints ritual that does not deal with the underlying fears and anxieties, leads to an ever more vigorous complaints procedure.

12. Many years ago, there was a Channel 4 programme called *Doctors' Mistakes*. What this particular hospital found was that, instead of going into denial and defence, when the doctors admitted mistakes and apologised publicly, suing rates went down, learning went up, and so accident rates went further down. Is there something that therapeutic bodies can learn from that?

13. Do complaints offer a sense of offering to regain potency that is perhaps misguided? We know a lawyer who has successfully sued therapists and said it did not bring closure for the clients and he will no longer do it. There was suffering for the therapist and not the outcome the client really wanted.

14. We have a complaints procedure about therapy, which does not seem therapeutic. Why? What is the need of the complainant? This is not about pathologising the client, but given as mentioned earlier about doctors' mistakes, then a system that enables this kind of inquiry and subsequent acknowledgment would seem more fruitful.

15. So, by extension the first step in a complaint is to ask the complainant what they want. If it were a product, it could be a replacement, or a fixing or a refund. For a relationship – what is wanted? If we again go back to doctors' mistakes, is it acknowledgement rather than an identification with the complaint that might be needed? How can the question: 'What do you need?' be held? In other words, the best support for the client might not be to pursue their client's grievance at face value.

16. Or it might be. This is not throwing the baby out with the bathwater.

17. I think our relationship to what therapy is all about reflects our attitude to complaints. If we think it is about understanding ourselves, rather than being fixed, then whatever happens is an opportunity to reflect. A complaints process in the helping professions could go the route of reflection rather than pursuing the right/wrong process.

18. And, of course, if we can't prove the therapy works, we don't get funding, so we really are caught in a double bind. There is a much bigger picture here about justification and money and fixing.

19. In divorce courts, there used to be an adversarial framework, which created much distress. It is now recognised that it is more useful that the couple be held, using methods like mediation. A complaints procedure that holds the practitioner and client would mirror the holding that is part of our work.

20. Supervision holds the therapeutic relationship. A complaints procedure could mirror that.

21. Society seems to be attracted to the Victim, Persecutor, Rescuer triangle. We can fall into replicating that with initially therapist as persecutor, client as victim and complaints procedure as rescuer. This then turns into complaints procedure and client as persecutors and therapists as victims.

22. Our work is about relationship and awareness and yet we can lose both foci in looking at complaints because it activates scripts like fairness, justice, power, betrayal and so on.

23. An understanding of parallel process is vital in our work. Can we apply this to complaints? Is there a replication of a client's or therapist's or complaints body's traumata being re-enacted? An understanding of some of the dynamics of shame in the Victim, Persecutor, Rescuer triangle could help with that.

24. Do both therapist and client have an image of a safe haven which gets betrayed by reality? Do therapists set themselves up to do more than we can, and thereby collude with a system that demands and blames?

25. I am back to looking at our personal countertransference and that of our profession. I believe that doing this can lead to less polarised positions and perhaps help us to embrace an understanding, inquiry process model rather than a right/wrong content model. This may help us work towards all parties being able to voice the feelings, unmet needs, values and expectations which might lie behind a complaint.

How green is your mind?[1]

Robin Shohet

This is an article I wrote in the mid 1990s. It marks the beginning of an investigation into thinking that is one of the foundations of our supervision work and shows how it can be applied outside the consulting room.

What people are doing in planting forests and saving the whales and so on is very necessary, and more of it should be done. Nevertheless, it is still downstream. Unless something is done upstream, that is, in the process of thought, it won't really work in the long run. (Bohm & Edwards, 1992)

There is nothing good or bad, but thinking makes it so. (Hamlet)

Suppose you were a car and your brain/thoughts/mind were the exhaust pipe. Every time you had a negative thought, *any* negative thought, criticism or judgement – about yourself, another or God – your exhaust pipe would give off fumes. Would you be polluting the planet?

I believe that pollution begins in the mind. *The Upanishads*, ancient Hindu texts, say, 'Where there is another, there is fear.' What I understand by this is that, as long as I see myself as separate and you as 'other', I will be frightened of you and our relationship will be polarised: if I am competitive, I fear you will upstage me; if I hate you, I will fear your attack; if I love you, I will fear you will abandon me. *A Course in Miracles* talks about special love relationships and special hate relationships and sees both as the same: both arise out of duality or a sense of separateness and therefore both exist in fear not love.

Fear, I believe, is the source of all pollution. Fear lies behind the greed which fuels our exploitation of resources – fear that I must get what I can before you do; and what I get will never be enough because my greed is fear driven and

1. This article first appeared in *One Earth, Issue 18, Summer 1995.*

therefore irrational. Logical argument has less power over us than our emotions do. For instance, everybody knows that smoking is not good for your health, yet people persist in smoking.

I think that some of the ecological movement underrates the self-destructive urge in each of us. According to psychoanalyst Harold Searles:

> Unconsciously we harbor the notion that since we do not immediately experience the ill effects of pollution and the like, it will not happen to us… Mankind is collectively reacting to the real and urgent danger from environmental pollution much as the psychotically depressed patient bent upon suicide by self-neglect. (Searles, 1972)

Searles connects the need for more power over nature, more industry and more technology with our desire to be in control of everything in order to compensate for infantile feelings of helplessness and powerlessness. These feelings can evoke rage which in turn evokes fantasies of destroying everyone – mother, father, siblings, the whole world – in order to gain revenge and prove our might. Unfortunately, as is not the case with a child, we actually have the power to make such fantasies come true.

I remember in my early twenties feeling quite depressed, hating anyone who was happy, and consciously thinking that I wished there would be a world war and everyone would be as unhappy as me and/or be destroyed. As I get older, I allow myself to feel more connected to others, but my own feeling of powerlessness and helplessness still evoke in me terrible thoughts of revenge. I have moved from being a fantasy bomb builder but am still a gross polluter when in such states. I have learned that one way of reducing the pollution I create is not to judge myself and to overcome the shame of acknowledging my shadow by publicly speaking and writing about it, as I am doing here.

In a book called *The Art of Hating*, the author, Gerald Schoenewolf (1992), looks at the whole business of hating, or, as I have described earlier, having negative polluting thoughts. He makes the following distinction between what he calls 'subjective' and 'objective' hate. When we hate subjectively, we are concerned with the immediate need to protect ourselves, to be right, to teach a lesson, to gain an advantage, to defeat an opponent or to revenge ourselves on an enemy. Objective hating, on the other hand, involves sharing our feelings of animosity in a way that aims to increase our contact, and does not lose sight of the humanity of the other. It requires an understanding of others, oneself and one's motives, and not to go into subjective hate when provoked.

When we are supporting a 'worthy cause', if we find ourselves feeling judgemental or ever so slightly superior, we can be sure we are into subjective hating. One of the characteristics of subjective hate is to deny our own aggression and to project it onto those deemed to be unenlightened. We become adept at provoking aggression in others in order to make our enemies look bad and ourselves look good. It is not surprising then that, when the subjective hating of the polluter meets the subjective hate of the environmentalist, a lot of anger is generated and very little in the way of solutions.

In a chapter called 'Us and Them', Peavey (1991) tells how she prepared for a meeting with the president of a conglomerate who owned a local napalm factory. She and her colleagues found out as much as they could about the president's personal life, relating to him in his human context, surrounded by the people who loved him and whom he loved. By the time the meeting took place, he no longer felt a stranger to them. Their aim was for him to see them as real people, not flaming radicals whom he could dismiss. They assumed he was carrying doubts inside himself about renewing a contract for his napalm factory and that they could voice these doubts in a non-antagonistic way. In approaching the meeting in this way, they had moved from subjective hate to objective hate and established a real, personal contact. The president did not renew his factory's contract.

Peavey asks some pertinent questions about the truths we must face in ourselves if we are to practise non-polarisation: ie. if we are to avoid creating 'otherness'. She realises that to work with social change without relying on the concept of enemies raises some practical difficulties. For example, what do we do with all the anger we are accustomed to unleashing against an enemy? Is it possible to hate actions and policies without hating the people who are implementing them? Does empathising with those whose actions we oppose create a dissonance that undermines our determination?

Saving our planet is as important a movement as there ever has been [this was written in 1995]. But unless I fully understand the mind of, say, the president of a napalm factory, I will be stuck in subjective hate and will therefore, in my own way, be as much of a polluter as he is.

The Indian sage Sri Ramana Maharshi commented that we thank God for the good things that happen to us, but not for the bad, and that is a mistake. I was shocked but I think I understand. As long as we divide events into 'good' and 'bad', we are at the mercy of our minds, caught in an endless cycle of craving for what we consider to be 'good' and having an aversion for what we consider 'bad'. This means that we constantly judge everything in terms of a limiting, dualistic frame of reference.

How does all this relate to Ecology?

a) The seeds of destruction are in the mind and in the emotions. Telling people about the effects of pollution is even less effective than anti-smoking campaigns. Polluting the world does not bring us instant or direct feedback the way smoking can. Revenge can be an important component as much in those who pollute as in those who, in their campaign against pollution, are simply hiding their subjective hate behind a 'worthy cause'.

b) A green campaign will, I think, be more effective if it includes some recognition of the divisive quality of human feelings and the human mind.

Even as I write, I am aware of creating a new division in my own mind – between all those who have 'greened' their minds as well as the environment versus those who just deal with the environment – a new hierarchy/duality.

c)   When I look inside myself, I see how deeply polluting I am in my thoughts, regardless of my green credentials. Acknowledging this is a useful way of balancing any moral superiority I may try to claim. Perhaps it is true to say that anyone who is not enlightened will be polluting. Ramana Maharshi's ashram was run with great precision. Nothing was wasted. This was not because it was a movement, or a conscious attempt to save resources, but a natural byproduct of an undivided mind.

d)   This does not mean there should not be a Green Movement. I simply want to remind myself (again) that, whenever I think I am right, I can be at my most bigoted and most unable to reach out to those who oppose me, because of the degree of my subjective hate.

I do not know if the Green Movement has adequately addressed this issue of inner pollution and it may be one of the reasons why it is not more effective. To change the president of the napalm factory, Fran Peavey had to work very hard on an inner level to release her subjective hate. I know I have not reached that state. My inner world is still full of 'goodies' and 'baddies'.

A recent minor incident in my life indicates how big an investment there is in the world for us to polarise. I was rung up by someone making a television programme against circumcision because I fitted all the criteria they were looking for. I am Jewish, male, articulate, have relived the trauma of my own circumcision in therapy and decided not to have my own sons circumcised. We were arranging dates for televising when I said (influenced, I think, by writing this article), 'You need to know that I can only be 95 and not 100 per cent certain that I have made the right decision. It could be that in later life my sons will be angry with me for robbing them of a tradition. If I say I am 100 per cent certain, I will, in my own way, become as rigid as those who fervently support circumcision. My wish would not be to convert or be converted, but for my 5 per cent of doubt to meet with a pro-circumcision person's 5 percent of doubt so we can dialogue and increase both our doubts and thus create more middle ground.' At this point the interviewer said he would have to consult his boss and would ring me back. He never did. My fantasy is that my unwillingness to polarise on this issue would not make good viewing.

I would like to end with an anecdote that amuses me and with which my unloving self identifies. Many years ago, I went to listen to Paul Solomon, psychic and healer. He related the story of how the CIA became interested in him because they wanted him to help them tap the secrets of the KGB. When asked if he could do it, his reply was, 'Sure. Anyone can do it. All you have to do is love the KGB more than you love yourselves.' The secrets of the KGB remain intact.

References

Bohm D, Edwards, M (1992). *Changing Consciousness*. San Francisco, CA: Harper.

Peavey F (1991). Us and them. In: Zweig C, Abrams J (eds). *Meeting the Shadow*. New York, NY: Penguin/Putnam (pp202–206).

Schoenewolf G (1992). *The Art of Hating*. Lanham, MA: Jason Aronson.

Searles H (1972). Unconscious processes in relation to the environmental crisis. *Psychoanalytic Review 59*(3): 361–374.

Using improv as a therapeutic and supervisory technique: a beginner's view[1]

Robin Shohet

Since 2015, I have been running improv workshops for therapists, supervisors and people in related fields. As a member in an improv group, I often feel out of my depth, but knowing I have survived (even though sometimes it feels terrifying) enables me to identify with people who are also just beginners.

I start the workshop by asking people to pair up and introduce each other without saying a word of truth. I love the paradox here, because of course the character we invent says a lot about us. As one participant new to improv said, it hijacks the unconscious. She invented herself as a Spanish princess, complete with accent and haughtiness and, for a moment, I really believed she had been one before she became a therapist. In another pair, a hitherto very proper woman became a prostitute and oozed sexuality. She asked rather nervously, 'What does that say about me?' and we agreed not to analyse. This is very important, as it will tend to make us less likely to be spontaneous.

Keith Johnstone, in his classic book *Impro* (1979) (he calls it impro rather than improv) writes:

> Students need a 'guru' who gives 'permission' to allow forbidden thoughts into consciousness… They agree that for years they have been suppressing all sorts of thinking because they classified it as insane.

Improv is all about being in the moment and cooperating. Johnstone writes that the improviser needs to understand that his first skill lies in releasing his partner's imagination and accepting the offer your partner has made. There is a wonderful game where two people are asked to sell something that the audience has decided. Say it is pink elephants. One (Mary) starts with reasons why everyone should have a pink elephant, and then at some point the other (Fred) enthusiastically

---

1. This paper is a shortened version of an unpublished thesis for a Diploma in Supervision, which is available by writing to info@cstdlondon.co.uk

says, 'Yes, that's right, Mary' and develops her idea. Whereupon she in turn says, 'Yes, that's right, Fred' and continues. Knowing your partner will enthusiastically accept whatever you say and develop it releases the imagination, and the audience loves seeing them combining and getting more and more absurd.

Johnstone's book is full of really wonderful insights into the human mind, as he watches how people block and accept both their partners and parts of themselves. I only know of one book that specifically relates improv to therapy; it's called *Rehearsals for Growth* and it's by Daniel Wiener (1994). Alison Goldie, in her excellent *The Improv Book* (2015), has the words 'Improvisation for Theatre, Comedy, Education and Life' on the front cover. Yes, it is for life. When I hear people say they have not laughed so much in years, this is the kind of therapy I want to be associated with.

For supervision

I have extended its use into supervision by asking the supervisee to present their client in gobbledygook (nonsense sounds). The supervisor acts as a translator of this gobbledygook to an imagined audience if it is a one to one session, and a real audience if it is a group.

Example

The supervisee, Lynn, is asked to think of her client and speak to an audience (real or imagined) in gobbledygook. As Lynn speaks, the supervisor/translator (Frank) becomes very haughty and arrogant and, as he translates Lynn's gobbledygook, he tells the audience how magnificent he is and it is really beneath him to even bother to talk to them.

They stop after about a minute and Lynn shares that her client is a chief executive who is very used to being in control, and that carries over into their sessions with his talking down to her. Lynn is getting very frustrated. In her gobbledygook she has portrayed her view of her client – namely, his perceived arrogance. Frank, who knows nothing about her client, has picked this up in the way he has translated her gobbledygook.

Frank suggests a different scene and that Lynn say the first line that comes into her head. She plays being a homeless old lady. She asks for a blanket. Frank plays a heartless care worker (embodying an aspect of the client) and says, 'We don't give blankets out before 8pm.' Lynn begs, and the supervisor softens and says that he could not break the rules but would give her a cup of tea. They are both moved.

Through playing that role, Lynn got in touch with her client's vulnerability, which she had blocked out. She was sure that would have an impact on future sessions with him.

Below is a summary of benefits taken from Wiener, which I believe are all relevant to therapy, supervision, coaching, life.

1. Playful. Frees imagination.
2. Encourages empowering exploratory behaviour.
3. Expands emotional range.
4. Can be used for assessment.
5. De-emphasises verbal – uses another channel, so good for children.
6. Corresponds with rules for healthy interpersonal functioning – attending fully to others, aligning oneself with others (accepting offers), and supporting others to be right or look good.
7. Enables people to see social norms and impact on them and others.
8. Opportunity for new narratives.
9. Sharpens observational skills – particularly non-verbal.
10. Status work – a good tool for understanding power in relationships.
11. Use of self in therapy, taking risks.
12. Can challenge robustly as it is fun.
13. Encourages spontaneity.
14. Breaking conventional logic.
15. Giving up control.
16. Using voice and body.

References

Goldie A (2015). *The Improv Book*. London: Oberon Books.

Johnstone K (1979). *Impro: improvisation and the theatre*. London: Faber & Faber.

Wiener D (1994). *Rehearsals for Growth*. New York, NY: WW Norton & Co.

Residential supervision training
Joan Shohet

We end this section on resources with a brief description of a residential course. The description by a course participant illustrates the transformative potential of supervision and supervision training.

We have been running the courses residentially for the past five years. The first two courses – the Core Course and the Seven-Eyed Model – fit neatly into the weekly structure of courses run by the Findhorn Foundation, a spiritual, educational centre and global eco-village in the north east of Scotland.

The combined Core and Therapeutic Course, which takes place in the last week of January, starts on Saturday afternoon and runs through to Friday afternoon at 4pm. It follows, in many ways, the same timetable as the London courses, with three days for the Core and three for the Seven-Eyed Model. It is held within the rhythms and rituals of the Findhorn Foundation, which are offered by the Building Bridges department, which hosts private courses like ours. There are daily meditations and also Taize,[1] yoga, Five Rhythms, a hot tub and usually a Burns Night supper celebration, all of which are open to course participants. Participants eat in the community dining room and do one KP (Kitchen Party) clean-up shift.

Tuesday, between the two courses, is when participants take part in an 'Experience' day hosted by Building Bridges, where they may experience attunements, some aspects of the daily work of the community and a work party out in the gardens or woods surrounding the community. Another tenet of community life are the Angel cards.[2] At the beginning of each course we start

---

1. The Taize community is an ecumenical monastic fraternity in Taizé, Burgundy, France. Over the years, members of the Findhorn Foundation have brought songs back from the Taize community and incorporated them into the community's spiritual practice.

2. Angel cards are a set of 72 illustrated cards, each depicting a unique angelic quality with a word and a picture. They can be used for support in many different ways. You can choose an Angel card on your birthday or other special occasions or select a weekly or daily Angel to bring inspiration to work, school, an activity or a relationship.

with a short attunement, followed by all choosing an Angel card, which, as with all such tools, can gently and humourously support, challenge and interrupt our core beliefs. These are the Angel cards drawn at a recent group: Compassion, Adventure, Play, Balance, Release, Honesty, Depth and Surrender.

The experience of the training delivered residentially is perhaps best conveyed by a participant, Sue Haycroft, who offered the following. We have included this account because of how well it describes the connection between supervision and life, which is one of the themes of this book.

> A residential week in Scotland, feeding mind, body and soul; meeting like minded fellow beings, learning new skills, and expanding horizons. Who wouldn't wish for that? But beware... this might just change your life, as it did mine.
>
> This course was a new approach to learning and possibly to living. A way of learning based on the ultimate belief in the potential of all, each in our own unique way.
>
> The validity of experience over theory and the desire to live from our own authentic heart.
>
> Appreciative Inquiry, the freedom to dream, and the structure of the Seven-Eyed Model, all central facets of life and supervision.
>
> Uncovering our own blocks, our own blind spots, our core beliefs and the radical idea that in any given moment it is all 'just data', in a safe, holding environment, meant that both personal development and exploration took place hand-in-hand with the practical application of the art of supervision.
>
> For that is how we were encouraged to view supervision – as an art form, a process that would inherently lead to growth and a depth of living and working if we could fully enter the process.
>
> This course, ostensibly about supervision, but reaching far beyond that, stretched and challenged me to open up to the real me; to come face to face with the core me from whom perhaps I had strayed too far.
>
> Findhorn, with its own defining spirit, was part of this mix, and the integration of the threads of community living within the therapeutic learning make this course, in my eyes, completely unique.
>
> I found parts within me previously lain dormant. I learnt truths about myself that my body had held but had never been raised to consciousness. I exposed some pretty central core beliefs that had caused blockages and blind spots for several years. I saw things within me that saddened me but also gave me hope. I learnt to be more me. I learnt to take risks. I learnt to challenge longstanding beliefs and fears and I had so much fun. I learnt that to share me, to be really present, and to listen intently meant that something different happened; that dynamics change and new experiences can occur.
>
> Sounds like therapy? Sounds like supervision? Sounds like life...

Name index

Subject index

Other books on supervision
from PCCS Books

Clinical Supervision Made Easy
(second edition)

Els van Ooijen

ISBN – 978 1 906254 674 (2013)

Clinical Supervision Made Easy is a practical book for supervisors and supervisees that offers the 3–Step Method as a guide to effective supervision. This method is not linked to any particular theoretical orientation or philosophy, so it can be applied in any helping context irrespective of the profession of the worker. The three steps are: 1. What does the supervisee need from this session? 2. How can this be brought about? 3. What has been learnt and what needs to happen next? The book is written in a relational, experience-near and conversational style with many helpful examples, suggestions and techniques, based on the author's considerable experience of giving, receiving and teaching supervision.

Available at www.pccs-books.co.uk

Other books on supervision
from PCCS Books

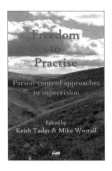

Freedom to Practise:
Person-centred approaches to
supervision

Keith Tudor & Mike Worrall

ISBN – 978 1 898059 59 2 (2004)

'This book is a thought-provoking and engaging addition to the literature on supervision. The editors have a vast knowledge of the field and clearly and authoritatively state their philosophy of person-centred supervision. This provides the context for the subsequent chapters by different authors. These cover a wide range of issues and topics which will be of real value to all supervisors to whatever school they belong.'

Robin Shohet, co-author of *Supervision in the Helping Professions*

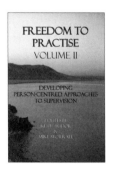

Freedom to Practise Volume II:
Developing person-centred
approaches to supervision

Keith Tudor & Mike Worrall

ISBN – 978 1 898059 97 4 (2007)

This book is the follow-up to the acclaimed *Freedom to Practise*. As the subtitle suggests, it develops the groundbreaking work in person-centred approaches to supervision begun by the first volume.

Available at www.pccs-books.co.uk

Permanent discounts
plus free UK postage and packing
available at
www.pccs-books.co.uk

Or call us to order books
+(44) 1600 891 509